BREAD OF HEAVEN

D0709815

BREAD OF HEAVEN

Ieuan Evans
and Peter Jackson

MAINSTREAM
PUBLISHING

EDINBURGH AND LONDON

Copyright © Ieuan Evans and Peter Jackson, 1995
All rights reserved
The moral right of the author has been asserted

First published in Great Britain in 1995 by
MAINSTREAM PUBLISHING COMPANY (EDINBURGH) LTD
7 Albany Street
Edinburgh EH1 3UG

Reprinted 1995 (three times)
This edition 1997

ISBN 1 84018 008 0 (Paperback)
ISBN 1 85158 786 1 (Hardback)

No part of this book may be reproduced or transmitted in any form or by
any means without written permission from the publisher, except by a
reviewer who wishes to quote brief passages in connection with a review
written for insertion in a magazine, newspaper or broadcast

A catalogue record for this book is available from the British Library

Typeset in Monotype Bembo and Gill Sans
Printed and bound in Great Britain by Butler and Tanner Ltd, Frome

I Mam a Nhad a'm ffrindau ar draws y byd

To my parents and those who have to suffer my moods, to my friends and friends to be

Contents

Acknowledgements

The authors wish to thank the following for their help and support in the preparation of this book:

John and Margaret Evans, Non Evans, Peter Herbert, Phil Davies, Gareth Jenkins, Allan Lewis, Roy Bergiers, Stuart Gallacher, Rupert Moon, Les Williams, Llanelli RFC, Alan Davies, Bob Norster, John Fairclough, Ieuan Harries, David Jenkins, Tim Atter, John Skeldon, Ian Rone, Jane Smith and all at Forthright Finance Ltd, Gareth Edwards, Will Carling, Brian Moore, Jonathan Davies, David Rogers of Allsport, Colin Elsey of Colorsport, Ross Kinnaird of Empics, Huw Llewellyn Davies, the *South Wales Argus*, the *Western Mail*, John Bredenkamp and Emma Twidale at Masters International, Akito Mizuno, Peter Barber, Julie Longden and Sheila James at Mizuno, Paul Leonard, Moira Davies and Gilly McCarthy at Cellnet, Bill Campbell and Avril Gray at Mainstream Publishing.

Foreword

BY GARETH EDWARDS

Throughout the autumn of 1984, people kept telling me of a newcomer who could run like the wind and sidestep like Gerald Davies. 'There's this young boy called Ieuan Evans,' they said. 'You want to go and see him.'

When I did, it became obvious why so many had spoken about him in such glowing terms. Quite by chance his parents had been sitting in front of me at Stradey Park that day and I made a point of introducing myself at the end of the match. 'You must be very proud of him,' I said. 'He's got a great future.'

Such a prediction did not require any powers of clairvoyance. Nor did you need to be a genius to appreciate that here was a young man of immense potential, and even if sport is strewn with examples of those who never fulfil it, I had no doubt about this lad. The question was not whether he would play international rugby but when.

In Wales we are quick, sometimes too quick, to put rugby players on a pedestal only to find that, all too often, they don't match our expectations. For a long time now, Ieuan has been on the highest pedestal of all and not even a cruel series of broken bones has knocked him off it.

He is truly a great player. Great tends to be a carelessly overused word in the vocabulary of modern sport and I certainly do not use it lightly. There are not many great players but there can be no denying that Ieuan Evans would have been a great player in any era. His electrifying pace and deft change of direction have brought thousands of spectators and viewers to the edge of their seats the world over. It is a rare gift and one which only the greats in any sport possess.

Had Ieuan been born a generation earlier and played in the seventies – a decade which brought Wales three Grand Slams and five Triple Crowns – he would have had enough opportunities to have pushed his reputation to still greater heights.

In some respects he has succeeded despite being in a team which, for the most part, was never quite able to give him the quality of support which we tended to take for granted during the seventies, and yet his record, eclipsing the one Gerald and I set, is there for all to see. It is no coincidence, therefore, that some of his very best rugby was played on successive Lions tours in Australia and New Zealand.

When I saw him for the first time all those years ago, I did not readily appreciate that one day he would be up there with the best in his field. There are some fine British and Irish wings, like Rory Underwood and Simon Geoghegen, but Ieuan has been a match for them all, including the French flyer Patrice Lagisquet and, of course, David Campese.

The important thing is to be renowned by your peers the world over and in that respect Ieuan stands out among contemporary Welsh players. He is, however, much more than an excellent player whose courage has taken him through savage setbacks. The sheer desire to play for his country is a quality which has pulled him through those horrendous injuries to his foot early last season.

As a captain who cared for his team and his country, he became an inspirational figure for young and old alike. That he carried out his many responsibilities with an unfailing dignity, even in the painful aftermath of having the job snatched from him, speaks volumes for the man and his character. What he wanted, more than anything, was to captain Wales at the last World Cup.

Ieuan Evans will go down in history as a great ambassador for Wales and for rugby union all over the world. I am proud to be associated with this, the story of his life to date. The last chapter of his playing career has still to be written and as the game rockets off into the unknown, people of his calibre ought to be in the cockpit to ensure that it doesn't run out of control.

Drwy gydol Hydref 1984, roedd pawb am sôn wrtho i am chwaraewr ifanc newydd allai redeg fel y gwynt ac ochr-gamu fel Gerald Davies. 'Ieuan Evans yw ei enw fe,' medden nhw, 'rhaid i ti fynd i'w weld e.'

Pan es i yn y diwedd, fe ddaeth hi'n amlwg beth oedd y rheswm dros y brwdfrydedd. Gellid gweld ar unwaith fod yma wr ifanc o botensial arbennig, a doedd gen i ddim amheuaeth o'r dechre y byddai'n cyrraedd y brig. Nid *a* fyddai'n chwarae i Gymru oedd y cwestiwn, ond *pryd*.

Dawn brin yw honno sy'n dod â thorf gyfan at ymyl eu seddi. Ond roedd hi'n eiddo i Ieuan gyda'i gyflymdra trydanol a'i newid cyfeiriad syfrdanol. Byddai wedi cael ei gyfri gyda'r goreuon mewn unrhyw gyfnod, ac mae'r ffaith iddo lwyddo i ddisgleirio, a chael ei gydnabod led-led byd, mewn cyfnod llwm i rygbi Cymru'n gyffredinol yn fwy o gamp fyth.

Ond blodeuodd Ieuan i fod yn fwy na *chwaraewr* disglair yn unig. Fel capten a boenai am ei dîm a'i wlad, bu'n ysbrydoliaeth i'r hen a'r ifanc. Daeth ei ddewrder, yn ymladd nôl ar ôl cymaint o anafiadau difrifol, yn esiampl i bawb, ac mae'r ffaith iddo barhau i roi o'i orau gydag urddas, hyd yn oed ar ôl y siom aruthrol o golli'r gapteniaeth, yn adrodd cyfrolau am ei gymeriad.

Bydd Ieuan Evans yn hawlio'i le yn deilwng yn oriel anfarwolion y gêm, ac mae'n fraint arbennig i fi gael bod yn gysylltiedig, mewn ffordd fach â stori ei fywyd hyd yn hyn. Rhaid aros am y bennod ola' mae honno'n dal heb ei hadrodd. Ond rwy'n siwr o un peth – fod rygbi'n hynod ffodus fod pobl o gymeriad a phrofiad Ieuan yn dal yno â dylanwad wrth i'r gem wynebu her y cfnod newydd sy'n agor o'i blaen.

CHAPTER ONE

The Little Chinaman

When they sat down to pick the Wales team to play France at Cardiff Arms Park on Saturday, 21 March 1964, the selectors left one wing position open, almost as if they were expecting a new arrival.

Being men of great natural vision, the Big Five had their reason for keeping the French guessing that week as the Five Nations Championship reached its climax. It had nothing to do with the latest deliveries in the maternity ward of Morriston Hospital in Swansea.

As events turned out, Dewi Bebb passed a fitness test which was just as well considering that Mr and Mrs John Evans's little boy was, for about the only time in his life, a bit too fast out of the blocks for his own good.

He appeared that Saturday alright, but so far ahead of schedule that he was not exactly in perfect shape, weighing in at a 'skinny' six pounds two ounces. 'He was underweight and yellow with jaundice,' his mother, Margaret, recalls. 'I thought he was a little Chinaman!'

Mrs Evans had spent long periods in hospital during the months before the birth of her first child, her husband, John, taking her on the short journey from their home in the village of Velindre in the Swansea valley – a place famous for its tin-plate works as well as Jones the Bat, disgracefully restricted to opening the innings for England in just one match.

The Evans baby had not been due for another three weeks when Ieuan arrived in a rush, thereby giving the rugby world the earliest possible notice of his capacity for taking people by surprise. How appropriate that Ieuan Cennydd Evans should have been born not only on the day Wales were playing at the Arms Park but on the day they completed an unbeaten record in the championship, the only one that season.

A home draw against France, secured by Stuart Watkins's late try and Keith Bradshaw's conversion, gave them a share of the title with Scotland. Under current scoring values it would have been enough to ensure that the infant Ieuan started the first week of his life with Wales acclaimed as champions in their own right.

Elsewhere that third Saturday of March, thirty-one years ago, at least three other notables were celebrating birthdays in various parts of the country, among them a footballer of a different kind. Brian Clough, his playing career truncated by injury, had begun at the age of twenty-nine to learn the art of soccer management at Hartlepool. A young Michael Heseltine was busy brushing up his Tarzan act in opposition to the Labour Government headed by Harold Wilson. Lord Oaksey was still riding the odd winner at thirty-five and in Trinidad a boy by the name of Alvin Kallicharran had turned seventeen. Soon enough the West Indies batsman would provide a small boy in west Wales with one of the outstanding memories of his childhood – hooking Dennis Lillee for six during the 1975 World Cup final at Lord's.

By then Ieuan was up and running and, like boys the sports world over, he dreamt of emulating his idols who were then making their mark on the international stage of the seventies. For a while, he couldn't quite make up his mind who he was going to be, Gerald Davies or Johann Cruyff . . .

To say I was mad on sport as a boy would be a serious under-statement. Ever since I can remember, I wanted to play rugby, soccer, cricket, tennis and race cars, all invariably at the same time. Depending on the season and the mood, I would be Gerald or Johann or, just occasionally, George Best.

When it came to the really serious stuff of big-time matches after school on the fields behind my home, I was always Liver-pool, Leeds and Manchester United. In the summer I had my Bjorn Borg racquet and whenever we played cricket, I would be Viv Richards or Clive Lloyd. I saw them when the West Indies came to Swansea during that very hot summer of 1976 and on the day I was there they scored over 300 between them.

My earliest sporting memory is of my father taking me to see

Northern Ireland play Wales at the Vetch Field in Swansea. It was round about my sixth birthday and I remember being offered the choice of either going to the match or to Billy Smart's circus. It was a no-contest.

George Best was playing in my own backyard and I wasn't going to miss that for anything. While my mum took my sister, Non, to the circus, my dad and I went to the match. Now, I would never dream of putting myself in the same bracket as a genius such as George Best but we did have something in common besides playing on the wing.

We were both fairly small, or in my case very small. In fact, I was so small that my father used to blame my mother for giving birth to a dwarf! My ankles and wrists used to be so pitifully thin that if anyone had predicted that this scrawny specimen was going to play for Wales, he would have been carted off by men in white coats.

Ever since I can remember there were huge arguments in the Evans household over food. More often than not they would degenerate into blazing rows because I never used to eat properly and would resist all attempts to be forced into doing so. All I was ever interested in was the wrong sort of stuff – fish-fingers, beefburgers and beans and such like. Carmarthen wasn't exactly swarming with dieticians in those days. If it had been, they'd have been wasting their time with me.

My parents were forever trying to get me to eat the right kind of food which I dreaded. They tried foisting meat and eggs on me but I wouldn't touch them. I was so small that the rest of the boys used to call me 'The Mighty Atom'. I never lacked for guts, which was just as well considering that I was always having to tackle opponents who were invariably far bigger.

At Queen Elizabeth Grammar School in Carmarthen I was always the smallest boy in my class – all the way through to the sixth form when I began to fill out. By then I had taken a fair bit of punishment, and the other kids had all overtaken me in terms of size.

I used to get concussed quite often in those days and my mother would get very upset whenever I was knocked about. It wasn't much fun and it has left a mark which explains why I feel so strongly about the increasing emphasis that rugby now places on sheer physical power.

The proud boast that it is a game for all shapes and sizes doesn't really stand up any more. It was supposed to be a game for all sorts in my schooldays but it didn't save me from taking a few unnecessary batterings.

My concern has always been over the number of talented players the game loses simply because they are put off by their lack of size. Being battered during your formative years is not exactly designed to endear you to the sport. At that level, it is liable to be decidedly off-putting.

We had moved from Velindre to Cwmffrwd just outside Carmarthen when I played my first organised sport, at Idole County primary school. It wasn't rugby, but soccer. There were only twenty-four pupils there and so I had to go to a neighbouring village, Llangunnor, to play rugby.

I played scrum-half, outside-half, wing and a few other positions as well and I must have made an impression on someone because when I was ten years old they picked me as sub for the West Wales Under-11s against East Wales at the Arms Park. I had been there once before and it was an experience I shall never forget as long as I live.

Somebody up there must have been looking after me because the match in question turned out to be the one which produced what many regard as the try of the century – the one Gareth Edwards finished off for the Barbarians against the All Blacks in 1973.

Oddly enough, I can remember my father saying before the match that nobody wanted tickets for it because nobody knew what sort of team the Baa-baas were going to pick. They must have sold like hot-cakes once the team was announced because my dad couldn't get two together.

My seat was at the Taff end of the North stand, his was at the opposite end of the ground. It would be an exaggeration to say I couldn't see a thing but I was so small and I sank so far into my seat that I couldn't see the near touchline. I didn't see much of the Edwards try but I remember seeing Phil Bennett making it all possible with those wonderful sidesteps in front of his own posts.

I could hardly believe my luck – not that I was able to appreciate it at the time. I had seen my first game at the Arms Park and it turned out to be one of the greatest matches in the history of the game. In my blissful ignorance, I thought all games were like that. Little did I know!

It left an indelible impression. I'd been to see this magical acre of ground, I'd seen the legends – Gerald and Gareth – at work and I wanted to go back for more. Never in my wildest dreams did it occur to me that the next time I went back there it would not be as a spectator but as a player.

Back home, my next step was to captain the under-12 side at school. My rugby life then went on hold to such an extent that I turned to soccer instead. I joined Llanelli Football Club, played as striker and scored quite a few goals. I loved my soccer, still do, and I can see now how it helped me as a rugby player. It gave me two priceless attributes. It taught me balance and it gave me the vision to see the pitch as a whole – a sort of built-in radar screen which told me roughly who was where at any given time.

Those were wonderful days and, as a Welsh speaker, I couldn't have wished to have been brought up anywhere else in the world than in and around Pontardulais, initially, and then Carmarthen. It wasn't until my dad's job took us across the Severn bridge that I came to appreciate that there is no place like home.

We spent six months at Alveston, near Bristol, and I think it is fair to say I hated every minute of it. They called me 'Taff' at school, which wasn't very original. I didn't mind that but I did mind the impression they gave me in that part of the West of England that they didn't have a particularly high regard for anyone from South Wales.

Safely back home and still the smallest boy of my age by some inches, I began to make more progress as an athlete than a rugby player during my first year at grammar school. I won the Victor Ludorum, winning the javelin, the long jump and the 100 metres. I missed the 200 metres because the long jump was still in progress when they came under starter's orders.

Most of my school reports were of the 'could-do-better' variety, which was more than could have been said about my rugby until I reached the fifth form when it began to blossom. I had grown at long last and suddenly found myself the main man. I began to think I might possibly be able to do something after all.

Roy Bergiers, the school rugby master who had hit the heights as a centre with Llanelli, Wales and the Lions, must have been suitably impressed because he did something which was unheard of. He picked me, a fifth former, to play outside-half in the annual match against the old boys whose team included Ray Gravell, the man Twentieth-Century Fox couldn't buy!

Later, in my third year in sixth form, I captained the first XV throughout an unbeaten season. One match stood out, against Sir Thomas Picton School, which brought me up against the schoolboy star of the time, Kevin Morgan, who went on to play for Llanelli and Northampton. I had a good game playing opposite him in the centre. Another match which stood out happened to be the only one out of almost thirty that season which we didn't win.

A 13–13 draw against Gwendraeth Grammar School was the only blemish on an otherwise perfect record. We had beaten them comprehensively at home but the return match left us feeling we had been robbed by some rather dubious decisions made by the Gwendraeth referee. My father had a bit of a running battle with him and, over the years, I've had a running argument with Allan Lewis, then the school coach at Gwendraeth, who would have such a big influence on my career with the Scarlets.

There were other games during which I would beat four or five opponents and score tries. It was as if everything had suddenly fallen into place. I put together a string of performances, running in tries from 60 and 70 yards, beating five, six and sometimes seven opponents along the way.

I began to take my rugby so seriously that I would play three matches every Saturday – one for the school in the morning, a youth match in early afternoon and then I would be dragged off at half-time to play for Carmarthen Quins in what was then the West Wales League. It may all have been highly irregular given the restrictions on schoolboy players but I would have played four matches on Saturdays had there been more hours in the day. I was a very young eighteen, mentally and physically.

My name started to appear in the local paper. As a stand-off I scored a try against Waunarwlydd from 85 yards, taking a pass from a line-out and beating three men. I was then lucky enough to clinch the match and with it Quins' promotion by dropping a goal from 35 yards, as unusual then as it would be now.

Never at any stage was I daft enough to think that one day I might play for Wales. My aspirations were aimed at a much lower level. I thought I might be a half-decent player. I never really believed I would be anything more than that.

Luckily, I had a father who was always there to offer gentle encouragement without ever forcing his views down my throat. My dad had played first-class rugby on the wing for clubs in Wales and England, for Aberavon and Bedford. He knew more than a bit about it, therefore, and although I didn't know it at the time, because he never told me, he thought I had the ability to go far. He has been a major influence but never in the least bit pushy. He would never dream of going into the bar and start bragging about his son the way some fathers do.

However, the fact that I had a great bunch of mates and that I liked nothing better than going out on the town was not doing much for my future as a budding rugby player. Nor did a whole lot of pasties, beefburgers and Double Diamond do much for my athletic prowess. Not surprisingly, it had a mushrooming effect on my body fat. The time would come when I would have to curtail my social life if I was to discover how far I could really go. Unfortunately, it took a nasty accident and a rollicking from the old man before the penny began to drop.

CHAPTER TWO

The Carmarthen Cowboy

One of the more extraordinary aspects of Ieuan Evans's often fractured career is that he made it to the top at all, let alone stayed there for the best part of ten years. His overall record – more than 200 tries in fewer than 300 matches – would have been still more imposing had a whole series of savage blows not torn huge chunks out of it.

Almost invariably, they struck with a cruel sense of timing, every wretched twist of fate arriving, or so it seemed, just as Evans was about to raise his career to a higher plane. Their cumulative effect would have ruined a player of lesser calibre long before the worst blow of all – the grotesque ankle dislocation which tested a surgeon's skill and an athlete's courage as they can rarely have been tested before.

By then he had had to overcome not one shoulder dislocation but five, an average of one a year, which took such a toll that it is no exaggeration to estimate the cost in terms of lost caps as high as twenty-plus. The first dislocation forced him to postpone the launch of his international career by fully sixteen months. It happened towards the end of a glittering debut for the Barbarians at Newport, barely a fortnight before he was due to win his first cap, against Fiji at the Arms Park.

Two of his first five seasons in senior rugby had to be completely written off and it required a touch of the miraculous that he should only lose half of the 1994–95 season, confounding all those – some of them from within the medical profession – who feared he would never play again.

The first bad break came in the shape of a broken leg playing for Carmarthen Quins in August 1983.

What was supposed to have been my first season in the big time ended before it could begin. A supposedly harmless pre-season seven-a-side tournament went so horribly wrong that I finished up slumped outside a Carmarthen public house, my left leg in plaster, waiting for my father to take me home. I had so much to gain during that first season after leaving school and it had all been reduced to nothing.

One of the Llanelli officials, Glan Tucker, had suggested that I would be given a trial with the Scarlets. In my excitement at such a prospect, I thought a little pre-season outing would not go amiss, which only goes to show how wrong you can be.

Everything went smoothly enough until I tried to pass an opponent, caught my foot in a rut on the pitch and went down like the proverbial sack of potatoes. The rub-a-dub man came on and got to work with his magic sponge before making a startling prognosis which would have cheered me up no end had it not been for the pain in my leg. 'You're alright, now,' he said, trying to help me back to my feet.

He may have felt there was nothing wrong but I didn't need to be Einstein to work out that something wasn't quite right. I simply couldn't get back up again. They carted me off to hospital where they gave me the bad news. I felt pretty sorry for myself but not half as sorry as after my dad had finished with me. Not to put too fine a point on it, he was furious.

I had just put the crutches in the back of the car when he tore into me: 'What the hell are you playing at, wasting your time in a Mickey Mouse competition like that?' And so it went on in that vein, the most severe rollicking I have ever had in my life and that's saying something. When I'd taken as much as I could, I had a go back. 'Who do you think I am, an international?'

I'll never forget saying that and I'll never forget his answer. 'You could be,' he said. 'But not if you go on like this.' It made me think. I knew I was a fair player and I'd always dreamt of playing for Wales and here was my father telling me that I had it in me to make it more than a dream. It was enough to make me change my attitude. I didn't know how good I was but I was never going to be content to be a big fish in a small pond. Now

I was determined to see whether I could make something of myself.

I had left school with eight O- and three A-levels and I was still on crutches some six weeks later when I began a three-year geography course at Salford University. After Carmarthen, Manchester was a culture shock and a severe one at that. It was a difficult time but it would have been a great deal more difficult had I not been able to get home most weekends once the leg was back in one piece.

That summer I made sure I gave every sevens competition a wide berth. I also made sure I had the time of my life. Carmarthen has eighty-one pubs, or it used to have back then, and there were times, most frequently in the early hours of a Sunday morning, when I felt as though I'd crawled round every one of them! When I wasn't knocking them back, I was working to make sure I had enough to pay for my beer.

I alternated between being a farm labourer and a brickie's mate. I milked cows, shovelled manure, cut bricks and made hay in more ways than one. My father having baled me out twice, I had to do something to stop myself drifting back into the red at the bank. I must confess that Llanelli RFC gave me quite a bit of unwitting assistance in that respect.

They paid my travelling expenses from Salford and it's a long way from the north of England to the west of Wales. I would claim a rail fare and do my level best to hitch a lift back home, which meant getting up at six in the morning to catch the lorries as they left Manchester going in all directions. Some of the consequences were hilarious.

One driver, for example, took a wrong turning and found himself heading towards Leeds, whereupon he dropped me off without a by your leave. So there I was, stuck on a motorway in the middle of the Pennines and not having a clue where I was – which doesn't say much for a student of geography. Luckily, someone stopped fairly quickly and took pity on me with a 'You can't stand there, mate. Could get run over.'

What with my army fatigue jacket, kitbag slung over my shoulder, long hair and unshaven appearance, I must have looked a right yob. I wouldn't have given me a lift, that's for sure! I would not advise anyone to hitch-hike nowadays because the risks are simply too great but, back then, I had some memorable journeys as well as the periodic nightmare.

The fastest one, just over four hours, involved only two lifts. The first took me a little way down the M6, the second all the way to Carmarthen. The worst journey, on a lousy day in mid-winter, took me thirteen hours to complete! It involved eighteen lifts, the majority of them no more than ten miles and I must have walked almost that far following my thumb through Altrincham, Sale, Wrexham and all the way down through Wales to Llandovery.

Never mind, it meant I had a few bob in my pocket. The most important question for me at the time was to ask who was coming out on Saturday night. I'd go out with the boys at least once a week, old school-mates like David Roberts and Malcolm Rees, Nigel Morris, Chris Bowen, Marino Conti, alias the Mad Eyetie, Simon Rogers and Stephen Bryant, who still plays prop for Carmarthen Quins.

I was too busy having the time of my life to worry about training. I've always been more horizontal than laid-back so it was hardly surprising that my first experiences with Llanelli should leave me flat on my back and feeling as sick as the proverbial parrot. I was so terribly overweight and unfit that the Scarlets were on the verge of showing me the door before I could really show them what I could do if somebody gave me the ball and a bit of space.

During my first night at the club they had me doing sprints up a hill with the rest of the hopefuls pulled in from miles around. After three sprints, I threw up and made some feeble excuse about suffering from flu. I was the unfittest man in the squad by some distance. Allan Lewis, one of the coaches, sent me back to the dressing-room straightaway. 'You won't be going anywhere in this game,' he said. He was right, of course. But we still have a laugh about it.

They were about to tell me not to bother to come back. However, I'd played in the first trial and they had asked me back to play in the second so they decided to give me the benefit of the doubt, at least until they could see how many times I'd throw up in the second, much stiffer trial. They didn't think I would fit into their running style but I scored two tries and managed to force them into a rethink.

I must admit I did cut down on my beer intake but not by much. I could always sweat off the beer but my lack of condition primarily stemmed from the age-old habit of eating the wrong stuff. I was still into pasties, chips, burgers and so forth and, to make matters worse, the local paper did a piece on me because I'd admitted being partial to trash food.

That didn't go down too well at Stradey but, despite everything, they offered me a place in their squad for that season without the guarantee of any games. I thought they were playing a bit hard to get so I bucked the system and decided to have a look around at the alternatives. My father took me to see Brian Thomas, the director of playing affairs at Neath, after they had played a missionary match at Resolven. He offered me a trial at The Gnoll a few days later when I took my place alongside another newcomer, Paul Thorburn, and I scored five tries from the centre.

So there I was, training on alternate nights with two of the biggest clubs in the country. Neath picked me for their home match against Pontypridd on 22 September and I managed to score two of their three tries. It had not gone unnoticed at Stradey. 'Good game on Saturday?' Gareth Jenkins, the coach, asked, when I reported for training. 'Aye, not bad,' I said. Anyway, the following Wednesday I was playing in the centre for the Scarlets, at home to Gloucester, and who should I be playing alongside but one of my heroes, the one and only Ray Gravell. Every time I see him in company, he says: 'Now, tell them. Who did you play your first game for Llanelli with? And didn't I look after you? Who said you would play for Wales? They said I was mad at the time, but didn't I say: "Now, here's a boy who's going to play for Wales"?'

I'll never forget turning up to play in that first match, walking into the dressing-room and hearing someone singing in the toilet. The door was open, he had a fag in his mouth, was reading the programme and singing Dafydd Iwan songs. This was a living legend, the man who used to eat soft centres, the nicest person you could wish to meet. What a shame they don't have characters like 'Grav' around any more.

Anyway, the following Saturday it was back to Neath and straight into my first run-in with an international wing, David Trick of Bath, then among the best and fastest around. We hadn't been playing long when he signalled that he was going to run round me. Instead I ran round him, with the help of a hand-off. I wasn't in his class, really. I wasn't a flyer, by any stretch of the imagination, for the simple reason that I wasn't fit enough.

After flitting between the two clubs, I had to make my mind up the following week because it was Neath against Llanelli at The Gnoll and each club wanted me to play against the other. Before Neath had finalised their team, I told them I was joining Llanelli. Brian Thomas was very disappointed but gracious enough to wish me well. As it turned out, we lost a thriller, 31–28, but only because one man, as usual, made all the difference.

I had scored a good try when Jonathan Davies intervened with one of his dinky drop-outs followed by a big break. His pass gave Elgan Rees a clear run in for the winning try although my inexperience made it easy for him. Instead of staying out with my wing, I came in to challenge Jonathan. Had I stayed put, our full-back, Martin Gravelle, could have taken Jonathan and Elgan would then have had to beat me.

Nobody held it against me, and after a handful of matches I was running out to play a part in another of those great Stradey occasions which come to pass every so often. The Australians were on their way to a Grand Slam tour of the British Isles when they called in at Stradey before playing their Test against Wales. At the time I was jousting with Edward Ellis for the left-wing position. Phil Lewis had made the right-wing spot his own but his selection for Wales that Saturday allowed me to take his place against the Wallabies.

It turned out to be another famous Llanelli win over a

touring team, maybe not as famous as the epic win over the 1972 All Blacks but pretty famous all the same. In all truth, I had a poor first half before managing to redeem myself, not by scoring a try but by running in the opposite direction to make a tackle which ultimately clinched the match. Matt Burke, the Wallaby full-back, had broken clear from halfway. Luckily, I caught him from behind on the twenty-two and their last chance had gone.

I knew all about how Delme Thomas and his team had beaten New Zealand. I was eight years old at the time and pretty upset that my dad had decided, not unreasonably in retrospect, that I had to spend the day in school and, therefore, he couldn't take me to the match. Max Boyce had sung about how they drank the pubs dry and I reckon my father did his bit in that direction. I'd read all about the match in the years since but not even that could prepare me for what I experienced the day we beat the Wallabies.

No club has a greater capacity for beating touring teams and that had been shoved down our throats in the weeks before the match. We were only too happy to embrace it and when the day arrived the atmosphere crackled to such an extent that you could sense something special was going to happen. We met at Ashburnham Golf Club and Phil May, as captain, hammered home the point that history was within our grasp and that this was too good a chance to let slip.

Alright, so it was only the Australian mid-week team but you can only beat what's there and it was still an amazing experience. Naturally, the Aussies felt more than a touch miffed about losing. They don't like it when anyone beats them and this time they were annoyed with the referee and with some of our tactics. Too bad. We were too busy having a good time to let anything spoil the occasion.

Thankfully, my sense of direction on the field was rather better than it was off it. Once, for example, I travelled down from Salford to a mid-week match at Bristol and got so hopelessly lost that I ended up walking miles to the ground. The rest of the team began to accept it as a common occurrence. I tended to be a bit of a space cadet in those days, living in my own world.

They used to call me 'The Carmarthen Cowboy', but in one sense I knew where I was going even if nobody else believed me.

It was as if I was making up for lost time. I kept scoring tries and before the end of the season some influential rugby writers were beginning to push my cause. John Billot of the *Western Mail* seemed to take a shine to me, and my first opportunity to show what I could do in a Welsh jersey arrived in the final weeks of that first season with my selection for Wales 'B' against Spain at Bridgend. I was on a field trip to Denmark with the university which meant that my parents had to contact me and the Welsh Rugby Union fly me home which certainly impressed the other students.

We had a powerful team, with players like Paul Moriarty of Swansea and, not for the first time that season, I found it all a bit too easy. I did something I had never done in a proper match before and scored six tries but, in all honesty, I didn't really have to work very hard for them. The other wing, Arthur Emyr, now the Head of Sport at BBC Wales, had scored three himself before I barely had time to blink.

My opposite number on the Spanish side was a bull of a man whom I only had to tackle twice – which was twice more than I would have liked. Fortunately, he wasn't able to stop me but I can never thank Martin Gravelle enough for what he did that evening. In the ten years since, I have never had the good fortune to play with a full-back quite like him. He may not have played for Wales but he was a magnificent player. When it came to spotting a gap and putting you clean through it, there was nobody to touch him. The timing of his pass was so perfect that he kept putting me into space, just as he had done for Llanelli all season. As an attacking full-back, he had few peers. It was just a shame that he didn't have the physical presence to justify his elevation to the highest level. What Martin had was style and style was what Llanelli was, and still is, all about.

Being at the western end of the Welsh rugby belt may be a disadvantage in terms of attracting sponsorship but it is a positive advantage in providing a huge reservoir of support throughout what used to be Pembrokeshire and Carmarthenshire. It makes

Llanelli the biggest club in Wales, a club which more than any other instils players with an *esprit de corps* normally associated with the most adventurous French teams, or at least it did until a couple of seasons ago.

At Llanelli I knew I would always get plenty of ball and that playing for them would be the fastest route to a cap. The backs at Stradey held all the aces. The forwards were simply there to provide us with the ball and we were expected to score tries. They demand a lot at Llanelli but they have a right to do so and they reward us with a support second to none. No matter how far afield we went in those days, our travelling support would, more often than not, outnumber the home club's.

Style means more than how you play the game. It also means how you behave when you play it. The first time I played at Twickenham, against the Harlequins, I scored a try from ninety-eight yards. I'd been chosen at full-back and I was standing so far behind the rest that I was doing my Peter Shilton impersonation between the posts when the ball came my way. I picked it up, beat a couple of men, chipped over the top, dribbled ahead and scored beneath the posts.

I was too knackered to do anything for the next half hour but my delight was such that I couldn't contain myself. I remember making a whole show of scoring, fist in the air and all the trappings. Gwyn Walters, the famous referee and great man of Stradey, was watching and afterwards he chastised me gently, pointing out that it really wasn't the done thing to display such exuberance. I took his point.

In that same match, I had another of my rollickings, this time from the captain, Phil May. I had been having a running battle with a big lump of a lad on the Quins wing by the name of Simon Hunter. At one stage it got a bit hairy and Phil took me to one side and gave me a very stern two-word order: 'Grow up!'

A more emotional conversation had taken place between us at the end of that first season. We had reached the Cup final against Cardiff and there were only minutes left when David Evans chipped over me and Gerald Cordle ran through unchallenged for what would almost certainly be the winning try. I cried. I thought I had let everyone down and Phil, like the good captain he was, came across to console me in the corner while the conversion was being lined up. I was just about inconsolable. Nobody was more relieved than me when Gary Pearce won it for us with his never-to-be-forgotten drop goal in injury time.

By the end of that season I had established myself as the club's number-one wing. I was getting fitter but I had a long way to go and it wasn't until Peter Herbert joined the club and revolutionised attitudes to fitness that I finally began to get to grips with it. By then I'd had another summer in paradise. July was my party month and I tackled it with such enthusiasm that when the sevens season got under way the following month I must have been carrying a bit of excess baggage.

The point was rammed home by a wag in the crowd at the Snelling sevens at Rodney Parade in Newport. 'Hey, Evans,' he called out. 'Just hit 'em with your gut . . .'

CHAPTER THREE

The Cold Shoulder

Tuesday, 22 October 1985, dawned without the merest hint of a warning that it was to be one of the more traumatic days in the life of the future captain of Wales. What began as just another humdrum day in the lecture room at Salford University would end in calamitous circumstances in the casualty ward of the Royal Gwent Hospital in Newport.

An emergency summons to represent the Barbarians gave Ieuan a ready excuse to shoot back home in such a hurry that, for once, he dared not risk thumbing his way down the motorways. His initiation into the most exclusive of all touring clubs proved to be the prelude to an accident which wrecked Welsh plans to cap him without further delay.

Phil Bennett had already acclaimed him as 'the new Gerald Davies'. Earlier that year, Evans's performance in the first Welsh Cup tie, for Llanelli against Llandovery, had the former Lions captain rushing into print in glowing terms. 'Some players have class written all over them and this kid has class as well as tremendous acceleration,' Bennett wrote. 'I believe the Scarlets have unearthed a new Gerald Davies.'

The first few weeks of the new season could hardly have gone any better. I had struck up a productive centre partnership at Stradey with a promising young player by the name of Nigel Davies and the newspapers were touting me for greater things. And then, not for the first time, fate took a hand and decreed otherwise.

I was in the middle of a morning lecture at the start of my final year at Salford when I took a phone call from Gareth Davies in his capacity as a Barbarians committee man. Robert Ackerman had withdrawn because of injury and they wanted me to take his place in the centre against Newport. 'Can you get down in time?' Gareth was asking me and I said: 'You bet I can. Count me in.'

The chance of playing for the Baa-baas was not one to be missed and when I explained my position to the authorities at the university I don't think they understood what I meant. I was thrilled to bits at the prospect, so I made my excuses and caught the first available train. I went straight from the station at Newport to the ground and met the rest of the team.

Bleddyn Bowen played alongside me in the centre and we had a brilliant attacking full-back in Huw Davies who, despite his name, was then an England international. I had scored two tries, laid on a third and was in the process of making another for Huw when it happened. I went round the opposite wing and flipped a pass back inside in the split second or so before I ran out of space. As I did so, my marker grabbed me by the arm and swung me round.

I was in too much agony to notice that Huw had taken my pass and scored. Nobody had any reason to believe I was hurt so, as I sat there on my backside, a few of my team-mates slapped me on the back, not realising that my right shoulder was hanging off. They tried to put it back into place on the pitch to no avail. I then had to wait for what seemed like an eternity for the ambulance to arrive and when it did they wouldn't give me any relief for the pain.

As if that wasn't bad enough, I also felt distinctly neglected. It would not have been much to expect somebody from the Barbarians Football Club to have come with me to the hospital or, at least, to have inquired as to how I was. Gareth Davies did come to the hospital once the after-match formalities were over. My injury was serious enough to have put the kibosh on my immediate prospects of an international cap and yet still none of the Baa-baas hierarchy thought it worth asking me about how I felt. I was pretty annoyed about that for a long time.

Their failure to accord me that simple courtesy has always rankled. I thought the way they treated me was a disgrace. Their pomposity disappointed me and perhaps it is no great surprise that they should now be struggling to attract the top British players. They gave me the impression that they took us for granted. They never seemed to miss a chance to ram it down our throats that we should feel privileged to be invited to play for the Barbarians.

I certainly felt privileged but I also felt badly treated. As a result of that first experience, I changed my attitude. I thought: 'If you're going to use me, then I'm going to use you.' I did play for the Barbarians subsequently, but only because it was in my interests to do so. For instance, when they asked me to play at Leicester that Christmas I took advice before accepting. It suited me to play because I had to prove my fitness for the forthcoming Five Nations series. Otherwise, I wouldn't have bothered and there have been one or two occasions since when I've turned down invitations to play for them.

I got home to Carmarthen that night purely by chance and certainly no thanks to the Baa-baas. David Newton, a friend of mine from back home, had watched the match and then called at the hospital to see how I was. He waited a few hours until they put the shoulder back in place and then gave me a lift home.

At least I got a Barbarians jersey out of it. You are only entitled to keep it if you play against international opposition but I don't think they had the heart to ask for mine back. It's a shame that my début should have left a sour taste because I admire the Barbarian ethos about entertaining at all costs. Just being asked to play for them filled me with awe, but they make it clear that if you abuse the club, you'll never be asked to play for them again. Unfortunately, that's been quite a turn-off for a number of players.

The first contact I had from the Barbarian club after the Newport match was when the honorary secretary, Geoffrey Windsor-Lewis, asked me to play in the showpiece Christmas fixture at Leicester. By then I had got over my dejection and my shoulder trouble, or I thought I had. Little did I know that it was going to be a recurring problem which would have a severe effect on curtailing my career.

Daft as it may sound, the initial damage to my shoulder was caused when I attempted a bicycle-kick during a knockabout game of soccer at university. I had to go to hospital and carry it around in a sling for three weeks, which did not go down at all well back in Llanelli. I had gone at least a fortnight without someone giving me a rollicking when Gareth Jenkins, the Scarlets coach, gave me a right going-over for being so stupid.

It took me the best part of two months to recover from the first dislocation. Thankfully, I picked up where I left off right away, scoring twice at Cross Keys just before Christmas and again in the traditional Boxing Day game against London Welsh. I then headed for Leicester and my reunion with the Barbarians and again people were telling me that I only had to keep clear of injury to make the Welsh team for the start of the Five Nations.

This time I failed to negotiate the first twenty minutes. Again it all happened innocently enough. Stuart Potter, the Leicester centre, tried to take me on the outside. I had him in my sights and made the tackle, only for his knee to catch me on the shoulder. It took three people to put it back into place, one doctor sitting on my chest while two others completed the operation.

The entire Five Nations championship, starting with England at Twickenham, had been wiped out at a stroke. John Devereux was chosen instead and all I remember about that night at Leicester was peering out through a haze of pain-killers at a television set and feeling quite impressed that I was considered important enough to warrant a mention on *News at Ten*.

In the months that followed my weight ballooned above fourteen stone, which gives an accurate idea of how I coped. It was a case of saying: 'There's nothing I can do about it so we may as well have a party.'

There wasn't anything to be gained by brooding over the fact that I had almost certainly missed out on eight caps, the Fijian match, the Five Nations and the South Pacific tour at the end of that season. For a while I felt very sorry for myself and sorrier still when I realised how difficult life can be, especially when I had a dissertation to write as the climax to my degree course.

My subject matter was entitled 'Social and Economic Change in the Tawe Valley, 1951–1981'. My mother had to draw all the maps for me and type all the rest. Finishing university gave me the opportunity to train more regularly, and that summer Llanelli allowed me to put my geography degree to some practical use by setting off on a three-week tour of Australia and Fiji.

It was a really good trip despite a bloodbath of a match against the Fijian national team in Suva. Fiji was marvellous, except for eighty minutes of pure mayhem on the pitch. To say they knocked seven bells of you-know-what out of us would not be overstating the case and I'll never forget seeing Phil May being brutally chopped down in a line-out, and all because of Laurance Delaney.

Laurance was having some real gyp from the opposition prop at every line-out. He kept saying to May, our captain: 'I'm going to have to let him have one, Phil.'

'No, don't do that, Laurance. It'll be alright.'

'No good, Phil. He's got to have one. Next line-out, I'll have him good and proper.'

'Alright, then.'

True to his word, Laurance let him 'have one'. Ironically, Phil caught the backlash. One of the other Fijian forwards responded to the Delaney dig with such a bang that Phil went down like a giant redwood. Fortunately, the nasty stuff didn't spoil my solitude out on the wing and when I returned home late that August I had a feeling that 1986–87 was going to be my season.

It started with a special match in memory of the late, great Carwyn James and I was lucky enough to score three tries from the centre, playing against some star-studded opposition. I was sharper than I'd ever been. Peter Herbert had taken over fitness training at Stradey and at last I was in some sort of shape, but again not as good as I ought to have been.

By that time I had established myself as the number-one wing at the club. Now I was battling it out with Glen Webbe for Wales, and the absence of any pre-Christmas internationals meant I had to wait until the New Year. The cap which had eluded me until now went on eluding me even after I had been named in the Wales team for the opening match against Ireland at the Arms Park. How ironic that after all the shoulder trouble my cap should still be in a deep-freeze, snow forcing the match to be postponed. And so I had to wait another fortnight for as tough a baptism as anyone could wish for, France at the Parc des Princes. I was chosen on the left wing and although we lost, 16–9, I felt we would probably have won had it not been for Paul Thorburn breaking his collar bone just before half-time. The game passed in a flash and I felt reasonably pleased with my contribution but, naturally enough, no such occasion would have been complete without the obligatory rollicking.

This one came about because, despite waiting so long for my cap, I was nowhere to be seen when the president of the Welsh Rugby Union, Des Barnett, was congratulating me on winning it at the formal presentation ceremony. While that was going on in a private room upstairs at the Hotel Concorde St Lazare, I was downstairs in the bar celebrating with a couple of friends from Carmarthen whom I had spotted as we came off the bus returning from the stadium.

Anyway, the upshot of it all was that the president had to send out a search party for me in the shape of the late Rod Morgan. He was not at all amused to find me in the bar when the president had been calling me forward along with the other new cap that afternoon, Kevin Phillips from Neath. Kevin had received his cap when I rushed upstairs and made a rather breathless entrance amid titters of laughter from the rest of the team.

I tried it on for size and discovered it was slightly less than a perfect fit. I wore it for a while, as is the custom, and then made sure I tucked it safely away in my bedroom before we all left for the after-match dinner. I took it home and gave it to my parents, never imagining that some eight years later the Welsh Rugby Union would be promising another cap to mark my fiftieth appearance.

At last I had achieved my great ambition and a fortnight later I was achieving another, helping Wales beat England at the Arms Park which is probably the only good thing to be said about that particular match. It was controversial, even by Anglo-Welsh standards, right from the start when a punch from Wade Dooley, alias the Blackpool Tower, broke Phil Davies's cheekbone. It did nothing to improve his looks at a time when he needed all the help he could get in that direction!

There had been some bad blood in the press during the build-up and some of that spilt on to the pitch. I don't know whether England were wound up too tight but their captain, Richard Hill, was passionately anti-Welsh. It was even suggested that his wife, who was expecting at the time, stayed away from the match to ensure that the baby was born in England. Richard was a tremendous competitor – which was reflected in his track record, especially at Bath – but he was rather too aggressive on this particular occasion.

The match certainly didn't impress the hierarchy at the English Rugby Union. The following Monday they suspended four players for what they called over-vigorous play – Dooley, Gareth Chilcott, Graham Dawe and Hill. Some people have expressed surprise that the Welsh Rugby Union took no such action. Maybe the video would prove otherwise but I felt all the skulduggery came from the other side. There again, I am a little biased.

Relationships between the Welsh and English players at that time were not good. There hadn't been a Lions tour for six years and therefore they had virtually no opportunity to mix and get to know one another. Wade, I know, regretted what happened, not least because he had his police career to think about and I don't suppose hitting a fellow officer, as Davies was at the time, went down at all well with his chief constable.

In those days, the Welsh public took a home win over England for granted. Certainly, we had a great record then and there was no doubt that the Cardiff factor helped pull us through some very tight matches. There was a feeling that we could be forgiven losing to everyone else provided we beat England. It was a view which was given some regrettable credence by Clive Rowlands later that year in his role as our World Cup manager after we had been hammered by the All Blacks in the semi-final.

Someone asked him where Wales went from here and Clive replied with some relish: 'Back to beating England next season!'

It turned out to be a rather unfortunate remark because there is a great deal more to it than that. Everyone wants to beat England, of course, and nobody takes more satisfaction from that than I do but you also have to look at the big picture beyond that fixture. Any thoughts we had that year of a Triple Crown vanished up at Murrayfield where I came in for some stick from more than one source.

A twisted ankle forced me out of the match in the first half-hour by which time I'd had a pass, which was more than I got against England. Bobby Windsor, for one, was not the least bit impressed. The old Lions hooker from Pontypool is not backward at coming forward when it comes to slagging players off. He felt I should have scored and went blasting off about it, saying he'd heard that this Evans bloke was supposed to be quick, but he's not quick enough to catch a bus in bottom gear.

I remember the match for a more amusing exchange between the referee and our pack leader, Bob Norster. It concerned Peter Francis, the Maesteg prop who had been called into the match at the last minute after Stuart Evans had gone down with an injury. Our scrum was in all sorts of trouble from the start and poor Peter had been shoved up in the air when the ref, Keith Lawrence of New Zealand, said to Bob: 'I'm not happy with your loosehead prop.' Bob gave him a withering look and said in an agitated voice: 'You're not bloody happy . . .'

Unwittingly, Bob also provided another amusing moment during the next match, at home to Ireland. He was galloping towards the Irish line from their twenty-two and it looked as though nobody could stop him. Bob certainly thought so because he began to go through the full repertoire of celebrations ten yards from the line before he realised, to his horror, that he might not get there. I've never seen anyone change appearance so dramatically in a split second but he made it, if only just.

I scored my first try for Wales in the same match. Robert Jones made a break, Richie Collins popped up at his shoulder and gave me such a superb pass that all I had to do was catch it and roll over. It was one of the very few things we did right on an afternoon when Ireland proved, as they have done with alarming frequency, that there's no place like the Arms Park for an away win. We wrote it off as a bad job and vowed to beat them a few weeks later when it mattered a bit more, at the World Cup.

By then, after a few months on the dole, I had even got myself a job, working for the National Trust in their public relations department and tootling round the country in the little brown van which came with the appointment. I helped design various brochures for the Trust but I would be less than honest if I described the job as onerous. Suffice to say, I got a cracking tan that summer, became a crossword addict and generally had the time of my life.

CHAPTER FOUR

Whingeing Wallabies

Rather like those other well-known geography students, Christopher Columbus and Vasca da Gama, The Carmarthen Cowboy set off on his first overseas mission with all the eager anticipation of an explorer uncertain of what he would find on the other side of the world.

It would be the first of five such Antipodean adventures in the space of six years which would take him to the heights of achievement and the depths of despair; from a sense of elation to one of shame at witnessing a rugby nation collapse all around him.

The Land of the Long White Cloud would all too soon become the Land of the All Black Nightmare and Evans would be left wrestling with the grim conclusion that the best Welsh players of his time had been reduced to so much cannon-fodder. Worse still, they were to be subjected to the same degradation off the pitch as they were on it. Some may have been happy to jump ship. Evans's fierce pride in Wales and Welsh rugby made him scornful of those who took the easy way out, and yet his first experience of New Zealand offered no hint of the horrors which lay ahead.

The inaugural World Cup had opened on a golden autumn day in Auckland with the finest team of its generation mowing down Mario Innocenti and his brave but hopelessly outgunned rugby innocents from Italy. For Wales, it began a few days later against familiar opposition in a distinctly unfamiliar setting on the other side of the planet.

It didn't take a genius to work out why they call Wellington 'The Windy City'. How strange that we should be playing one of the home countries there, twelve thousand miles from home and kicking off at something like three o'clock in the morning,

39

British Summer Time. It would have been stranger still had the Irish been allowed to beat us at opposite ends of the world in a matter of weeks.

Being drawn together in the same pool alongside Tonga and Canada meant that we were both seeded to reach the knock-out stage when the real tournament began. Winning that first game was imperative if we were to go beyond the last eight. The winner could reasonably expect to be playing England in the quarter-finals whereas the loser was left with the booby prize of running smack into the pre-tournament favourites, Australia.

It turned out to be pretty much par for the course as Wales–Ireland matches go which meant it was anything but pretty. In other words, not much of a game but we scraped through it to win 13–6. If the locals found it a poor advertisement for the Five Nations championship, which they most definitely did, we couldn't have cared less.

We had a good team in the making which was going to get better fairly rapidly. In Jonathan Davies, Robert Jones, Adrian Hadley, Stuart Evans and David Young we had players who were not only the best in Wales but the best in Britain, by some way.

Others, like John Devereux, Paul Moriarty and Bleddyn Bowen, were fast developing into outstanding players in their own right. And yet the best of them were allowed to drift away, mostly to Rugby League. In Jonathan's case nothing was done to stop him which, in my opinion, was little short of a national scandal. He was, after all, a national treasure. When I think how little the Welsh Rugby Union did to keep him and how much they ought to have done, it fills me with a mixture of sadness and anger.

None of us was to know how soon we would be going our separate ways as we travelled a long way south to the next match at Invercargill, the oyster capital of the world; a place so remote that it almost feels as if it is at the bottom of the earth.

The Canadians were waiting there for us and whatever else they may have lacked as potential winners of the World Cup, it certainly wasn't a belief in their own ability. What they were going to do to Wales was nobody's business. We seized upon their bumptious attitude, turned it into a motivational force and set out to show them that talking a good game is one thing, playing it is rather different. The result was that we dominated the match from start to finish.

Invercargill may not be the number-one fun place in the universe, what with the tumbleweed blowing down Main Street, but Homestead Stadium offers a beautiful playing surface, as good as I have seen anywhere. When I first set foot on it, I remember thinking: 'If you can't play on this, you can't play on anything.'

I was not to know I would be lucky enough to score four tries, something which I later discovered no Welshman had done in a full international since Maurice Richards against England back in the sixties. I should have gone one better and finished with five. I would have done if a scissors move with John Devereux hadn't gone wrong.

Like two fishermen talking about the one that got away, we had a 'friendly' argument about it in the dressing-room until I finally took into account the fact that 'Crazy Horse' is considerably bigger than me. I therefore thought it wise, on this occasion, to agree to disagree.

The next match, Tonga at Palmerston North, took us from almost one end of New Zealand to the other. I sat this one out and Glen Webbe took my place. He scored a hat-trick, which would have been memorable enough in itself even without his producing one marvellous try from his own twenty-two. That he scored it without knowing a thing about it, because he was in such a concussed state, spoke volumes for his courage.

Glen was in such a bad way after the match that he kept looking round the dressing-room, a blankly bemused look on his face. The only person he recognised was his close friend, Mark Ring. 'Hey, Ringo,' he kept saying. 'Who are all these people? Where is this place, anyway?' And then he'd shake his head and mutter: 'What am I doing here?'

It was no wonder he didn't know where he was. He had been hammered by one of the most brutal tackles I have seen on a football field of any description. A Tongan Exocet is not at all a pretty sight. This bloke flew at him in such a blind fury that he might have taken Webbey's head off. How he was allowed to stay on the field, I shall never know.

We paid a high price for winning that one. Glen had been thoroughly checked at the local hospital before being allowed to rejoin the team, albeit briefly. He wasn't the only casualty unlucky enough to have to catch an early plane home. Stuart Evans, one of the cornerstones of our campaign, also had to be invalided out of the tournament because of a broken ankle.

John Rawlins, the Newport prop, came out as his replacement and never in the history of modern sport can anyone have gone so far for so little. After a thirty-two-hour flight from London, John stepped off the plane in Brisbane where we were preparing to play England in the quarter-final. He went straight to the training ground, changed and, after two minutes, he had torn a hamstring. Why he wasn't given at least the rest of the day to overcome his jet lag, only the management can explain. Poor John's chance of a bit of glory had gone before he could even win himself a cap.

The sudden front-row crisis caused a lot of head-scratching before the selectors unearthed a real gem on the spot. Dai Young, who had gone to the World Cup as a fan, responded to the emergency in such an amazing way for a nineteen-year-old that he gave the impression he had been playing international rugby all his life.

For the second time in a matter of months we had beaten England – and more decisively than during that ill-tempered affair back in Cardiff. The English had been touted as a good outside bet for the World Cup. Their early games had gone well but their performance that day in Brisbane was one of their worst. Once again, we had spoilt the party for them.

Robert Jones scored a great try and we won with something to spare: 16–3. As a game of rugby, it had precious little else to commend it and yet again the locals were quick to let us know they were less than fully appreciative of our combined efforts. Not to put too fine a point on it, they gave us an unmerciful slagging in the papers.

Again, it didn't say much for Five Nations rugby, not that we gave two hoots about that at the time. On the contrary, we felt rather pleased with ourselves. We were through to the semi-finals, we had built up a terrific team spirit and the management had given us two days off in Surfers' Paradise.

We made the most of it in the certain knowledge that whatever experience awaited us back at Ballymore in the semi-final on Saturday, it wouldn't be called paradise. Nobody was foolish enough to underestimate our task. Never before had I seen a team to compare with the All Blacks of '87, and I have not seen one since.

They had crushed everyone in sight – Italy, Fiji, Argentina, Scotland – and now it was our turn to stem the black tide, if only we could. Like the rest, we were overrun by the sheer intensity of their power game. I knew they were good. I didn't know they were *that* good. That side was something else.

No Welsh team had ever been beaten like that before. The scale of the defeat, 49–6, broke all records which lasted only until we played them again the following year when they made sure of topping fifty points on both occasions. It left us feeling shell-shocked. Not only did we lose the match, we lost the fight, too; a technical knock-out followed by a less than technical one.

The upshot of it all was that Anthony Buchanan, the Llanelli prop, went down in World Cup folklore as the first man to be knocked out of the main supporting bout a few minutes before his team were knocked out of the main event. Wayne Shelford should have been sent off for that.

Had the refereeing then been as strict as it was at the last World Cup in South Africa, there is no way he would have been allowed to reappear in the final the following week. The fact that he was the greatest No. 8 of his time ought to have had nothing to do with it.

There is no doubt that Huw Richards, the Neath second row who, as a champion sheep-shearer in New Zealand, obviously knew a thing or two about the opposition, started the whole ruckus. Buchanan's only crime was to get up at the wrong moment whereupon he was hit by a sledgehammer of a blow from Shelford, a real pearler which Mike Tyson would have been proud of.

Shelford should have walked even though Richards began the aggro by thumping one of the Whetton twins. Anthony got up in a way which made him a dead ringer for one of those rubbery weebils. He was certainly the right shape to bounce back up, but in no shape to continue. His legs had gone.

Phil Davies grabbed him. 'Hold on to me, Phil,' Anthony said, 'I can't stand up on my own.' Had he gone down a second time, they'd never have got him back up.

Richards was sent off and Shelford escaped any punishment for his part in a nasty little sideshow which, I hasten to point out, made not a blind bit of difference to the result of the other, more one-sided, contest. The mood afterwards was one of absolute despondency. We had been taken apart by a superior force but nothing could excuse the enormity of our beating.

The result took a lot of digesting and I remember traipsing off to the after-match function in no mood for any frivolity. I could not for the life of me understand why Paul Thorburn should stand up and start to sing 'Always look on the bright side of life'. Lead balloons have gone down better. We disowned him at that point. Paul had an unfortunate habit of doing the wrong thing at the wrong time, as we were to see the following year.

Meanwhile, back at the hotel in Brisbane, Bryan Robson, the England soccer captain, had seen it all on television. I had met him before, during my Salford days when I went for treatment at Manchester United's training ground. We had a long chat during which our hooker, Alan 'Thumper' Phillips, bet Bryan, then playing for a Brisbane club, that France would beat the Blacks in the final. Back home in Carmarthen a few months later, I switched the television on one night for *Question of Sport* and who should pop up wearing an All Black jersey but Bryan Robson.

Despite what they had done to us, it slowly began to dawn that, in a small way, we had lived to fight another day; that our World Cup wasn't quite over and that we could still finish third, albeit a long way short of the gold medal category.

We licked our wounds, regrouped and flew back to New Zealand for the third and fourth place play-off against Australia in Rotarua, an interesting town famous for its sulphuric geysers. For this one, we came armed with a sulphuric geyser of our own, stamped 'Made in Swansea'.

Richard Webster had taken the summer off from his job as a brickie to see a bit of the world and follow Wales. The All Blacks had had such an effect on our resources that he went straight in against the Wallabies for his first cap in exactly the way Young had done against England a little earlier.

On our way to Rotarua, the team coach stopped off in the middle of nowhere so the boys could have a little light relief. Bleddyn Bowen, as good a practical joker as any, came running out of the only shop for miles around, shouting to Richard that a reporter was on the phone from back home wanting to talk to him about his first cap.

Well, 'Webby' got into such a panic about it that he begged someone else to take the call on his behalf. When asked what message he wanted to be relayed, he said: 'Tell the boys in the Nag's Head I'll be home soon!'

Pitched into the back row at next to no notice, he made an immediate impact on the match which, of course, was typical of a player who would have been one of the greats but for such a terrible run of luck which meant something like five knee operations. The play-off started with David Codey, the Wallaby flanker, being sent off for kicking Richard.

It was my first international against Australia and they were all thoroughly ungracious about the whole thing. Their coach, Alan Jones, made some bitter comments before and after the match about the standard of refereeing. He also said that it was a nothing game and that nine times out of ten they'd have stuffed Wales, anyway.

It was also my first match against an opponent who would turn out to be an old foe, David Campese. Like the rest, he didn't have much to say afterwards. So much, I thought, for rugby's great freemasonry and all that business about sharing a beer with your opposite number. The Wallabies didn't make any effort to mix – not that we were too fussed about that.

We were very happy with our own company. We had finished third and it made a change to have the whole of New Zealand on our side. They wanted the Aussies beaten and they didn't much care how the beating came about or who administered it. As it proved, we gave them real value for money with a cracker of a match, Thorburn's touchline conversion of Hadley's corner try winning it for us in magnificent style, 22–21.

If nobody had been too sure whether the World Cup would be a good thing for the game, then there was no doubt by the end that it was here to stay. It was also clear that it would change the sport as never before, raising its profile worldwide and exposing it to millions around the globe, a great many of whom did not know one end of a rugby ball from the other.

For Wales, third place was better than anyone could have expected. We had beaten the tournament favourites and nobody will ever convince me that they didn't try. An Aussie team not trying? Do me a favour! We had picked ourselves up from the biggest dusting down we had ever had and played very well.

We took that team and that spirit through to the Triple Crown the following season, in what should have been a Grand Slam, starting at Twickenham. But one thought kept gnawing away at the back of my mind as we flew home from New Zealand: in twelve months' time we would have to go back there and play the All Blacks all over again. Not once, but twice . . .

CHAPTER FIVE

Merlin the Magician

Ieuan Evans has never been one for half measures. Even at such an early stage of his career as the start of his second international season, he had dislocated his right shoulder three times and scored six tries in one match on two occasions, twice more than any of his contemporaries, including Rory Underwood.

Six tries for Wales 'B', even if they were against a bunch of Spanish novices, and six more for Llanelli in the Welsh Cup suggested that his was a special talent. Four against Canada in a remote corner of New Zealand was fairly unusual, too, but it wasn't until Scotland came to Cardiff for the second round of matches in the 1988 Five Nations championship that the world at large realised that Evans was truly descended from the Welsh rugby gods.

Only someone from a celestial plane could have ghosted through the Scottish ranks the way he did that afternoon. This was more than an artful dodger with a nifty line in picking the most intricate lock. His wizardry sent Bill McLaren into such raptures that the disbelieving commentator acclaimed him as 'Merlin the magician'.

It was, by anyone's yardstick, one of the great individual tries of the decade. In one long, blinding flash he had given meteoric expression to that most hackneyed of rugby clichés, the one about Welsh flair. The eight-year-old boy who had been enchanted by his first visit to 'the magical acre' had earned the right of admission to its highest circle.

You can meet some very interesting people at Los Angeles international airport. Who should we bump into there, on our way home from the 1987 World Cup, but Tom Jones.

Disembarking from the Auckland flight for a thirty-six-hour

stopover, we found ourselves confronted by a queue at immigration which looked as though it was stretching halfway round California. I was resigned to spending most of the day shuffling along at six inches an hour until my companion, the ever-resourceful Mark Ring, decided he would speed the process up in his own inimitable way. In other words, we jumped the queue, by at least two hundred yards!

Not surprisingly, we got heckled by a heck of a lot of people and at one stage it appeared as if our impatience would cause a bit of a disturbance. Safely through passport control, we went for a stroll while waiting for the rest of the party to make their painstaking way through. We walked past a bar and Mark said: 'Look who's in there.'

If it wasn't Tom Jones, it was certainly his double. Anyway, before I know it, Ringo's gone straight up to him with an opening line which might have suggested that he'd known him all his life. 'How's it going, then, Tom?' he says, bold as brass.

I don't think Mr Jones knew exactly who we were, but he certainly recognised the badge on our blazers and knew where we had been playing. 'Congratulations on finishing third in the World Cup,' he said. 'Better than any of the other British teams.'

At this stage Mark was beginning to think that our chance meeting with the Jones boy would lead to a big party at Tom's place up in Beverly Hills and that he would push the boat out for the whole squad. I did not share his optimism, but that did not deter him from dropping enough hints about us having thirty-six hours to kill and not much to do.

Alas, no such invitation was forthcoming. In fact, Jones the Voice didn't even buy us a drink. We bought him several instead because Tom literally did not have two cents to rub together. He had just come back from celebrating his fiftieth birthday with family and friends in Pontypridd and apologised, a little awkwardly, for the fact that he 'didn't have a bean'.

Well, if royalty never carry anything as common as money around with them, why should Tom Jones be any different? He was with his wife and we ended up plying him with four or five beers. It was worth every single dollar if only to see the look on the faces of the other players as they walked past and saw us holding court. You could see them nudging one another and you could almost hear them saying: 'Look at Ieuan and Ringo with Tom Jones.'

Tom was diplomatic enough not to make any reference to the semi-final against the All Blacks and he was very wise to resist any urge to invite the Welsh team back to his place. Patriotism has its limits and I wouldn't have run the risk of turning thirty rugby players loose in my house. Never mind, it had been an amusing interlude on the long haul back to Carmarthen.

I enjoyed that summer like no other and, when September came round, I was ready for what would turn out to be the season of my life. The 1987–88 campaign was like no other and, I suppose, the same could be said, if for vastly different reasons, of the New Zealand tour which followed it. As coach, Tony Gray had a slightly laid back approach to the job which I, for one, found refreshing.

He believed implicitly in the Welsh way of playing and he gave the players a certain latitude to play it off-the-cuff. Such a policy paid off handsomely with the Triple Crown and, very nearly, the Grand Slam which we were to miss by the narrowest of margins.

Once upon a time when I was a small, under-nourished boy, Wales winning a Triple Crown was almost an annual event which, in those days, was no exaggeration. They had won it four times in a row towards the end of the seventies but then there had been nothing for nine long years. We had that at the back of our minds when we kicked off the Five Nations series at Twickenham in January. We could not have wished for a better start.

A memorable match for a variety of reasons – not least for Jonathan Davies giving Micky Skinner what must have been the biggest runaround of his life. The very large English blind-side flanker is a great sledger and he was at it right from the start, warning Jonathan that he was going to give him a 'real boshing' if he dared to go down the blind-side. 'Jiffy' didn't mind that one little bit. He had a natural arrogance on the field, a belief that he was the best and the opposition had better look out.

He didn't just leave Skinner floundering, he made a complete fool of him. 'Jiffy' toyed with him from start to finish. Before the end he had taken the Micky out of Skinner so often that if anyone got 'boshed' it was the Fat Boy, as he is fond of calling himself. 'Jiffy' set him up a treat on several occasions, dancing rings round him in such a way that Skinner could never lay a hand on him.

This was Will Carling's first home match as an England player and it was good for him to be given a quick reminder of the facts of Anglo-Welsh life even if, most regrettably, they are rather different now than they were then. Two excellent tries by Adrian Hadley gave our season such a flying start that the Crown and the championship became a real possibility.

On top of everything else, we had found a new hooker, Ian Watkins of Ebbw Vale. He came on for an injured Kevin Phillips at a time when we had been struggling in the line-out. Ian's first throw homed in on its target so perfectly that Bob Norster took it two-handed. That one moment gave us such a lift that from then on there was never the slightest doubt we would win. We never looked back for the rest of the season.

I had played three times against England in less than twelve months and we had won them all. A lot of Welsh people took that for granted back then. Well, it may be quite a while before Wales beat them three times in a row again, never mind within one calendar year. However, back in New Year 1988, we were beginning to think we had something special and that we could win.

The next match, Scotland at the Arms Park, was to prove that we did, indeed, have something special. It was, without the shadow of a doubt, the best game of rugby I have ever played in – a classic encounter during which the match ebbed and flowed until we emerged as breathless winners, 25–20. Great is a much-abused word but this truly was a great match, played in a unique atmosphere which only the Arms Park can generate. There was never a dull moment, which is more than can be said about the vast majority of international matches.

Scotland had by then built a team which in two years' time

would go one better than we did that season and achieve the Grand Slam with a famous victory over England at Murrayfield. They scored first at Cardiff that day and opened up quite a lead before Jonathan scored a truly fantastic try. He grubbered through, gave Derek White, the formidable Scottish No. 8, a ten-yard start and seemed to catch him within fifteen to get the touchdown. That is not intended in any way to be a criticism of White, rather an illustration of Jonathan's phenomenal pace. Only he could have done it, not simply because he had this explosive acceleration, but only he had the audacity, cheek, nerve – call it what you like – to attempt such an outrageously difficult ploy. No wonder we called him 'Jiffy'. He had, and still has, the arrogant self-belief of a true champion. He was probably the most talented player I played with or against and, believe me, that is really saying something. What a shame that by the end of that year he had been hounded out of the country, but more of that later.

His try against Scotland was a one-off. In a topsy-turvy match, I managed to follow it with an individual burst of my own. Whether that, too, was a one-off is for others to judge. I will never score a better one if I play for another ten years, that's for sure. Mark Ring fed me early and when I got the ball, about fifteen yards in from the right-hand touchline, there were so many Scots around me I didn't think I would get very far.

Gavin Hastings was the first to make a challenge. I had reached the Scottish ten-yard line when he came up flat and tried to push me towards the touchline. I could see what he was trying to do, so I came in off my right foot and I did exactly the same thing to dodge the next man. It was then that I began to think I had a real chance of going all the way.

Everything was happening in a flash but, once I sensed that a try was possible, the ball was tucked well and truly under my armpit. I wasn't going to let it go. I just kept stepping inside all the time, past Roy Laidlaw, past John Rutherford, I think, and by the time David Sole grabbed my ankles, I was falling over the line for the try. 'Fancy being caught by a prop,'

Jonathan said afterwards. 'And we thought you were quite quick!'

Bill McLaren's commentary about 'Merlin the Magician' will do for me. I'm not the emotional type but I don't mind admitting I do become quite emotional about that. Whenever I feel low, I watch it on video and suddenly I feel a lot better. I get a tremendous buzz when I see it, or when someone says it was the best try he, or she, had seen.

Until I got the ball for that try, I hadn't really had much of a pass to do anything with, let alone score. Opportunities present themselves so rarely at international level that you have to be ready to try and make the most of them when they come along, knowing that it is likely to be the only chance you'll get.

The Scottish tries that afternoon were all extremely well worked. Ours, by contrast, were very much the product of individuals prepared to back a hunch. It is a constant source of satisfaction to me that Jonathan and I should be remembered for that game. We have been close friends for many years and I am particularly proud to be godfather to his son, Scott.

The excitement of the Scottish match had only just died down when we took off for Dublin and what we hoped would be the last stop on the twisting road to the long-lost Crown. I came close to spending most of that Saturday afternoon as a spectator. An early clout left me feeling groggy, a clout caused by someone's knee catching my head after I had come into the line. I managed to play through what was unquestionably our worst eighty minutes of the championship.

Luckily, Paul Thorburn had a magnificent game. As well as kicking the winning penalty from wide out on the twenty-two in injury time, he then made a crucial mark on the line with a huge garryowen and the whole Irish team screaming down on him. Rock solid when the chips were down, he won the match for us and, with it, the mythical Crown.

Dublin being my favourite port of call, we celebrated in style thanks largely to that most genial of hosts and bon viveur, Hugo MacNeill, the Irish full-back. He took a few of us on a grand tour of Leeson Street and, no matter which bar or club we called into that Saturday night, it was always the same, a bottle of champagne on the house wherever we went. Needless to say, I was feeling a lot less than a million dollars when we flew home the next day.

To have won something at last gave us a sense of achievement on the journey back to Cardiff. We were, however, already looking ahead to France and the Grand Slam, which no Welsh team had won since 1978, the year Gareth, Benny and Gerald all hung up their boots.

On the big day, the weather was not untypical of the Arms Park for mid-March – wet and thoroughly unpleasant. It was the last thing we wanted. We had played better rugby than the French during the weeks running up to the championship decider. We wanted to spread the ball wide and play to our strengths. The conditions would not only make that virtually impossible but suit the French plan to keep it tight.

I scored a try which Ringo keeps arguing with me about, but it was mine, definitely! Despite that, it was one of those horrible days where I hardly touched the ball throughout the match, apart from the try which cut their lead to 10–9. In scoring it, I damaged a hamstring and missed the final few minutes of a match which brought me head-to-head with the fastest man I have ever had to mark, Patrice Lagisquet, the Bayonne Express. Luckily, I managed to prevent him getting up too much steam.

In the end there was just the one point in it. So near and yet so far. It left us thinking that we had been short-changed, that we had not done ourselves justice. Still, you make your own luck in sport and our failure to make enough of it explained the feeling of anti-climax which pervaded the dressing-room.

There was still one more big occasion left for me that season, the game against Neath in the Cup final. Llanelli's appearance after a three-year gap guaranteed the Arms Park another full house and, even if I say so myself, there is no doubt that the Scarlets and their huge travelling support made the final a real event.

We had at least twenty thousand there that day to see us regain the Cup, their massed ranks swelling the attendance to 56,000, then a world record for a club match. The sight of the Arms Park bedecked in scarlet splendour inspired me to a flyer, the first of my Cup final tries arriving in the first minute after I caught an attempted clearance from the Neath scrum-half, Chris Bridges.

I made the most of that weekend. A few dirty All Black clouds were beginning to loom on the horizon . . .

CHAPTER SIX

Lambs to the Slaughter

It must have seemed like a good idea at the time, a tour of New Zealand which, with a bit of luck, would prove that what the All Blacks had done to Wales the previous year really was too bad to be true. Four weeks in the hardest school of all were designed to remind the natives that Wales were no longer a soft a touch as they had been during the World Cup semi-final in Brisbane twelve months earlier. It could be argued that this time, if anything, they were an even softer one.

Far from completing a swift rehabilitation, the trip plunged the Welsh game into an almost recurring state of relapse. Wales had gone out as Triple Crown winners and joint champions of the Five Nations, expecting to give the best team in the world a reasonable run for their money. Their systematic destruction, beginning with the game against Waikato, had such a demoralising effect that Tony Gray was sacked upon his return – too many of his colleagues on the general committee of the Welsh Rugby Union conveniently overlooking the fact that he had been the only Welsh national coach of the eighties to win anything.

That a constant supply of reinforcements had to be flown out to cope with repeated casualties did not say much for Welsh fitness to cope with the physical intensity of such a tour. Six players went home and of the eight newly capped during all the mayhem, two were never heard of internationally again: Tim Fauvel and Jonathan Mason. Of the remainder, only Mike Hall stood the test of time.

Within six months of returning home, Jonathan Davies had gone north, to be followed by several more who clearly decided, with ample justification, that they wanted to play for more than just a love of the game. Far from being a passing phase, their pummelling from pillar to post marked the start of the worst four years in the history of Welsh rugby.

As if anxious to keep pace with an ever-changing but ever-losing team, the WRU lurched from crisis to crisis. Their clandestine role in the South African centenary celebrations of 1989, for instance, degenerated into a national scandal with secretary David East and president Clive Rowlands resigning in protest at unofficial Welsh involvement. Rowlands later changed his mind and, while all that was going on, the movement north became more than a trickle.

Six more followed Davies to Rugby League – Jonathan Griffiths, John Devereux, David Young, Paul Moriarty, Mark Jones and Rowland Phillips. Hard as they tried, they knew from personal experience that Wales in New Zealand in May–June 1988 was no hard-luck story but depressing confirmation that the gap between the haves and the have-nots had widened to a chasm.

All Blacks, old and new, could hardly believe their eyes. Graham Mourie remembered how Wales used to be, how New Zealand won at Cardiff in 1978 by the skin of their teeth with a penalty which still evokes painful Welsh memories of how they fell victim to a Machiavellian plot. 'When I played against Wales, they knocked you down and sent you flying backwards,' Mourie said. 'Welsh tackling is not what it used to be.'

Their defensive record, conceding twenty-eight tries in four matches alone, leaves no doubt that he was putting it politely. John Hart, the Auckland coach, was not bothered by niceties in arriving at the damning conclusion that Welsh rugby was 'in the pits'. Draughty, dreary hotel accommodation reinforced the suspicion that they really had become second-class citizens.

The results were scarcely good enough to be second class. Wales won two of their eight matches, conceded more than 100 points in the two Tests and ended up with a negative try equity of eighteen to one. Just as well, really, that they were still worth only four points.

When they lost to North Auckland in the final provincial game before the last Test, Wales found a new line in poverty which struck a chord with one spectator. Their failure to cope with a modest team a long way down the provincial pecking order behind Auckland, moved him to produce a bugle and sound 'The Last Post'.

The horror story began with the first match and unfolded on such a regular basis that it became almost a daily event. Beaten by provincial New Zealand teams in the two opening matches, we took flight to the South Island and landed in Dunedin at the start of the week running up to the first Test.

What happened there proved beyond all doubt that there would be no escape from the horrors. The hotel was cold, so cold that every single member of the squad went to bed in his tracksuit. If the Otago winter didn't prevent us from sleeping, then the location of the hotel most certainly did.

That first morning we were woken at 5.30 to discover that we were stuck in the middle of an industrial estate next door to a sawmill. As if that wasn't bad enough, the food tasted as though it had come from the same place! It was so appalling that we were left wondering what kind of hotel they would have booked us into had we finished bottom of the Five Nations championship instead of joint top.

Stuck in dire hotels, often miles from anywhere, and saddled with an itinerary which would have taxed the Lions never mind Wales, we were left with one inescapable conclusion. We had been sold down the river by our own Union. The longer the tour went on, the more angry we became at the fact that someone back in Cardiff had given official approval to the whole sorry business.

The fixtures – five top provincial teams and two Tests in a matter of four weeks – were ridiculous. Even Grizz Wyllie, the All Blacks coach, said so. He made the point that New Zealand would never have accepted the kind of itinerary which was foisted on us.

Traditionally, a touring team is permitted the comparative luxury of a not-too-difficult opening match so they can get the show on the road. Instead, we were pitched straight in against Waikato, who were then in the process of building a team which would become national champions.

We had no chance from the start but, if the schedule had been a touch less hostile and the hotels a touch more hospitable, the damage might not have been as severe. Make no mistake about it, this tour set Welsh rugby back years.

That first beating, by Waikato at Hamilton, shook us to such an extent that we could never recover. We had become lambs to the slaughter. The batterings we took all over the length and breadth of New Zealand left such deep psychological scars that some players never had a chance of recovering.

It is impossible, even now, to quantify the cost to Welsh rugby. We lost so many players as a direct or indirect consequence of that tour. Even those of supreme self-confidence, like Jonathan Davies, were shaken to their foundations by the experience. The crushing defeats shook us all to the very core.

We had arrived believing ourselves to be the best team in Europe and, as such, we would command a bit of respect. Losing the first game was a major blow. It was close enough, but there was no getting away from the fact that we had lost. Some of us were beginning to think: 'Good God. What next?'

Wellington wasted no time providing the answer and, from then on, there was never any chance of salvaging anything from the wreckage. In Wellington we ran into four All Blacks, including full-back John Gallagher who had made such an impact at the World Cup, but it was a Tongan who caused more damage than anyone else.

I had never heard of Emosi Koloto before. A massive No. 8 who scored two of Wellington's six tries in their win by 38–22, he turned professional a few months later. His signing by Widnes, a few months before Jonathan Davies joined the same club, meant that at least one relieved Welshman never had to worry about trying to tackle him again.

Wellington also marked the start of what became a very long casualty list. The depression was already deep enough before the tour captain, Bleddyn Bowen, broke a wrist. It meant that I played under three captains in as many weeks. Bob Norster took over from Bleddyn for the first Test and when he gashed his knee Jonathan stepped in for the second Test, running almost the full length of the field for a try which at last stopped the All Blacks in their tracks.

By then a team, which only weeks earlier had gone within an ace of winning the Grand Slam, had tried to compete with the best and been found seriously wanting. Collectively, we were forced to question our ability as international players to perform at that level.

We had no way of competing against a team who had perfected the power game and taken it to staggering new heights. We had hoped to live off scraps of possession but, without a pack capable of competing, we were always going to be too busy manning the barricades to be able to do anything else. A few Welsh pop guns were never going to be anything more than a minor irritant once the All Blacks began firing their heavy artillery.

The Test matches were horribly one-sided, the first one so much so that all I could do was try to tackle Terry Wright on four-man overlaps. Not once in that match at Christchurch was I given the ball in an attacking position, yet Barry John made me the Welsh man of the match because I made three try-saving tackles. It was as farcical as that.

After that first Test, people were queuing up to go home. Their response disappointed me greatly. A few jacked it in there and then. I had not seen such a defeatist attitude before. There was a queue outside the doctor's room every morning and we had an open ticket for players going home on the first available London plane.

At one stage we were calling all sorts of people out in their place. Some of those who went home early were relieved to the point of being light-hearted, as if they had escaped from the front of a war zone. I suppose I, too, could have made my excuses, cut my losses and headed for home without having to stay to the bitter end.

My shoulder, the left one for a change, had been giving me a fair bit of trouble. I could have signed off, but I was determined to stay and see it through. I don't like injections of any kind, least of all of the cortisone variety, because they tend to hurt. I had three jabs in my shoulder after the first Test and stayed on the ship, even if by then we were sinking fast.

Despite manful attempts to find a silver lining, morale was sinking almost as fast. It hadn't been helped by the refusal of an experienced back-row forward to join the party. Cardiff were in New Zealand at the same time and, when Richie Collins was badly injured during the second match, we asked Gareth Roberts to take his place. For whatever reason, he refused, which in a time of adversity was a shame and my Llanelli colleague, Gary Jones, came out instead to win his first cap.

If ever a team was beaten before the match started, it was Wales on that trip. The grim reality of our predicament was such that it was solely a matter of keeping the score down. It worked, briefly, in both Tests but once one or two players had gone off with injuries, the floodgates opened and the All Blacks exploited that with a ruthlessness demanded by Wayne Shelford.

Nobody taking a close look at our domestic game will have been surprised that our tackling wasn't good enough. Nine times out of ten it doesn't take a lot to bring a player down in our club rugby. We are capable of making terrific tackles but we don't do it week in, week out. In New Zealand we simply weren't used to taking the knocks involved in having to make consistently heavy tackles.

They were so ruthless that when Jonathan Mason won his only cap as a late replacement in the second Test at Eden Park, his brand-new Welsh jersey never survived the first ruck. Thankfully, Mason did. When he reappeared, it was as if he had been put through a shredder. A promising young player, he was one of the many who suffered a crisis of confidence and it may be more than coincidence that Jonathan never played for Wales again.

New Zealand can be the most unforgiving place of all. In addition to the daily dose of pumpkin soup and awful stodge served up as food, in some of the worst hotels in the world, we also had to contend with being torn to shreds in the papers as well. One of them gave us marks on a scale of one to ten after the first Test. One player was given nought and the average was no higher than four.

I felt dreadfully embarrassed by it all and never more so than at the after-match functions. They tend to be more brutal in their comments, less subtle than we would be in similar circumstances. We all took a particular dislike to Gary Whetton in that respect. He took the mickey out of us in one speech and then made it fairly clear he did not wish to waste his time talking to us.

How you conduct yourself in victory is every bit as important as how you conduct yourself in defeat. We tried hard at times to make the best of a bad job and reminded ourselves that it was only a game after all. We never quite convinced ourselves about that, despite composing a song about Jeremy Pugh, entitled 'I'm the King of the Swingers'.

The Neath prop used to be renowned for talking the best game of all without ever quite getting round to backing it up with a bit of action. This is the man who once pulled out of a training session claiming he was suffering from 'jogger's nipple'!

It would have been bad enough had the horrors ended the minute our jumbo took off at Auckland on the long haul home. True to form, the Welsh Rugby Union made a crisis out of the drama, ensuring in the process that the rest of the world had something more to laugh about that summer.

CHAPTER SEVEN

Why I'd Have Gone North, Too

When the remnants of the Welsh Triple Crown team limped back home, their new captain decided that drastic performances called for drastic action. Jonathan Davies – one of the very few to emerge from the tour with his reputation enhanced – thought it might be rather useful if he could address the annual meeting of the Welsh Rugby Union.

Anxious to open some line of communication between the dressing-room and the committee box, he merely wanted to say his piece in the hope that they would learn from the experience so as to eliminate any danger of making the same, catastrophic mistakes again. It would not have been unreasonable to assume that such an offer would have been readily accepted and Davies given a full hearing as a matter of some urgency. The Union might even have learnt something from what he wanted to tell them about where Wales had gone wrong and how they could at least begin to put it right.

The AGM came and went without a solitary word from the person at the sharpest end of the public floggings all over New Zealand, the one whose phenomenal try had given the All Blacks a fleeting glimpse that all was not yet over.

'I couldn't have been treated with more contempt if I'd suggested digging up the National Stadium and planting potatoes,' Jonathan wrote in his autobiography. 'My request to be allowed to address the annual general meeting on the subject of what to do about being wrecked in New Zealand, where we were laughed at and called the worst major touring team ever to visit there, was dismissed out of hand. At least, that's what I must assume because I didn't get the courtesy of a reply.

'I really couldn't understand their attitude. After all, it was the players who suffered the real humiliation. The administrators back home were no doubt hurt and demoralised by our failure, but how could they possibly not want a first-hand account from the men who came face to face with a superior rugby force and perhaps saw how we could do better next time?'

Ieuan, sharing the same sense of hurt at Kiwi jibes and Welsh inadequacy, was asking the same questions, not knowing then that he would be repeating them over and over again amid mounting anger before, during and after the next Welsh tour – an even more humiliating experience, not that that seemed possible after what he and his colleagues had just been through.

He has no doubt that the Union's refusal to grant Davies a hearing gave him another hefty nudge in a northerly direction. Grant Fox heard the news at home in Auckland with audible disbelief. The All Blacks stand-off has long maintained that that rebuff, more than anything else, led to his opposite number turning professional.

What he has to say on the subject reinforces Ieuan's view that Davies was 'hounded out'. 'Jonathan had so much to give to rugby union and was deeply committed to giving it,' Fox said. 'He was rejected like a peasant. Here he was, Wales's finest player by the length of the Taff and with the stature among the players of the game at all levels to be heard and heeded. The rejection cut deeply into his soul and I have no doubt that was the real beginning of his Rugby League career.'

The Welsh Rugby Union did what they always do in difficult times: they appointed an investigative panel. Ray Williams, revered as a coaching organiser who kept ahead of the game for most of the sixties and seventies, did not bother to hang around for the verdict. He resigned as secretary in September 1988 in a dispute over salary.

In the same year Wales lost two international players to League, Adrian Hadley and the phenomenal David Bishop, the nearest thing I have seen to a one-man team. Twice as many left the following year – Davies in January, Paul Moriarty in March, John Devereux in August and Jonathan Griffiths in September.

Three more internationals, David Young, Allan Bateman and Rowland Phillips, left the following year. Imagine how much worse it would have been had Ieuan Evans gone, too. He very nearly did and would have done had fate not intervened. How ironic that his future in

Union should have been secured in a painfully tortuous way by the fourth of the five shoulder dislocations which caused him so much grief for so long.

I have never admitted this before and it pains me to admit it now. I have never wanted to play Rugby League, nor have I ever solicited any approaches from any of their leading clubs.

Welsh rugby was in such dire straits after the New Zealand tour that if someone had made me a decent offer at that time I would have taken the money and gone north. It is a measure of the disillusion I felt that I would have been prepared to cash in my chips and play a game which I have never had any ambition to play.

The Welsh Rugby Union was guilty of such recurring mismanagement that we stumbled from crisis to crisis. We had become a laughing-stock. I could not believe that a nation which had given the world so many great rugby figures over the years should have been reduced to such a shambles.

As if that wasn't bad enough, we have this appalling habit of washing our dirty linen in public. Many nonsensical decisions were made. Awarding caps for an alleged 'international' against the Barbarians that October was another, cheapening the most cherished prize of all. Heaven knows, it had been cheapened enough by some of the charades which had taken place on the field.

Nothing, however, made more nonsense than the sacking of Tony Gray as coach. In the months following that ludicrous decision, we went from bad to worse as a national team until it became hopeless. Whenever nobody thought it could possibly get any worse, France wiped us off the face of the earth in Paris at the end of the 1989 championship. Any team spirit, any semblance of togetherness had gone.

John Ryan, Gray's successor as coach, was battling away as best he could but it was a case of the blind leading the blind. One half of the team didn't know what they were doing. The other half should never have been there in the first place.

It reinforced my fear that I had become stuck in a bottomless

Learning the art of leadership: captain (third from left) of the Under-12 team at Queen Elizabeth Grammar School, Carmarthen, during the 1975–76 season

Captaining Wales for the first time on the night they switched on the floodlights at the Arms Park, 4 September 1991. From left: H. Williams-Jones, D. Evans, A. Emyr, E. Lewis, P. Davies, K. Moseley, Glyn Llewellyn, R. Collins, L. Delaney, M. Griffiths, K. Waters. Front: L. Evans, M. Hall, R. Jones, M. Ring, I. Evans, A. Clement, S. Gibbs, G. Jenkins, A. Booth, M. Morris (David Williams)

Winning on the big stage for the first time: me with my Mum and Dad after the Llanelli–Cardiff Welsh final, 27 April 1985

Capped at last. I was called out of the bar for the presentation in Paris. A good job that the Welsh Rugby Union president, Des Barnett, saw the funny side

Bedford RFC c.1963, with a Welsh flier on the wing (back row, far left), my father, John Evans (The Bedfordshire Times)

Posing in ancient garb, as the first Welsh rugby superstar, Arthur 'Monkey' Gould, might have done a century ago (Sian Trenberth)

Showing Brendan Mullin a clean pair of heels during Wales's Triple Crown clincher in Dublin in March 1988 (Colorsport)

Try again! (The South Wales Argus)

Flying past Rory Underwood for the most famous Evans try of all — Wales 10, England 9 — at Cardiff Arms Park, 6 February 1993 (David Rogers, Allsport)

Merlin the Magician at work. Beating Gavin Hastings, I cut a swathe through the Scottish ranks and David Sole's tackle comes too late to stop me. It was said to be one of the tries of the decade. Wales v Scotland, Cardiff Arms Park, 20 February 1988
(Allsport/The South Wales Argus)

Flying the flag at the end of the series. I am surrounded by Englishmen (from left) Rory Underwood, Dean Richards, Rob Andrew and Brian Moore (Billy Stickland, Allsport)

The Evans version of the Big Hit, on Grant Fox during the first Lions Test against New Zealand at Lancaster Park, 12 June 1993 (Ross Kinnaird, Empics)

Mean and moody. The Carmarthen Cowboy, complete with short-lived moustache

Among my souvenirs: at home with my Mum and Dad (David Rogers, Allsport)

black hole. There seemed no way out other than to turn professional. Fortuitously, as it turned out, no such escape route existed because by then I had dislocated my shoulder for the fourth time.

Once again a match at Leicester had proved my undoing. I had gone there with Llanelli on the last Saturday of October in reasonably buoyant mood, looking forward to the chance of helping Wales redeem their fortunes after the summer fiasco by winning the pre-Christmas matches against Western Samoa and Romania.

Everything had gone without a hitch that season until Steve Kenney, the Leicester scrum-half, grabbed me by the sleeve as I collected a chip kick and hurled me round. I thudded into an advertising board on the side of the pitch with such an impact that I knew something had gone. The Welsh team doctor, Bob Leyshon, told me I was lucky it hadn't been my neck. Had that been the case, my entire rugby career would have been over there and then.

If the first three shoulder dislocations had cost me a stack of caps, then the fourth at least ensured I would stay in the game, for the time being at any rate. Had I been fit at the time I would have been as vulnerable as anyone else to League offers. Maybe it was all for the best; not that I could appreciate the sentiment during that most depressing period leading to the end of a grim series of matches in the Five Nations that season.

I had had three offers to turn professional before and since but no Rugby League club in its right mind was going to splash out on someone who was currently a long-term casualty with his arm in a sling. At that time, whenever anyone mentioned Ieuan Evans, they thought of a dodgy shoulder.

One club in particular knew better than any the cost of splashing out on a Welsh international only to see him bust his shoulder in the first few minutes of his first match. As a student at Salford back then, I'd gone to Odsal that Sunday to watch Terry Holmes make his much-heralded entry into the professional ranks for Bradford Northern against Swinton only to see him being helped off the field. That must have left a lot of

League clubs wondering that if one of the really hard men of Welsh rugby couldn't take it, then what did that say about the rest?

By the time I recovered from the Leicester accident, Jonathan Davies had shocked the rugby world by signing for Widnes Rugby League club. There was no doubt that the New Zealand tour had affected him as badly as it affected everyone else. Romania achieved a famous victory at the Arms Park just before Christmas and the consequences of that result were to have such a further demoralising effect that the best outside-half in the game would never take centre-stage at the Arms Park again.

The team had lost its way and there were those in high places who seemed only too quick to try to pin some of the blame on Jonathan as captain, a role which he had taken over in an emergency in Auckland the previous summer.

The fear gnawed away at him that they were plotting to strip him of the captaincy and maybe drop him as well. All it needed was someone from the WRU to pick up the phone and reassure him about his place and his importance to the long-term strategy of the team. Not only did they not do that, but when Jonathan turned up for squad training one night after the Romanian débâcle, none of the selectors spoke to him. Not unnaturally, he thought something was afoot.

He was, therefore, ripe for plucking when Widnes came knocking on his door. By then, he had had enough. Doug Laughton, the Widnes coach who later went to Leeds, persuaded him that his future lay in the north of England and the prophet who felt he was suddenly without honour in his own land decided to make himself secure financially and opt for someone who really did appreciate what he had to offer.

Jonathan phoned me the day before he met Laughton and he phoned me again just after he had signed. I had lost a kindred spirit and, if I had been in any fit state to attract a similar offer, I'd have gone, too. As it was, I went north at the first available opportunity to see his first match and I still got there in time despite losing my way around Merseyside – another case of the geography graduate not knowing his geography!

Timing is often the most crucial aspect of any League offer. Fortunately, my offers came at a time when no amount of riches was going to distract me from achieving my ambitions in Union. You cannot put a price on a Lions tour and you most certainly cannot put a price on captaining your country.

Featherstone Rovers very nearly did.

Hull had made discreet inquiries two years earlier. I gave them no encouragement and it fizzled out. St Helens were more persistent. Joe Pickavance, their chairman, went straight to the point in a typically blunt, north-of-England way. 'Right, lad,' he said. 'Let's talk turkey.'

We spoke for a while but, to be honest, there wasn't much turkey to talk about. I had no intention of going and I wasn't going to waste his time by asking for the moon. The Saints offer was a good one, a four-year deal worth £135,000 which, back in 1989, would have been a record for a Union signing.

It was very flattering to think someone thought I was that good but I kept thinking of those things in rugby union which money couldn't buy. The bottom line was that I had no intention of going north. I was new to international rugby and I wasn't going to jack it in after one season. At that stage I was some way off being disillusioned.

Every man, of course, has his price as the All Blacks were soon to discover when they woke up one morning at the end of that season to the news that John Gallagher had signed for Leeds. A month or two before his transfer went through, Featherstone made me an offer which was too good to turn down without a lot of very serious consideration.

It was the biggest deal I ever had – £175,000. There would have been a signing-on fee of £40,000, the rest over a period of four years and a job as a rep. with Scottish & Newcastle Breweries thrown in. All I had to say was 'yes'.

Had they made the offer a few months earlier, I would not have taken much persuading. Unfortunately, or fortunately, depending on your point of view, the Lions were going to Australia that year and I had set my heart on making the trip.

As a small boy I had been brought up on tales of the Lions and

I wasn't going to miss it for all the tea in China or, to be more accurate, all the brass in Featherstone. I thought long and hard about their offer before deciding to resist. Once again, it was a matter of timing.

I know that most of those Welsh players who went north have missed out, to a larger or lesser extent, in terms of unfulfilled careers in Union. Jonathan Davies, for instance, would love to have been a Lion. In a perfect world, he would have been and then turned professional. But it's the old story about the penny and the bun. You can't have them both. There is a price to pay for everything.

Jonathan would joke about using his influence in northern circles to fix me up with a lucrative contract. The last offer I had was again from Featherstone, in 1991 after the shameful tour of Australia. They must have thought they had got their timing right. They would have done had I not been presented with something money simply cannot buy, the captaincy of my country.

It would have been a lot less traumatic had we been able to turn the clock back and reclaim all those who had been lost to League during the worst years in the history of the game in Wales. The cumulative effect of losing so many good players cannot be overstated. Jonathan was only one, albeit the best of all.

There were others, like John Devereux and Dai Young, who were also the best in the British Isles in their respective positions – as they proved for the Lions before taking the road north. Paul Moriarty would certainly have been a Lion had he stayed.

When Dai went to Leeds, we didn't just lose a tight-head prop. We lost our scrum. With Paul, we lost a flanker who had everything it took to become one of the outstanding back-row forwards of the nineties. He was the very model of the big, athletic, versatile back-five forward in such demand the world over.

We were sadly lacking players of his physical stature, ball-carriers who could smash through tackles. Paul had so much going for him but, for reasons beyond my comprehension, he had fallen foul of the coach, John Ryan. Gray, the man who had taken us to the Triple Crown the previous season, was now no longer good enough and was discarded, ironically, by the very general committee of which he was a member.

It was almost as if there had to be a knee-jerk reaction among the rank and file of that committee, as if their only policy was to change the coach, change the captain, change the team. They either refused to recognise or acknowledge that the root cause was embedded far deeper than that.

Sadly, there were people on the WRU then who simply were not capable of making the right decisions because they were too parochial, too insular or just plain short-sighted. As the old saying goes, there are none so blind as those who will not see.

How could you have officials from small clubs with no real knowledge of world rugby making decisions which affected the national team and, more often than not, affected it for the worse? At least now, under the chairmanship of Vernon Pugh, QC, the Union is at last tackling a problem which should have been tackled years ago.

Their refusal back in the late 1980s to streamline the decision-making process and get to grips with the real problems left me wondering whether we were not living in some sort of self-imposed isolation, as if we were happy with our own little lot.

Well, we would fill the Arms Park twice a year and we'd still get twelve thousand or so when Llanelli played Swansea. The bar takings would be up. So what was all the fuss about? A case of 'nothing to worry about, boys'.

At a time when our rivals were planning ahead and learning from the likes of Australia and New Zealand, too many of our people seemed more concerned with ensuring they had their supply of free tickets and hotel accommodation for international weekend junkets. Old habits die hard, in some cases very hard.

At the 1995 Annual General Meeting of the WRU, which took place seven days after the World Cup final, delegates made more noise about what stage the senior clubs should enter the Swalec Cup than the state of the national team. They also spent a lot of time arguing the toss about whether the divisions of the Heineken League be extended to sixteen clubs.

What planet are these people living on? Don't they know that we're stuck in the bottom half of the second division of world rugby, or doesn't it bother them? This is our national sport, for goodness sake. I find it very hard to take, and harder still considering we have been out of the first division for so long.

And yet, back then in the winter of 1988–89 they would tell you there was nothing to worry about, that Welsh rugby was still in a healthy state. Going into a new Five Nations campaign, there was plenty to worry about on the field and none of it was the least bit healthy.

CHAPTER EIGHT

A Match to Cap the Lot!

When it comes to the principle of capping players, the Welsh Rugby Union is undoubtedly in a class of its own, and not merely because of a tendency to go chucking them about left, right and centre.

Those who never cease to be baffled in their search for an answer to the mysteries of the practice will be considerably more baffled by the following two indisputable facts. They concern matches played at Cardiff Arms Park in the mid-seventies and early nineties.

On Wednesday, 27 November 1974, Wales played New Zealand, which in those less commercialised days was about as near to a World Cup final as you could get. The Lions had conquered South Africa as never before that summer and now almost half their untouchable Test team were back in their natural habitat, ready to subject the rest of the Five Nations to Welsh rule.

This was the Wales of J.P.R. and J.J.; Merve the Swerve and The Duke; and Gareth and Benny. The gang were all there that day and a few more, too – among them Ieuan's old schoolmaster, Roy Bergiers, and Gerald Davies, who had been unavailable for the Lions because of studies at Cambridge. And then, for good measure, there were Lions in the making, like Terry Cobner and Trevor Evans. They would still not have enough to overcome an All Blacks team commanded by Andy Leslie and featuring three straight out of their Hall of Fame – Bryan Williams, Sid Going and Ian Kirkpatrick.

An imposing international cast by anyone's standards, except that the Welsh Rugby Union decreed that it was not, officially, an international and that, therefore, no caps would be awarded. Ludicrously, Wales were billed on the programme as 'A Welsh XV'. Never before can so many great players have been sent out against the supreme rugby nation – well they certainly were then – under such a belittling title.

The New Zealanders had spent that autumn in Ireland helping the natives celebrate their rugby centenary and dropped in at Cardiff on the Wednesday, *en route* to London and the traditional tour finale against the Barbarians, at Twickenham. The International Board, even more difficult to fathom then than in more recent years, excelled themselves by allowing the game to take place but, for some inexplicable reason, there could be no caps.

So we fast-forward sixteen years to 6 October 1990 and another 'international' at the Arms Park. Wales, their Lions now dwindling dangerously close to extinction, were playing the Barbarians and there would be no need for the Union to await instructions from the International Board as to whether caps should be awarded.

How, after all, can you cap a player for appearing against a club team, albeit an exclusive one? Quite easily, if you happen to be the Welsh Rugby Union. The very organisation who had refused to give caps for a full-blown international against the All Blacks then chucked them out to all and sundry in the Baa-baas match, as if they were about to go out of fashion.

On the contrary, the Welsh cap had, at that time, never become more fashionable. In less than four years between the start of the New Zealand tour, in May 1988, and the end of the Five Nations, in March 1992, they capped no fewer than seventy-five players. J.P.R. was not gilding the lily when he spoke then about caps being thrown about like 'confetti'.

During a period so volatile that every day seemed to bring some sort of trauma, Wales had four coaches – Tony Gray, John Ryan, Ron Waldron and Alan Davies. Between them they selected, or helped to select, five different teams in four seasons. These were the pack-'em-in, chuck-'em-out years.

So many were rushed in and rushed straight back out again, presumably on a selection whim, that it is not difficult to assemble an entire team of Welsh internationals who lasted, at best, no more than a few weeks and who, more often than not, were discarded after one international match, never to be brought back.

No wonder Ieuan Evans, as one of the few fixtures in a team

changing with a bewildering frequency, found it almost impossible to keep track of the comings and goings. The Rugby League foxes may have wrought periodic havoc in the chicken coop but that, alone, does not explain why selection amounted to such indecent numbers.

Only a recurring state of panic could have resulted in so many being wheeled in and passed out. It is a damning indictment of the selectors that during those four seasons they ran through as many as fifteen players without giving them more than one proper international, as opposed to the spurious one against the Barbarians.

Some, like Aled Williams, deserve to be more than one-cap wonders. Others will probably confess privately that they were lucky to get one. The full list, Baa-baas excluded: Mark Davis, Richard Diplock, Alun Edmunds, Luc Evans, Tim Fauvel, Wayne Hall, Jonathan Mason, Stuart Parfitt, Phil Pugh, Alan Reynolds, Ken Waters, Aled Williams, Owain Williams and Richard Wintle.

Even back in the seventies when the team picked itself, players, whether they were on the inside looking out or the other way round, took nothing for granted. 'Not with the Big Five,' they'd say. 'It's hard to know what they're thinking.'

By the time the selectors were ready to tell the players the team for the first match of the 1989 championship, it was safe to assume that none of them had a clue what they were thinking.

The team for the first match, Scotland at Murrayfield, was announced at five-thirty one Monday morning as we made a bleary-eyed exit from our New Year training camp on the Costa del Sol to Valencia Airport for the flight back to Cardiff.

To my considerable surprise, I was down to play on the right wing, even though I knew I could not possibly be fit in time. My shoulder had not fully recovered from the bashing it had taken at Leicester some ten weeks before. I couldn't tackle a bag, let alone some hairy Scotsman screaming down on me like a latter-day Rob Roy.

Mike Hall took my place in Edinburgh and scored a consolation try, which was about all we got out of a match which the Scots, with Craig Chalmers in rampant form at outside half, ran away with to win 23–7. The writing was on the wall and by the time we had finished our next match, there was no wall left to put any writing on.

Ireland came to the Arms Park and, as is their custom, won. There was nothing unusual about that, nor was there anything unusual about the manner of our performance which could be summed up in one word, dire. It really had got that bad.

At that stage there were people playing – too many of them – who should never have played for Wales. New faces were appearing so often that some had gone before I could really get to know who they were. To learn that we picked the equivalent of five teams in four years is one of the most revealing statistics of that particular period.

In their desperation, the selectors were often guilty of abandoning their principles and taking panic measures in the hope of appeasing an ever more sceptical press and public. Every so often the newspapers would chuck in the odd, wild suggestion, no doubt just to get people talking.

Unfortunately, none of their suggestions were too wild for the selectors. More often than not, they would end up picking them, like a drowning man clutching at a straw. At times it was impossible to understand their thinking. Logic tended not to be their strongest suit.

The forthcoming Lions tour to Australia gave the championship a competitive edge, an added significance. There was so much to be gained and, being one of the last out of the starting blocks that year, of all years, was a decided disadvantage. I had come back for the Irish match but no one could have been the least bit impressed by any aspect of such a scrappy affair.

The match turned on a try that should never have been allowed. David Irwin, the Irish centre, knocked-on before Paul Dean picked the ball up and went over. The referee, Roger Quittenton, had been caught on the blind-side and awarded the try in all good faith. I know touch-judges can only intervene on foul play, but it's a pity neither of them could have tipped the wink about what had happened that day.

Nothing goes right when you're down on your luck but once

again we only had ourselves to blame, not the referee. As a team we were caught in a deep whirlpool; a team stripped of confidence and spirit. Not for the first time, I was desperate for someone to shine a light and show us the way out. France in Paris did nothing to lift the darkness.

Serge Blanco, a star player if ever there was one, had one of those dream games where everything bounced up into his hands. By the time Blanco had done everything there was to do in his Welsh benefit match, only England stood between us and one of the few indignities still to befall Welsh rugby during this painful time, a championship whitewash.

To go from challenging for a Grand Slam one March to being within eighty minutes of losing all four matches the following year, took some doing. There was, alas, a grave danger that we were about to achieve precisely that.

England turned up at the Arms Park promising to do as everyone else had done and give us a good hiding, while conveniently overlooking the fact that they hadn't given us a hiding, good, bad or indifferent, at home for more than a quarter of a century. It poured down exactly as it had done twelve months before and this time it was exactly what the rain doctors had ordered.

Paul Turner, drafted into the team that year at the age of thirty to fill the void left at outside half, played like someone who had waited all his life for this one chance which, in his case, was absolutely true. As Robert Jones peppered England with box-kicks as only he could, Paul increased the bombardment, ensuring the English weakness under the high ball would be exploited to the hilt.

One such kick in foul conditions led directly to the winning try, an up-and-under which left Rory Underwood and Jonathan Webb in such a dither that all Mike Hall had to do was pounce on a loose pass chucked with reckless abandon behind the English line. By literally throwing it away, England had rescued us from the ultimate fate of a championship whitewash.

How ironic, then, that our only win that season should coincide with another furore, provoked in a manner which many considered to be a classic case of the skipper shooting himself, and Welsh rugby, in the foot. I was to learn soon enough from personal experience that it is all too easy for the captain, especially one living in the fishbowl environment of South Wales, to develop a sense of paranoia.

There are times when captaining Wales is about as high-profile as you can get within the Principality and, consequently, you learn to take the rough with the smooth. Like it or not, you are up there to be shot at. If the team win, you are a national hero. If they lose, you are apt to be regarded as a bit of a charlie. Very rarely is there a happy medium.

Hurling an obscene gesture in the general direction of the press box as you leave the field after a match against England is not the best example of how to win friends and influence people. No reason could be strong enough to justify that sort of behaviour. It was a gesture made at totally the wrong place at totally the wrong time, in front of 56,000 inside the stadium and as many as five million more watching all over the British Isles on television. That a hefty percentage of that audience were children left no doubt as to the damage done to the image of the game.

Paul Thorburn had gone into the match feeling frustrated and more than a little hurt at what he felt was a lack of support from the Welsh press in general, and one member of the national press in particular. Stephen Jones, a Welshman from Newport and proud of it, too, had written a piece in the previous week's *Sunday Times*, saying he hoped Wales would lose because the shock of a whitewash would bring the WRU to its senses and ensure, or so he hoped, that the right remedial action be taken.

It was known that Paul was going to have a pop about that in his speech at the after-match dinner at the Angel Hotel. Instead, he let his emotions get the better of him without thinking through the consequences of what he would say. No Union can invite a journalist, or anyone else for that matter, to the dinner, as Wales had done with Jones, and then have the captain ask him to leave because he thinks he is 'the scum of the earth'.

In the rough and tumble of international rugby, players and

journalists often have lively, heated differences of opinion – what they refer to in the diplomatic world as 'full and frank discussions'. The journalist has his say in print, the player has a go back and most of the reporters on the rugby circuit will take it on the chin.

Paul's comments were unfortunate, to say the least, and most unbecoming of the captain of a national team. There are always ways of saying things. Often it's not what you say, but how you say it which matters and I think Paul was lucky to get away with it.

Other countries, seeing their captain behave like that, would have dumped him there and then and, no doubt, there were raised eyebrows that he survived to captain the team in Canada that summer. There was a siege mentality within Welsh rugby at that time: a case of trying to batten down the hatches and limit the damage.

For strictly selfish reasons, my anxiety that weekend was over whether I had done enough to warrant selection among the thirty players the Lions would announce that following week for the tour of Australia starting in June. There had been lots of rumours all season about who would be going, who might be and who wouldn't.

Because I had been given so few opportunities, it was a case of hoping for the best. I knew I needed a good game against England but, if I was going to impress, it would have to be in a purely defensive capacity. If I found myself denied the chance to show what I could do going forward, I could at least make the most of going backwards, which I did, once catching that flier of an English wing, Chris Oti, from behind.

By the Sunday night I was already on my way to Australia. I had not counted my chickens, nor had anyone given me any classified information. I went off with Robert and Devs and a group of other British and Irish players to play in the Sydney sevens. After the last year or so, it was a real tonic to be given a reminder that rugby really is a fun way of seeing the world.

CHAPTER NINE

Apologising to Campese

David Campese might never have lost a home series to British opposition had he not taken a liberty with the wrong man in the wrong place at the wrong time – Ieuan Evans in the Sydney Football Stadium on Saturday, 15 July 1989.

He had spent his rugby life specialising in the priceless knack of making something out of nothing and the world at large had marvelled at his ingenuity, but they had never seen anything as outrageous as Campese attempting to run the ball out from behind his own line, in the middle of a deciding Test against the Lions and against a wily Welshman to boot.

Against a lesser opponent, he would probably have got away with it, if not clean away over the distant horizon, then certainly, without it developing into the national catastrophe it became once it dawned on the Aussies that their greatest match-winner had, in effect, thrown the Test series down the drain.

Campese saw the sort of opportunity only he could see. Before he could exploit it, Evans had forced him to off-load, a pass chucked over the shoulder with such abandon in the general direction of full-back Greg Martin that the predatory Welshman had only to make sure he fell on it. The goose had been cooked before it could even get into step.

With a little help from fate, Evans had taken on the smartest operator the game has ever seen and outwitted him in his own backyard. If he doubted the significance of what he had done when the series ended half an hour later, with that try making all the difference, he only had to listen to the wrath of Australia coming down like rolling thunder on Campese's head.

His description of what was going on in his mind at that time confirms that Evans had outfoxed him. 'There was space and time to get out from our line and attack hard, perhaps as far as halfway or even further,' Campese wrote in his book, *On a Wing and a Prayer.* 'But I felt sure Evans would come with me, to leave Martin a free run outside me. I suppose, subconsciously, I didn't attack the situation as hard or as directly as I would have done had I been alone.

'Of course, the outcome would not have been so dire had my pass been respectable but it was hardly the world's greatest by any stretch of the imagination. The ball caught Martin on the shoulder, I think, and Evans fell on it over the line. There was no way Martin was to blame, it was completely my fault. The orthodox thing to do would have been to belt the ball into touch, of course, but then orthodox methods have never appealed to me very much. Besides, any normal player could have done that. I still believe the idea was perfectly sound. It was just that the execution went wrong.'

In Campese's moment of anguish, coach Bob Dwyer made a point of going across the dressing-room to comfort him. The player was less than happy with his colleagues, claiming that none bothered to make a similar gesture. His captain, Nick Farr-Jones, certainly did in unprecedented fashion with a letter to the *Sydney Morning Herald* published the next day.

Dear Sir,

Not only as captain of the national team but as an Australian, it disturbs me to hear and read the constant, and at times vilifying, attacks by rugby followers and the press on one of our greatest sportsmen, David Campese.

Campo's blunder last Saturday was careless and costly. But few of the Australian players would be satisfied with their performances, including myself. Campo will hopefully learn by the mistake and the whole team, I am sure, will not only show the tremendous spirit in Australian rugby but will improve on individual performances when matched against the might of New Zealand in August.

To Campo, I say: Yes, one bad mistake on Saturday which I know you will learn from but, mate, if I was a selector you would always be one of the first picked, with no handcuffs or chains to inhibit you.

Nick Farr-Jones

The repercussions of a defeat from which Australia recovered to win the World Cup two years later did not end there. The Lions had become Public Enemy No. 1. Bob Dwyer, the Wallaby coach and, as such, one of the most admired figures in the game, called them 'at times the dirtiest team I have ever seen in international rugby. I say this because their use of foul tactics was not occasional but a common and consistent theme of their play.'

What Dwyer wrote in support of his accusation added up to a powerful condemnation of the Lions under Finlay Calder's captaincy. 'The Lions were different,' he wrote in his autobiography, *The Winning Way*. 'With them, dirty play was a persistent, deliberate, all-embracing tactic.'

He also revealed that the Australian Rugby Union had written a letter of protest to the four home unions in Britain, enclosing a video of the nasty bits. 'I understand that the rugby authorities in Britain chose to ignore the complaint,' Dwyer said. 'A year or two later, one of the Lions players on that tour cast a revealing light on the affair while speaking to an Australian administrator. Asked about the foul play his team had engaged in, he said: "It wasn't all of us. It was the English coppers." The player, it goes without saying, was not an Englishman.'

After winning the first Test, Farr-Jones had warned his team that the second match would be 'twice as hard. If we give these blokes a sniff, we're going to be in trouble.' He cannot have imagined then that, if anything, he had understated the case.

Farr-Jones has told how his opposite number, Robert Jones, had stood on his foot as he went to put the ball into the first scrum and that they 'began to wrestle. Next thing I knew, Finlay Calder came off the scrum and belted me.'

The Lions had, unwittingly, done the Wallabies a favour. They had exposed a soft underbelly and it is a tribute to Dwyer and his henchmen that they learnt the lesson so swiftly that barely two years later they had walked off with the World Cup. As Dwyer put it himself, using the sort of language not to be found in a Lions picture book: 'They exposed our vulnerability, mentally, to the kind of bully-boy tactics they employed.'

Out on the wing, one man had been quietly minding his business except when Campese chose to bring it his way. Ieuan Evans returned home to Carmarthen that summer on top of the world, as well he might. He had made it all the way to the summit as one of the élite wings in the world. The trick would be to stay there, to survive the test of time in the years ahead and that would be difficult enough without the cruel handicap caused by yet another dislocated shoulder. Was there to be no end to his misery?

Despite that there was much more still to achieve but already he had come a long way from Idole County Primary School . . .

When I scored that try, I did something I had never done to anyone on the rugby field before or since. I gave David Campese a dose of the verbals and regretted it immediately.

Sledging may be a fairly common practice these days, but it has never been my style. What made me give Campo a mouthful is something for which I cannot find a satisfactory explanation. I can only put it down to the enormity of the occasion without offering that as the slightest excuse for my behaviour.

A lot of sportsmen use words like pressure and tension when they stray from the straight and narrow and while there is something in that, the great thing about sport at the highest level is learning to cope with whatever it throws at you without losing your cool. In other words: get on with the game.

Nobody knew anything about this particular incident except the two of us. It wasn't as if I had been trapped by video committing some foul deed, caught with my trousers down, figuratively speaking. No, this was a very minor incident in the grand scheme of things but there was no escaping the fact that, in a hot-headed moment, I had let myself down. I had behaved in an unsporting manner and I felt rather ashamed of it.

Campese had annoyed me in a perfectly legitimate sense. My annoyance was at allowing him to sell me a dummy which gave him the time to gain oceans of territory for his team. When he threw that ball over his shoulder and I fell on it for a try, all my pent-up fury came out. It shouldn't have done, but it did.

I should have appreciated that he would have felt bad enough about what had happened without my coming along and adding insult to injury by putting a verbal boot into him. It troubled me to such an extent that as soon as I got to the after-match reception I made a beeline for Campo, took him aside and apologised profusely for what I had done.

He wasn't in much of a mood to discuss the niceties of the game which, in the circumstances, was understandable. I could only hope that he had accepted my apology as a genuine indication of how much I had regretted shooting my mouth off at him.

I had gone into that deciding Test with a basic line in strategy, to sit on Campo, never imagining that it would have such a spectacular impact on the match. When Rob Andrew went for a drop goal during the second half with the Lions 15–9 in front and the match hanging in the balance, I was out on my wing.

By the time the ball had bounced well wide of the posts and Campo had picked it up and begun to run with it from behind his line, I was virtually on top of him. If it had been any other player, he would have dotted the ball down and gone for the obvious option of a drop-out. Obvious was the last word you would ever associate with David Campese.

No one knew what he was likely to do next. I remember reading once that he reckoned not even his own team-mates could possibly know what his next move would be because he didn't know himself! You could watch him like a hawk, think you have him hemmed in and then suddenly he'd be gone like a puff of smoke.

All sorts of things were racing through my mind when he started to run from his own line. I managed to force him to chuck the ball behind him, to where he thought his full-back would be waiting to take it and break out. Something which we mere mortals would reject as too great a risk, Campese would think nothing of and proceed to astound players and spectators alike by showing them how it could be done. But this, even allowing for his amazing talent, was a fairly dodgy ploy.

It took Greg Martin so completely by surprise that the ball went to ground and I couldn't believe my luck or my eyes. Estimates as to how far I had to go to score that try vary. Resisting all temptation to stretch a point, I have to say that it was no less than six inches and no more than two feet.

The match provided me with a rare double, bagging a bunny and Campese in a matter of minutes. There had been a stoppage early in the second half when I became aware that the crowd was in a state of high amusement over the antics of something. I looked up at the giant screen at one end of the stadium and could see a rabbit moving behind me. I turned round and caught it which certainly did no harm to the Merlin reputation. Handing the rabbit to a spectator for safe-keeping, all I needed to complete the illusion was a black hat. Maybe Campo should have recognised there and then that nothing was going to get past me.

As tries go it was a bit of a freak alright, one of those once-in-a-lifetime moments when you wonder what you have done to deserve the luck, and perhaps that holds the secret to the whole thing. That one incident proves the value of chasing every ball, no matter how hopeless it may appear. What happened in the Sydney Football Stadium that day proves there is no such thing as a lost cause.

A wing will spend most of his life chasing in vain but, once in a blue moon, fate has a habit of rewarding persistence. Once in a blue moon manna from heaven will fall and you have to be wide awake to make sure that it falls into your lap.

In sport, as in life, you work for your luck. Gary Player, the great South African golfer, made the point when he chipped in off the green at a tournament many years ago. When someone in the gallery chided him about a lucky shot, Mr Player turned round and smiled. 'You know, it's a funny thing, my friend,' he said. 'The harder I practise, the luckier I get!'

A lot of water has flowed under a lot of bridges since the Lions left Australia but, for me, there will never be a tour to hold a candle to that one. Believe me, that tour was great in every respect – the players, the morale, the places, the hotels. Everything. No freezing bedrooms on this trip and no need for the Lions to make their tracksuits double up as pyjamas, as we had done with Wales in New Zealand the year before.

Wherever we went in Australia, they treated us like royalty.

They knew that to have the Lions in their midst would raise the profile of rugby to new heights from its position as a distant third to League and 'footie', Aussie Rules. This was the start of the Wallaby boom and it was good to be a part of the evangelistic movement, even if they were to make us pay for it at the next World Cup.

I could never talk enough about the 1989 Lions. It was such an event that, for a start, I got myself fully fit for the first time in my life. At long last, under Peter Herbert's expert tuition at Llanelli, I had recovered from all the junk food bashings to which I had willingly subjected myself over the years.

A series of individual tests in London prior to departure left me in no doubt that I was still not in the best condition. There were six weeks to go to take-off and the tour manager, Clive Rowlands, made it clear that he would like to see me fitter when we assembled for the flight.

For every day of those six weeks I trained as never before. The Lions demanded nothing but the best and I wasn't going to give them any cause for complaint, least of all over my physical state. For once, the delights of Carmarthen and a boys' night out were shoved to an all-time low in my list of priorities.

Some people contend that the Lions are outmoded, that there can no longer be a place for them in an increasingly hectic schedule dominated more and more by the World Cup and the need of individual countries to concentrate on long-term preparations. If I could slap a preservation order on the Lions, I would do so tomorrow. It would be such a crying shame if they were to be abolished and future generations of players would never begin to know what they had missed.

Until I went on that tour, I had not had an opportunity to get to know players from the other three countries. Had it not been for the Lions, I would never have met such unforgettable characters as John Jeffrey, Dean Richards and Mike Teague, 'Iron Mike', of whom more later.

Brian Moore is another interesting character. I had never met him until we shared a room during the trip and we had a number of lively discussions. Thoroughly enjoyable they were, too. Like him or loathe him, one of the most appealing things about Brian, and I accept that he doesn't appeal to everyone, is that he speaks his mind.

He is not afraid to say those things publicly which most players would hardly think about privately. He reads a lot of military books and perhaps that's where he gets some of the ideas for the psychological warfare which he has been known to wage from time to time on the back pages, either against the RFU or whoever England happen to be playing.

Being a lawyer, he will have thought it all out and calculated that the printed effect of his comments will, in some small way, assist England's cause. The French were at Twickenham last winter shortly after a certain Manchester United footballer had become rather more annoyed with a spectator than I had been with Campese. Brian's line likening the French rugby team to fifteen Cantonas, 'brilliant but brutal', was powerful stuff. Vintage Moore.

And then there was Donal Lenihan. He might not have made the Test team but the Lions would never have made it without the Irishman's magnificent leadership of the mid-week team, the celebrated 'Donal's Doughnuts'. Mid-week teams of lesser calibre can easily fall by the wayside as we were to witness on the next Lions tour, in New Zealand, four years later.

Donal and his mid-week team not only gave 100 per cent for every minute of every match but in doing so they saved the tour from coming apart at the seams. Canberra, in between the first and second Tests, was without doubt the turning-point of the tour. We had gone there to play Australian Capital Territories with everyone in dire need of a lift after losing the first Test by a heavy margin of 30 points to 12.

At one stage at Canberra the locals were so far ahead that another score and they would have been out of sight. The 'Doughnuts' dug deep and turned the game on its head, winning 41–25. When we needed it most, they had shown that we did, after all, possess the inner strength to come from behind and win the series.

Four players were rewarded for their performances with

immediate promotion to the Test team – Wade Dooley for Bob Norster, Mike Teague for Derek White, Scott Hastings for Mike Hall and Jeremy Guscott for Brendan Mullin. Like the grand player he is, especially on the grand stage, 'Jerry' responded as to the manner born, a sensational try helping us to square the series.

No sooner had we completed the job back in Sydney the following Saturday than we were being slated as the dirtiest team ever to tour Australia. Of course, you just can't win with the Aussies. If you lose, you are derided as a bunch of lily-livered Pommie softies. If you dare to win, it's because you are a bunch of bully-boy thugs. Older students of the Anglo-Australian sporting scene will probably say that was pretty much par for the course.

Now, make no mistake about it, we were a hard side and after that first Test we were certainly not slow at coming forward. Bob Dwyer is right when he talks in retrospect of the Wallabies not being as 'hard-nosed' as they needed to be.

The pack won us the series and they started winning it in the first moments of the second Test. After losing the first one, we had to give them a dose of their own medicine. We wanted a physical contest. I am quite prepared to admit, too, that we wanted to antagonise them, provoke them, put them off their game.

At the first scrum, Robert Jones stood on Nick Farr-Jones's foot as he put the ball in. It started a fight which, as it turned out, was exactly what we needed. We wanted to show them that we were fired up and that we weren't going to be messed about. We figured the best way of doing that was to start a fight so they would realise that this time we really meant business, that there would be no backing off and they had better look out.

Like it or not, rugby football at international level is based on physical intimidation. We intimidated the Aussies in that second Test, no doubt about it. We had the players to do it, like Dean Richards and Mike Teague.

The Wallabies didn't like it one bit. Apart from Tim Gavin, their powerful No. 8, they didn't have the players who could take a good kicking. As for Dwyer's charge about us being the dirtiest team of all, I reject it completely. There is a world of difference between seeking a physical encounter and, as he alleges, using dirty play as a 'deliberate tactic'. Some of the Aussies suggested that we had reactivated the '99' call which the Lions had used in South Africa in 1974 when everyone would pile into the opposition. There was no question of that ever being used by us in Australia.

What we did was not overly aggressive. I have witnessed a lot worse in a lot of other places. Apart from Dai Young kicking Steve Cutler on the head, I cannot recall one particularly bad incident. No, the only 'crime' we were guilty of under Australian rugby law was to come from one-down to take the series.

The Wallabies showed how well they had learnt from life with the Lions by making life a misery for each of the home countries in turn. By 1991 they had become a class act from back to front, very worthy winners of the World Cup and, just as importantly, terrific ambassadors for the game wherever they went.

I shall never forget the 1989 Lions; the trip of a lifetime. It would not, I suppose, have been complete without another dislocated shoulder. It went for the fourth time during the last match of the tour, a special, extra fixture in Brisbane against a combined Australia–New Zealand XV, the Anzacs.

It all happened innocently enough with what I thought was a routine tackle on Michael Lynagh. It could have been worse, I suppose, in that it could have happened at the beginning of the tour, but I'd have been happier if it hadn't happened at all. Four dislocated shoulders is more than enough for anyone and this one would take a whole season out of my career. Once again I had been kicked in the teeth just when it seemed that the world had become my oyster.

At least I came home satisfied in the knowledge that my reputation had been enhanced. I returned a better, more confident player than I had been on departure. Apart from that bump in the last match, the whole tour had worked wonders for me. I had no doubt now that I could hold my own with anyone, anywhere. I no longer had anything to fear.

Socially, players with whom I was on little more than nodding acquaintance before the tour had become friends for life, not that the adventure was without its dangers. Dai Young, for example, almost lost his life in a white-water rafting accident one day when I was underwater elsewhere out on the Barrier Reef with one of the white shark fraternity. Scuba-diving with John Jeffrey is not for the faint-hearted, especially when he creeps up behind you and catches you by the flipper.

Something went wrong with Young's apparatus one day which meant he kept floating to the surface. His attempts to get back down to me doing my Jacques Cousteau bit on the seabed had to be seen to be believed. And then there was the Cocktail Club, an extremely exclusive little band composed of J.J., myself and a few other fearless founder members.

We would meet every Saturday evening in a bar in Darling Harbour on the Sydney waterfront and proceed to order a series of exotic, multi-coloured concoctions. The only thing about the Cocktail Club is that whenever I bump into any of them on the circuit, I know I'll have a thumping headache the next morning.

CHAPTER TEN

Headless Chickens

While the series-winning Lion licked his wounds, Wales spent the winter of 1989–90 doing things they had never done before. A gruesome collection of records added up to the first Welsh whitewash in the Five Nations championship.

Coaches came and went, as did managers and selectors. Players rolled off an imperfect assembly line into the team in ever-increasing numbers and many rolled back out again almost as soon as they had arrived. The only constant factor was to be found in their failure to win a single game that season.

New Zealand, first up at Cardiff that November, proceeded to win at the Arms Park by a record margin, 34–9, no surprise given that they had already done so by larger margins in Brisbane, Christchurch and Auckland during 1987 and 1988.

The previous season Wales had avoided losing all four champion-ship matches by coming from behind to beat England in their last game. This time there was to be no salvation. Losing at home to France in January was no disgrace. England at Twickenham four weeks later most certainly was.

Not even J.B.G. Thomas, the doyen of rugby journalists who had seen it all from the year dot, had experienced anything like this. 'The Welsh display,' he wrote, 'was so poor as to be beyond comprehension.'

John Ryan thought so, too. He resigned as coach, more or less on the spot and, in the wake of their burial at HQ, it was not entirely inappropriate that Wales should turn to men in black. Ron Waldron, the senior architect of Neath's rise to the front of the Welsh game, took over against Scotland, stopping the rot if not the losing run.

Only Ireland could save them now. The last time Wales had gone to Dublin it was to win the Triple Crown, but there would be no eleventh-hour reprieve as there had been twelve months earlier, only the grim reality that it had all become a pointless exercise.

Ieuan Evans could only sit and suffer and share the sense of depression deepening over the South Wales rugby belt; its rich seams, if not exhausted, then in serious decline. His shoulder cured once and for all by surgery, Evans was back for the 1991 championship. Given Wales's inability to provide him with any sort of service, it was like trying to run a Rolls-Royce without petrol.

The records kept on tumbling. Losing at home to New Zealand by a record score was bad enough. England following suit that January was harder to swallow – not only had they won but they, too, had done it by what for them was an unprecedented distance, 25–6. Scotland in Edinburgh offered no respite, 32–12 amounting to the heaviest defeat Wales had suffered at Murrayfield.

Ireland at home brought some relief but not much, a 21–21 draw at least checking the sequence and the spectre of another dose of whitewash. France at the Parc des Princes was a landslide, not merely the biggest Welsh defeat in Paris but their biggest in any Five Nations match.

No propagandist, however demented, could call the Neath experiment a success. Three Neath players – Paul Thorburn, Kevin Phillips and Mark Jones – were in the team bequeathed by Ryan. Waldron more than doubled the number for his first match, adding Allan Bateman, Brian Williams, Jeremy Pugh and Gareth Llewellyn.

Others followed rapidly, Chris Bridges, Glyn Llewellyn, Martyn Morris, Alun Edmunds, the durable John Davies and the outstanding Scott Gibbs. All told, Wales picked fourteen Neath players in successive seasons. Phil Pugh, brought in against the All Blacks and then excluded, had been capped pre-Waldron and another Neath back-row forward, flanker Rowland Phillips, was to go north.

Meanwhile, the roller-coaster which had taken Wales's number-one player into the stratosphere in Australia was on a rapidly downward spiral. For the second time, fate had conspired to rob him of an entire season.

Llanelli were three weeks away from their big game against the

All Blacks and, after what he and his team had done to us on their paddocks down under, I was anxious to welcome Wayne Shelford and company to Stradey. Home advantage, for once, would be very gratefully accepted.

There remained the small matter of my right shoulder and whether it would stand up to the first test of the 1989–90 season which also happened to be the biggest. There was only one way to find out and so on the final Saturday before the Blacks came to town I was back in the Scarlets first team for the match against Neath at Stradey.

Having suffered enough, I felt that I had more than paid my dues and that it would simply be a matter of proving my match fitness. That I had a tendency to bust the shoulder every other year, invariably during an away match somewhere in England, bothered me not in the slightest. It should have done because within thirty seconds the shoulder had gone again, for the fifth time in four years. I knew it couldn't go on like this, and that the major surgery required would wipe me out for the entire season. The Lions had given me a new belief in myself and, given a clean bill of health, I felt I could have raised my game to a consistently higher level. Instead, it was all over before I could start.

The next Monday I was in Morriston Hospital in Swansea, back where I was born, for a three-hour operation on the socket carried out by surgeon Bob Leyshon. It would cure the problem once and for all but it would take time. After seven days in hospital, the long, laborious process of rehabilitation began, by which time the All Blacks had been and gone.

They won wherever they went in Wales, and in all kinds of weather. The wind was getting up for hurricane force at Stradey and threatening to cause so much damage that a temporary stand was considered too hazardous for human occupation and there was even talk of the match being postponed until the Sunday.

Going downwind in the second half, the boys thought they were in with a real chance but Shelford's pack controlled the game as only they can with the result that we were completely shut out. The wind wasn't the only freakish thing about that day. It was the first time Llanelli had drawn a blank in a home match for fifteen years and there was I, stuck in my hospital bed, unable to do a thing about it.

The one consolation about the international the following Saturday was that Wales had reduced the size of the defeat to 34–9. All the tries came from the All Blacks but by the end of the tour they were beginning to face the outbreak of something which had by then reached epidemic proportions in Wales. For the first time, New Zealand players were being lined up by Rugby League clubs.

It meant that the awesome World Cup-winning team had begun to break up. John Gallagher went to Leeds at the end of that season, Craig Innes was to follow him there and two more backs, John Timu and John Schuster, went to League in Australia. For Wales, this was what they call an on-going situation.

Having experienced all the frustrations and traumas of the previous year, I found myself on the outside looking in when the Five Nations got under way. Being a long-term casualty, you have to take a detached stance, get on with your work and keep your distance.

I certainly did that when Wales went to Twickenham for their second match after losing a high-scoring home match against France, 29–19. One consolation about being injured is that I could indulge in a good old-fashioned international weekend in the company of my pals from Carmarthen. We stayed at a hotel in the West End, saw the lights of London and travelled out to Richmond on the morning of the match eager to sample the atmosphere.

So we headed for the Orange Tree and got settled in for the afternoon to such an extent that I gave my ticket to a friend. It wasn't entirely a noble gesture on my part. Had I gone, as intended, I would have found the experience an uncomfortable one. I felt so upset at missing the whole season that I didn't really want to thrust myself back towards the limelight. I didn't want to expose myself to a position where well-meaning people would come up and ask me what I thought of the match.

In hindsight, it was just as well I did stay away, what with

Wales being beaten by a record margin on a day when Phil Davies was one of the very few to stand out. The fact that John Ryan had resigned by Monday morning said it all really. Ron Waldron took over – his track record at Neath made him the obvious choice.

By then the surgeons had assured me that my shoulder was healing nicely, that it would be stronger than ever and that I would definitely play again. There was always the fear at the back of my mind that all those dislocations might force me to retire but it was too depressing a thought to dwell on for any length of time.

Halfway through the championship there was suddenly a new sense of optimism that everything was about to be put right. The Wales team for the next match, Scotland at home, should have been wearing a hefty dash of black along with the red. In addition to the four Neath players already there – Paul Thorburn, Kevin Phillips, Gareth Llewellyn and Mark Jones – Waldron added three more, Allan Bateman in the centre and Brian Williams and Jeremy Pugh to form an all-club front row either side of Phillips.

They didn't last very long. Scotland won, narrowly enough, but there were ominous signs then that what worked for Neath at club level wasn't going to work in the more sophisticated environment of international football. Two more Neath players, Martyn Morris and Alun Edmunds, were drafted in for the last match, Ireland in Dublin. Unfortunately, it couldn't prevent the dreaded whitewash.

When I finally got going again with my brand new shoulder in September 1990, the Neath bandwagon was still rolling with more and more of their team stepping forward as candidates for the national team. We all hoped for Wales's sake that it would work, but the signs were fairly grim.

England had tried something similar, placing an abnormally heavy reliance on their leading club, Bath. When it made no difference to their results, they gave it up as a bad job. The plain fact of the matter is that the concept doesn't work.

Ron made a constant reference to 'organised chaos'. The

entire Neath philosophy was based on fitness, their ethos on 100 miles an hour rugby. You started running and you ran and ran and ran for miles and miles and miles. Often we would start with twelve laps of the pitch. It got to the stage where we would be knackered before we could start any of the skill drills.

We would often run four or five miles and then train. It would have been alright if we'd been going for the Olympic 5,000 metres and it may have suited the front-five forwards in improving their stamina, but for people in my position there was nothing to be gained from running long distances at one pace. The irony is that for all the work we were still not properly fit.

The real flaw in the Neath philosophy, however, was in its mentality. Neath frightened and intimidated their opposition. They played the game at a terrific pace and with the togetherness of a real team. An international team, even a modest one, is just as together and nine times out of ten, bigger and stronger. They weren't going to be intimidated by Neath.

At national level you are up against top-class internationals. They see things that much sooner, do things that much quicker and they always have that priceless extra split second or two of time to jump a couple of moves ahead. Running around like headless chickens was never going to be the answer. New Zealand play a total brand of rugby but they had method. There didn't seem to be any method with Wales. I was totally lost.

On the domestic front nobody could touch Neath. Llanelli or Swansea could beat them in a one-off game but nobody could match their consistency. They weren't the most talented but they were the most committed. Nobody liked going to The Gnoll because they didn't feel safe, not that I ever had any problems in that respect. They rattled up record scores left, right and centre but it has to be pointed out that their fixture list wasn't the strongest. They were playing a lot of poor sides.

It didn't mean that all their players were good enough to play international rugby. Neath had a good PR machine working for them and an awful lot of their players were promoted to the national squad – so many that there were one or two whom I didn't know. A lot of players, not just from Neath, were capped then as a result of panic-stricken measures.

During these seasons the uncertainty was such that players were constantly coming in and out of the Welsh set-up. A journalist would plug a certain player and before you knew it he was in the team. It had all become a bit of a charade because the selectors operating under the different regimes tended to allow themselves to be influenced too easily instead of remaining detached and relying purely on their knowledge and instinct.

At that stage I was very much an outsider. Ron had asked me whether I would be ready for the first match of that season, the so-called international against the Barbarians. I told him I wouldn't. I desperately wanted to be at the forefront of the Welsh resurrection after missing the previous season, but to have rushed my recovery would have been sheer folly, especially with the more important matches not starting until the New Year.

When I came back for the start of the 1991 championship it was to a new experience. For the first time I knew what it was like to lose to England and at Cardiff, too, where, according to legend, England never won. They did that day and the way they did confirmed all my fears that I was going to have to get used to playing international rugby without touching the ball.

Over the next two seasons I would be lucky to get more than one pass per game, if that, and then hardly ever in a scoring position. England outclassed us up front which was not surprising, considering that we didn't have a pack. Simon Hodgkinson kicked everything in sight and that was that. The only chuckle we had that day was to hear that England had refused to give any interviews. It had taken them nearly thirty years to win at Cardiff and now, when they really did have something to talk about, they had nothing to say. Funny people, the English.

Given our ball-winning capacity, my opportunities to run with the ball were always going to be few and far between, even without the restrictive game we were committed to playing. Paul Thorburn was one of the world's great goalkickers, magnificent under the high ball but he was not, by any stretch of the imagination, an attacking full-back.

Running was not his strength as I knew to my cost. His weaknesses did not suit my game, or any wing's game for that matter, which was why we couldn't play a fast, open brand of rugby. Paul's main deficiency was in coming into the line, or, to be more accurate, not coming into the line. It denied me the chance to attack the opposition which would have done wonders for my game. It was no coincidence that I should have played my best rugby on Lions tours, away from the mindset our players had fallen into; away from the restrictive game we were playing.

For the first time in my life I found myself having to swallow a very unpalatable fact. I enjoyed my club rugby for Llanelli but I no longer derived any enjoyment from playing international rugby. I could not understand the ethos, I could not understand the principles we were supposed to be playing by and I could not understand the team selection.

Why, people will ask, didn't I do something about it? I was, in all honesty, not in a position to do anything. I had just come back from a serious injury and I did not feel sufficiently secure or important to start laying down the law, however politely. I simply could not make demands after I had been missing for so long.

And so the awful frustration went on. I would play knowing that I could not possibly perform to the best of my ability because I was never allowed to do so within such a limited team framework. It baffled me because it was a contradiction of the finest traditions of Welsh rugby. The Welsh public have an innate preference for backs who run the ball as opposed to kick it, and yet we did precious little running.

Scotland at Murrayfield, with Craig Chalmers in superb form, was another big defeat, 32–12. At least we put a stop to the rot with a home draw against Ireland which included a thrilling Welsh try started by Mark Ring breaking out of the twenty-two and finished off by Neil Jenkins. However, France in Paris put paid to any notion that the recovery was under way.

Ron made repeated references before the match to Philippe Sella. Names were never Ron's strongest point so he kept calling him 'Young Buck Sella'. He thought Sella had a weakness which we could exploit by attacking him. We were talking about one of the all-time great centres and it seemed odd to me that his game was being questioned by the coach of what was, in all honesty, one of the worst Welsh back lines of all.

There was nothing more certain than that Sella would score. He did and France ran up their biggest score against us, 36–3. The bitter-and-twisted brigade, the ex-internationals who will slag anyone off if there's a quick buck to be made from the papers, had a field day. Constructive criticism, of the sort we had from people like Gerald Davies and Gareth Edwards, is perfectly acceptable any time. Rubbishing somebody in print because there's a few bob in it is something I abhor.

The French beating gave them more ammunition. We were well gone by then, lost in a giant maze. Worse than that, we finished up a complete and utter rabble. And soon, too soon, we would be heading for Australia . . .

CHAPTER ELEVEN

A National Disgrace

The most shameful weekend endured by any international rugby team began with the captain breaking down before the match. It continued with a mass breakdown on the pitch and ended with a dining-room fracas which inspired the headline: 'Woeful Wales Wallop Each Other'.

Paul Thorburn, devastated by the burden of leading Wales through their Australian nightmare during the summer of 1991, dissolved in tears during a private heart-to-heart with tour manager Clive Rowlands in his hotel bedroom before playing his last international. He had already decided to give it up as a bad job.

What followed was to make Wales, in the words of their demoralised captain, 'the clowns of international rugby both on and off the field'.

They lost the match by a margin without parallel for a fixture between senior International Board countries, 63–6. Australia scored twelve tries at a time when they were worth only four, and having put Wales to the sword they then sat back and watched a group of Welsh players fighting among themselves.

Their boorish behaviour unfolded in full view of dining-tables occupied by Wallaby players, officials and their wives. It degenerated into a fracas which left Mike Hall needing medical attention for a gashed hand caused by a broken wine glass. The tour management had no excuse for not pre-empting the trouble. I and at least one Australian journalist had warned them independently of what was brewing. Instead, they reacted when it was too late.

Thorburn sensed trouble from the moment a mini-rugby ball splashed into a soup bowl within damaging distance of a guest's wife. There was an undercurrent of ill-feeling which made this more than a harmless bit of post-match horseplay. The captain, by then in total despair, could only pray for the formalities to finish without an explosion.

'Kevin Phillips, who had been sharing a table with David Campese, though the latter had hardly consumed the same amount of beverage as our hooker, was about to create havoc,' Thorburn recounted in his autobiography, *Kicked into Touch.* 'I had seen it before and I knew trouble was brewing.

'First, Kevin wanted to have words with referee David Bishop and then Fred Howard of England. Kevin had a long-standing argument to settle with Fred after the Neath–All Blacks game at The Gnoll. Fortunately, I was able to usher David away and Fred found a safe haven somewhere else.

'Something was going to erupt that night because the temperature had been simmering for so long. Clive Rowlands and I attempted to step in, but there is little reason in drink and I joined Campese on the balcony. The skirmish which broke out was apparently short and sharp, the end result being a broken glass and Mike Hall's cut hand. Malcolm Downes, the team doctor, attended to the injury but the harm to Welsh rugby was incalculable.'

In his letter of resignation to the Welsh Rugby Union, Thorburn admitted that the pressures had 'become too great for me to handle'. He condemned some of the Welsh players for their disloyalty to coach Ron Waldron, for having no regard for pride or motivation, and of being the first to complain, bicker and find fault.

There were other squabbles, too petty for words except that they offer an insight into the whole shambling scenario. Lyn Davies, the BBC Wales reporter, was ostracised because his commentary of the New South Wales match, the one Wales lost 71–8, had upset the coach's wife.

The Wallabies scored eight second-half tries in barely half an hour – the first four in a period of thirteen minutes, the second four in eleven minutes at the end. Thorburn departed just before half-time but subsequently admitted that he, too, had lost 'all heart'.

The stress of the tour had taken its toll on Waldron, an honourable man who worked ceaselessly in the Welsh cause. His resignation on grounds of ill-health followed.

We were a disgrace to our country and to the game of rugby football. An utter disgrace. I would go so far as to say that this was the greatest single disaster ever to befall Welsh rugby. The New Zealand tour two years before had been almost a success by comparison.

This was a nightmare from start to finish. We arrived in Perth in the middle of a typhoon which was not the only experience to fill me with a sense of foreboding. To make matters worse we were stuck in a summer motel in a seaside resort in the middle of the Western Australian winter with no heating and a hurricane howling about.

The *Hi-De-Hi* setting would have been ideal for a family holiday in summer but we had come to attend to some very serious business, and the last thing we needed was to be stuck in a place where the beds were so damp that, if we'd stayed much longer, we wouldn't have been able to get into them for the watercress!

The lights kept going out and the food was so substandard we had to keep going to the nearest pizzeria to keep body and soul together in the wind, cold and rain. There we were, marooned miles from Perth with nowhere but a deserted beach twenty yards away.

When a photographer bowled up with a couple of surfboards and suggested Phil Davies and I pose for a picture, I went ahead when I ought to have known better. An alarm bell ought to have woken me to the possibility that the happy snap might just be used to set me up. It duly appeared in the *Western Mail* after one of our less than glorious efforts, giving the reader the impression we were having a whale of a time while insinuating that we should have been training harder. Ah, well, I could at least put it down to experience and make sure I did not fall into the same trap again.

As manager and coach, Clive Rowlands and Ron Waldron were at loggerheads from the word go. They disagreed on team selection and other crucial issues, like training. I didn't agree with some of it either because, again, there was too much emphasis on running. We would run to the training ground a couple of miles away, run more while we were there, round an Aussie rules oval — which is a lot bigger than a rugby ground — and then we would finish up with some extra running.

It was a dire time. Clive, having made his objections known, then went through the four-week trip aggrieved on the two most important matters of the tour. He was used to being centrally involved but felt from an early stage that he had been completely eliminated from the decision-making process. He felt he had been pushed out of the circle. Someone suggested they were at loggerheads before we left Heathrow. I don't know about that but I do know that Clive's relationship with Ron deteriorated rapidly.

If the two at the top couldn't see eye to eye, it was hardly going to make for a fun trip, but this one was doomed from the outset. We kicked off with a win, a win which everyone gets against Western Australia, and then lost the next match — not exactly the end of the world because Queensland, as they were to prove in the Super Ten, could justifiably claim to be the most powerful provincial team in the world.

We squeezed past the next state team, Australian Capital Territories, in the mud and rain at Canberra before walking into what I can safely say was the biggest humiliation of my life, which is not an easy thing to assess, given that I have had the misfortune to be a part of quite a few such humiliations.

That this one should have been inflicted by a state team made it worse than the rest. New South Wales hammered us 71–8 and for a non-international team to do that to an international team is nothing short of scandalous. That we should have performed so much better the previous Saturday in holding Queensland to 35–24 clearly calls the attitude of the players into question.

I played against Campo that day and he finished up with five tries, which I suppose gave him a bit of his own back for what had happened the last time we had been in opposition, in that deciding Lions Test two years before. I don't really know what he thought about Wales that day because they didn't want to talk to us after the match.

They didn't address us at all but, there again, why the hell should they? They had nothing to talk to us about. Instead, we had to listen to a barrage of abuse from those who did have something to say to us in the after-match formalities. It amounted to a non-stop flow of very patronising stuff, a general mickey-take by all and sundry. Being thrashed out on the field was by no means the end of our anguish.

When I look back on that day I sometimes have to convince myself that it wasn't all a bad dream and that instead of playing a rugby match we were filming a sketch for *Monty Python's Flying Circus*. John Cleese would have been in his element. If anyone had witnessed what I witnessed in the Welsh dressing-room before the kick-off that day, they would have been doubled up in laughter.

The dressing-room floors at the Concorde Oval in Sydney are ceramic and as such liable to be fairly slippery, all the more so when you are wearing boots with aluminium studs. Before the match we warmed up with a series of criss-cross drills which meant players had to run diagonally across the spacious dressing-room from all four corners.

Not surprisingly, some of the boys began to slip and pretty soon they were falling all over the place. These were great big blokes who, through no fault of their own, were liable to do themselves an injury. At first it was all rather disconcerting, then it got to such an embarrassingly funny stage that I could contain myself no longer. I sought sanctuary in the toilet where I attempted to hide while trying not to kill myself laughing at the sight of what was going on right in front of me.

When it started, I tried telling myself that, no, we weren't really doing this. It all seemed too incredible for words, forwards of six and a half feet and more were falling on the floor and people were shouting and yelling all over the place. I'm all for getting psyched up, but not to the extent where we were putting ourselves in danger.

Anyway, Paul Thorburn had to come and drag me out from the toilet. It was such pure Monty Python that it would not have looked out of place in the *Life of Brian*. Talk about the *Holy Grail*!

It was such an absolute farce. I had expected to see Brian Rix burst in at any moment and drop his trousers!

Out on the pitch we disintegrated into a shambles. Paul tried to rally the troops but he was totally powerless to do anything about it. The show had gone off the rails and plunged the depths and there was no way he could have brought it back. We could have taken the field that day with all six replacements, played with twenty-one men and still lost. Long before the end all communication within the team had broken down. Ron had always been optimistic but it was then that he realised how badly we were struggling.

During the week I did my best to lift spirits. Four of us, myself, Robert Jones, Scott Gibbs and Paul Arnold, staged our own exclusive pop video which caused a lot of laughs and, believe me, that wasn't easy. At that stage we all knew that the Test would be an exercise in damage limitation. Some limitation.

Even the Wallaby supporters seemed to realise what a rabble we had become and began heckling us at every opportunity. They treated us to the usual abusive chants and then they paid us the ultimate insult. They began laughing at us. Any ball we won and passed without dropping would be greeted by ironic jeers which served only to increase our sense of humiliation.

The worst stage of the match came in the second half. For a while they scored whenever they wanted to. We had neither the guts nor the determination to try and stop them. We were incapable of limiting the damage any more. Our resistance had gone. It was as if we were all in darkness; as if the lights had all been switched off which, come to think of it, I suppose they had.

I just wanted to escape there and then but there were formalities to observe and so we went to the dinner. The speeches over, some of us sat at tables, in my case chatting to Australian friends I had made during the Lions tour. Others took part in different 'discussions'. Naturally, a tour like ours had produced no shortage of critical material for the journalists covering the trip and a few of the players took exception to some of the articles, most particularly those written by Paul Rees, then writing for the *South Wales Echo*.

At this point I was talking to David Campese. Some of our players were drunk and the situation began to degenerate rapidly. A few bread rolls were thrown, then knives and plates were chucked across the room and couple of players were becoming louder and louder in their 'discussions' with Paul Rees.

Others began to realise something was going on and that Paul might be in some danger. Someone went in to pull Kevin Phillips away from him. There was a lot of pushing and shoving and bad language. Clive and Ron got upset at the unedifying spectacle unfolding before their very eyes, none of which was doing us any good as far as our hosts were concerned. They were bemused and saddened by the whole sorry episode.

Then Mike Hall had his hand cut quite deeply by some broken glass. The wound was bleeding badly so I dragged him downstairs to the medical room where he could have it stitched. For the players involved to have done that, knowing a number of journalists were there, was the height of stupidity. What a way to represent your country!

Once that had happened there was only one thing for it and that was to beat a hasty retreat out of Ballymore and back to the hotel. Morning and the flight home could not come quickly enough. By then Thorburn had been shot to pieces and it had an obvious effect on his form. Quite a lot of players had been crushed by this stage.

Some of them seriously questioned whether they wanted to play for their country again, whether there was any point in going on if it had come to such a sorry state. Our reputation the world over had been badly tarnished and that one Saturday caused more damage than any other single day in our rugby history. We had become a bad joke, a laughing-stock.

Before the end, Ron's health had taken a turn for the worse. He was looking ill and the strain had clearly taken its toll. On that tour, nobody could have worked harder to make it a success. A workaholic, Ron never stopped and I respect him for that. He is a very nice guy but it does not alter my opinion that his concept of international rugby was a mistaken one.

Then, after we had stumbled home from one farce into

another with the Welsh Rugby Union holding another of their special general meetings, Ron resigned for health reasons. In his place they appointed someone of whom I had never heard but of whom the rugby press thought very highly. Alan Davies, as an ex-England coach with Nottingham and the Midlands, at least would not be burdened by divided club loyalties and parish pump politics. That would be two very definite pluses.

Thorburn having retired from international rugby, the new coach asked for a meeting at the Holiday Inn in Cardiff with myself and three other senior players – Robert Jones, Phil Davies and Mike Hall. It was early August which meant that there was no time to be lost – not with a match against France coming up in four weeks time and, four weeks after that, the World Cup for which we were in something less than perfect shape.

I had no idea that Mr Davies was going to offer me a place in the team, never mind anything else . . .

CHAPTER TWELVE

Captain Cymru

Queen Victoria was still on the throne when Willie Llewellyn from Tonypandy became the first of a rare breed, nipping in at the end of the nineteenth century with four tries for Wales against England at St Helen's, Swansea. By the start of the twentieth century he had established himself as the first of another rare breed.

Starting against Scotland at Swansea in February 1904, he captained Wales from the wing for a run of five matches before bowing out of international competition at the age of twenty-six. He did so after the historic victory over the pioneering All Blacks, presumably working on the principle that it would all be downhill from there on, concentrating instead on his pharmacy in the Rhondda Valley.

The captaincy of Wales has been entrusted to so few wings over the decades that Willie's record stood the test of time for more than eighty years. Until Ieuan Evans was summoned to the Arms Park one morning in late summer 1991, only five other players had captained Wales from the wing.

Reggie Gibbs, a Cardiff shipowner who was by then steaming his way past Llewellyn's total with seventeen tries in sixteen matches, was the second, for one match only – Ireland at Lansdowne Road in March 1910. Rowe Harding, later Judge Harding, lasted a little longer, leading the team three times during the mid-twenties before the selectors decided that it probably wasn't the done thing.

John Rees was another one-off leader from the right wing, against Ireland at Cardiff in 1936. Post-war, the species almost became extinct. Ken Jones took charge against Scotland at Swansea in 1954 before promptly handing back inside to Bleddyn Williams for the next match.

Almost another quarter of a century passed before the captaincy went back to the wing with Gerald Davies's appointment for the second Test against Australia, at the Sydney Cricket Ground in 1978, at the end of a tour for which neither Phil Bennett nor Gareth Edwards was available. The injury to the official captain, Terry Cobner, made Gerald's choice a stop-gap but an eminently appropriate one given that it marked the farewell appearance of one of the legends. Needless to say, he responded to the occasion with a try.

Evans, therefore, completed a magnificent seven. He did so with some trepidation, not least over the practicality of captaining a team from a position on the periphery of the action rather than at the heart of it. He had not captained any team since his last year at Queen Elizabeth Grammar School in Carmarthen. They had swept all before them that season with the exception of one draw, so Evans could boast that he was bringing an unbeaten record to the captaincy, except, of course, that he has never been one to boast about anything.

As positions in sport go, the captaincy of the Wales team had at that time been sufficiently precarious to make soccer management appear secure by comparison. Evans bucked the trend, defied the odds to hold the position longer than any of the previous one hundred or so Welsh captains – longer even than the incomparable Arthur 'Monkey' Gould.

The original Welsh superstar, Gould captained Wales through five consecutive seasons for a total of eighteen matches; a record Evans was to stretch to twenty-eight. As a reminder that there is nothing new under the sun, Wales rewarded Gould with a testimonial which was more than they did for their captain a century later. Gould's fund was set up with the permission of the Welsh Football Union, as they were then known, whereupon the International Board intervened, upholding charges of professionalism levelled against the Welsh Union by their English, Scottish and Irish counterparts.

Their refusal to excommunicate Gould raised the very real doubt about Wales being drummed out of the International Championship and their matches against Ireland and England declared null and void. Gould averted the crisis by announcing his retirement at the age of thirty-two and a few months later, at a banquet in his native Newport, he was given a house in appreciation of his career.

Ieuan is still waiting for his . . .

The speculation began in earnest once the news broke over the first weekend of August that, following Paul Thorburn's resignation, Wales would need a new captain for the impending 1991 World Cup. The Australian tour having shattered his confidence, Thorburn's decision came as no surprise.

Robert Jones became the immediate favourite with a lot of heavy backing for Phil Davies, my captain at Llanelli. When the Welsh Rugby Union called me to the Arms Park one morning that week for a further chat with the new coach, I had no inkling that I was even a candidate for the job, let alone *the* candidate.

Alan Davies and I sat down in an office overlooking the magical acre. We exchanged pleasantries and then he said: 'Would you be interested in taking over the captaincy?'

Something like that hitting you as a bolt out of the blue takes some digesting. Alan knew the enormity of what he was proposing and understood only too well that I would need time to gather all my thoughts, stifle the initial surge of excitement and think it through rationally. In fact, he made it clear he did not want a decision there and then. He wanted me to go away and think about it and give him my verdict in good time.

I thought long and hard. Nobody needed to warn me about the strain entailed in the job of fronting the national sport. I had seen for myself what it had done to Paul Thorburn earlier that summer and I reflected also on the toll it had taken of previous captains, not least Jonathan Davies.

There was a lot of consultation to be done. I spoke to my parents, to my employers, to Jonathan, Phil Davies and my coaches at Stradey, Gareth Jenkins and Allan Lewis. What I was being offered was a rare privilege, so rare that people would willingly give their right arm for it. I would have given mine but I had to sit down and think it through.

It wasn't simply a case of my wanting to accept. I was very conscious of how the public would perceive my appointment; how they would react. It began to worry me. I found myself wondering: 'Are people going to laugh when I'm introduced as captain of Wales? Are they going to ridicule me? How are the players going to respond? Will they accept it?'

I had no knowledge of captaincy at senior level and I knew that wing was not exactly the most central place from which to supervise the running of a team. I was a little concerned during this period of intense speculation that I had not been given a serious mention until the day before the appointment was due to be announced.

It was with some relief that I read John Kennedy describe me in the *Western Mail* as the dark horse in the race. He probably knew that I was past the post and the thought that someone else knew I was in the running made me feel a lot better. I knew I was taking on one of the most demanding jobs in British sport and I was desperately anxious to make a success of it.

What I did not appreciate then was that my life would never be the same again. It changed my lifestyle completely. It took over my life to such an extent that it led to the break-up of my long-standing relationship with my girlfriend, Clare Peacock. We had been living together for four and a half years and would probably still be together had it not been for the demands of international captaincy and my obsessive desire to give it my undivided attention.

I knew I would be public property and that I would now be required to give of my time as the spokesman for the team. I could handle that provided I could make my captaincy count on the field and that meant inspiring those around me. The need to be on top form was even more paramount than if I was still just one of the team.

Alan had outlined his plans for the resurrection of Welsh rugby. He had jumped into the breach at short notice and taken the job only for as long as the World Cup which meant it would have to be done in a hurry. He told me that the new manager would be Bob Norster and that impressed me. Here was someone who had been largely untainted by the events of the last few seasons, someone who commanded huge respect in and out of the country.

From the very outset we talked about mending bridges. Relationships between team and press had been strained, to put it mildly, for some eighteen months. We wanted a far more open book which meant wiping the slate clean, starting afresh and getting the press corps on our side. I phoned Alan back to say yes, I would be delighted to accept the captaincy.

Even now, I cannot put into words the pride and emotion I felt at being awarded the captaincy of my country. It wasn't all a bed of roses, though. The downside reared its head very early and what I overheard stiffened my resolve to make sure that I was going to make the sceptics eat their words.

Some of the comments were hurtful, like: 'How the hell can Ieuan Evans be captain of Wales? It's a joke. You can't skipper a side from the wing.' I overheard the jibes from conversations in the street and it helped me develop a mental toughness without which I could never have survived.

My personality changed rapidly. The laid-back, Carmarthen Cowboy persona disappeared. I became far more positive in my attitude to people I had never met. Whereas before I would use the slightest excuse not to engage in conversation with strangers, now I soon learnt that I was very much public property. I was expected to talk to people, to project the image of Welsh rugby and I rapidly became less and less introverted. It took a conscious effort because I am basically a shy person. Unfortunately, some people mistook that for aloofness and arrogance.

I took the job seriously from the word go, perhaps a little too seriously, but that was the way I was going to do it. There is no doubt that it changed me as a person. I became more susceptible to mood swings. Clare suffered the backlash of those as did a number of my friends. Slowly, but inevitably, it affected our relationship for the worse.

The captaincy influenced me in all sorts of ways. I felt I couldn't go out and socialise the way I had done before. I had a role to play, an image to project and there was no room there for the old Carmarthen boy going out and getting sloshed the way he used to. Where I used to go out and think nothing of it, I stayed in and became increasingly less sociable.

On top of that, I would bottle things up until they began to eat away inside me. I showed my emotions a lot less and that affected me for the worse. I had lost most of my hair and what I have left is no doubt turning grey but I am not complaining. Nobody forced me to do it that way. I chose to do it that way because really it had to be all or nothing.

There can be no prouder moment for any human being than to be the leader of his country going into an international match at a stadium like Cardiff Arms Park with millions and millions of people watching all over the British Isles and beyond. Everything I did was designed towards that end.

When I walked into a packed Centenary suite at the Arms Park for my first press conference as Wales captain, nobody, least of all me, imagined that it was to be the start of something big, that it would run for twenty-eight matches and extend to receiving the Five Nations trophy from the Queen at Twickenham, of all places.

There were some very surprised reporters there that morning. None of them can have been more surprised than I was at suddenly finding myself in such an exalted position. This was my first press conference and it was like being chucked in at the deep end. All the interviews I had done prior to that were easy ones for television where the questioning never really got any tougher than a nice and easy: 'How's it going, then, Ieuan?' Now, for the first time, I was having to talk for the team as a whole. Despite being in a state of some apprehension, I enjoyed that first conference. I had had no training in how to deal with the media but I learnt a great deal very quickly. The rugby journalists were all very helpful and, over the years, fair enough.

After Australia, there were a lot of broken fences to be mended and I accepted that an important part of my job would be to go out of my way to be as co-operative as possible. We were never going to succeed without the press.

Inevitably, there was never any shortage of advice. I was given an awful lot which I didn't ask for. At times it felt as though it was being shovelled down my throat.. The world and his brother wanted to have his say, which was understandable. Everyone wants to pick the Welsh team and why should that be any different just because I had been made captain?

It's a national pastime, one in which I had indulged often

enough myself. Now I was virtually being given the opportunity to do it for real and that gave me a tremendous buzz. Alan and Bob picked the squad. Once that was done, I then helped select the team. I was asked for my opinion before the squad was chosen. When it came to the actual XV, I had a direct input. That meant selecting and de-selecting players, passing opinions on people I liked and knew, being a party to tough, unpopular decisions.

The ultimate in responsibility put an end to any lingering fear of my going to Featherstone or any part of northern England. The Yorkshire club had made their big offer a little earlier and there was a lot of talk within the squad about who would be the next to go after the Australian fiasco.

Once we were back home, events moved quickly. The Union held their special meeting, the captain resigned, then the coach. A new man was in charge and then I was offered this. Once that had happened, Rugby League ceased to be an option.

No sooner had I been appointed captain than I was leading the team out on to the Arms Park for the first time. France during the first week of September sounded rather out of sync but the match had been arranged to celebrate the floodlighting at the stadium, installed at a cost of £400,000. More to the point, it gave us the chance to test ourselves against class opposition a few weeks before plunging into the second World Cup.

France beat us and Serge Blanco scored another of his master tries in what turned out to be his farewell to Cardiff. If there was a better full-back, I never saw him. Wales seemed to hold an attraction for him which invariably turned out to be fatal as far as we were concerned. He played against us eleven times and lost only once, back in the days when I was still at school.

Although we lost, the performance was a much improved one and while it is fair to say that any performance would have been an improvement on the last one, we did enough to earn the encouraging reviews in the papers the following day. There was no doubt that people were willing us to do well and after the summer annihilation we had done better than expected with quite a few new faces. It wouldn't have been me had I not taken a bang on the shoulder which forced me off before the end, but at least it was not as serious as a dislocation.

And so to the World Cup. Four years earlier we had gone to the other side of the world and finished third. Here we were in our own backyard and we couldn't even make the last eight. Had the Davies–Norster alliance only been in place a few weeks sooner, I am convinced we would have avoided the catastrophe of failing to survive the first stage of the competition.

Western Samoa were always liable to be dangerous opponents. What we didn't know is that we had been stuck in the same group as the team who would prove the surprise packet of the competition. They took plenty of teams by surprise, starting with us.

They went all the way to the quarter-finals and in next to no time the All Blacks were picking off the best of their players, like Frank Bunce and Pat Lam. Losing that first game at the Arms Park on that depressing Sunday meant we had to win our two remaining pool games, against Argentina and Australia, to qualify. It didn't help that Mark Ring, our playmaker-in-chief, had not fully recovered from a blow to the knee during the French game the previous month. He was never really fit, not that I was 100 per cent either after my shoulder bang in the same match. The Argentinian tie brought me into direct conflict with Mark halfway through the game. When I took him off goalkicking duties, he threw his toys out of the cot.

Mark had missed a few and in a close game I couldn't afford to have him miss another. When the referee had given us the penalty in question, I signalled to the posts. Mark came up to take it and I said: 'No. Mike's taking this one.'

With that, I called Mike Rayer forward. 'Ringo' threw a temper tantrum which Mike found highly amusing. He duly slotted the penalty over without any bother. Afterwards, Mark told me he understood my decision. Somehow, I doubt whether he did. All that mattered was that we had won the game and now it was straight in against the team that had given us such a terrible beating only three months earlier.

Instead of 63–3 it was 38–3. An improvement, especially considering we had been taken to the cleaners in the line-out by the staggering count of 28–2. Nick Farr-Jones, on his way to lifting the World Cup at Twickenham a few weeks later, was generous during his speech at the dinner, saying it was nice to see Wales on the way back.

Well, we still had a very long way to go and nothing was going to alter the fact that we had been knocked out of the World Cup on home soil by an unseeded country. Next time we would have to qualify, another indication of how far we had fallen in world terms. We took a slating and the obituary of Welsh rugby was written and published all over the world. Like Mark Twain, I was going to show that reports of the death of Welsh rugby were more than a bit exaggerated.

CHAPTER THIRTEEN

Rumpole to the Rescue

It was never going to be anything other than a matter of time before the first 'incident' of Ieuan Evans's reign as captain of Wales landed at his feet. To be strictly accurate, it landed in a rather large heap not too far from his feet during the opening minutes of the opening match of the 1992 Five Nations championship.

The drama arrived in the crumpled form of Ireland's towering second-row forward, Neil Francis, and the referee was already taking a dim view of how he had come to be laid out in such a prone position. Fred Howard being the referee in question, Evans knew he had to do some very fast talking if Wales were to avoid starting the match with fourteen men.

Howard had a worthy reputation as one referee who took a consistently commendable hard-line attitude towards violent conduct, and Tony Copsey was in serious danger of being sent off before he could be presented with his Welsh cap. It was then that Evans discovered how much more there was to international captaincy than tossing a coin and exhorting the boys to get stuck in.

The other British and Irish captains lining up for the Five Nations in January 1992 had all been through the mill to a lesser or greater extent – Will Carling, Phillip Matthews and David Sole. Carling and Sole knew how it felt to produce the winning consistency demanded of a Grand Slam team. They had the comparative luxury of leading a settled team with an automatic choice of a Lion at No. 10 – Rob Andrew and Craig Chalmers.

Wales, in contrast, had gone through seven outside halves in the three years since Jonathan Davies packed his bags. Now they were on their eighth, Colin Stephens. Davies's transfer had such an effect on him that he suddenly found himself thrust centre-stage at Llanelli as an eighteen-year-old appearing not in any old jersey but in the revered No. 10 as worn by Davies, Phil Bennett and Carwyn James.

No player had had to grow up so fast and now he was being asked to carry an even greater burden, knowing that it had been too much for his immediate predecessors. They were many and varied, Wales turning initially to Bleddyn Bowen. Six more followed, in chronological order, Paul Turner, Tony Clement, David Evans, Neil Jenkins, Adrian Davies and Mark Ring.

After all that, they were no nearer filling the position. Now Stephens was about to make his application for the vacancy. He would at least make a winning start, thanks in no small way to his captain's powers of persuasion.

My first championship match as captain of Wales had only just begun when I found myself in the throes of a crisis. An Irishman had been knocked down, the Dublin crowd were baying for blood and one very worried Welsh player was about to be sent for a bath, even though he'd barely had the time to work up a sweat!

Tony Copsey had chinned Neil Francis, the big Irish second row, in either the second or third line-out of the match and, judging by his body-language, Fred Howard was about to send him off. It was then that I found out how much it pays if you can reinforce your captaincy with a breathless impersonation of a defence lawyer, a sort of Rumpole of the Bailey done on-the-hoof.

Perhaps, on reflection, my defence was more in the spirit of Petrocelli and the NYPD! After the most desperate pleading I have ever done for anyone in my life, the English referee granted Copsey a stay of execution. I would hesitate to say that I completed my first match-winning performance without needing to touch the ball, but we would almost certainly have lost the match had 'Cops' been told to get on his bike.

It was just as well that M'lord did not know the circumstances which led to Francis being knocked down. We knew beforehand that if we were to have a real chance of getting out of Lansdowne Road with a win we would have to keep Neil quiet because, on form, he is one of the best line-out jumpers in the world. The line-out being little better than a jungle, you try and get away with whatever you can.

The first line-out or two confirmed our fears about Francis. The pack decided something would have to be done about him and Copsey volunteered. He would be taken care of. Tony was the ideal man, all elbows and arms, an awkward customer, one whose attitude never caused me any problem, your honour. He would willingly give everything for his adoptive Wales, so he let Francis have it at the next line-out and I could see Neil hit the floor. Whether it was a punch or an elbow I could not be sure but whatever it was, Copsey caught him good and proper. Fred called him over at once in a very stern manner and I rushed over right away and launched into the defence of my man. I used every excuse I could think of and a few I hadn't thought of. 'It's his first cap, ref. First minute of the match. Very physical. Always the same with the Irish. Fred, you can't send him off, not for that.' And so I went jabbering on in much the same vein.

For that match, as an experiment, Fred had been wired up to the television commentators so he could keep them informed on every decision as he gave it. At the start he looked to me to be on the verge of sending Copsey off. I'm not saying I influenced him but at one stage he covered his microphone up so no one could hear the exchange.

He had put the fear of God up both of us before letting Copsey off with a severe warning. Really, that episode won the game for us. Ireland in Dublin, more than any other Five Nations away match, is a physical encounter. The Irish are never backward at coming forward to dish it out, so you have to get in first and stand up to them. Without Copsey, we would have lost that match.

Francis carried on, but the wind had been taken out of his sails and we shaded it, 16–15. There was a public outcry that Copsey had been allowed to stay on the field and Irish supporters did not feel any better about it a few weeks later when one of their referees, Stephen Hilditch, sent two of the French front row off against England in Paris.

People tend to forget the number of times we've been on the receiving end of a low blow. The England match in 1987 and Shelford's big right hand in the World Cup semi-final that same year are two cases in point. I know what it's like to be on the wrong end of some fairly ferocious rucking and I use the term rucking very loosely.

As I've pointed out before, it is an intimidating game at international level. After a while it becomes second nature. You learn, often by bitter experience, where not to be at any given time and how to protect yourself. No, in this case I felt we deserved the rub of the green, if you'll pardon the pun.

In the dressing-room afterwards, Copsey was suitably grateful for my pleading on his behalf. He was the first Englishman to qualify for Wales under the six-year residential rule, having studied in Cardiff and then stayed on to make a career for himself with Llanelli. As a good old Essex boy from Romford, he had a 'Made in England' tattoo on his backside. When he thanked me for helping get him off the hook, I said: 'Just make sure you get another tattoo on the other cheek, one that says "Refined in Wales" . . .'

Thankfully, I never had cause to push my luck to such an extent again on behalf of a player in trouble for taking the law into his own hands. Maybe it was just as well because, if the referee was really determined, then nothing I, or anyone else was going to say, would make a blind bit of difference.

My old pal, Anthony Buchanan, would have stretched my skills as a budding defence lawyer beyond breaking-point had I been around to leap to his defence one dark, mysterious night at Northampton. We had played our annual match there and the English club's renowned hospitality guaranteed the usual, raucous Saturday night. Northampton were always superb hosts and it's a great shame that such an Anglo-Welsh fixture has been lost, along with many others, but that's another story.

Returning to our hotel fairly late and a little the worse for wear, Anthony decided he'd had enough and that he would go to bed. He was sharing a room with Phil Davies, so he asked for what he thought was the key to his room and bowled along the corridor, bouncing from wall to wall as he went. Opening the door, he could see a shape in the bed next to his and assumed that Phil had turned in.

Thoughtfully, he decided against switching on the light for fear of disturbing his room-mate's sleep. Then when he is about half undressed, Anthony calls Phil by his nickname, 'Tulip'. At that point, sheets and pillows are hurled across the room and a very irate, frightened human being leaps to his feet.

The world's top snooker players were staying at the same hotel and the man who Buchanan has mistaken for his second-row colleague turned out to be none other than Eddie Charlton, who in addition to being a snooker star happened to be a former Australian boxing champion. Eddie was about to let him have one, thinking he was some sort of overweight burglar, whereupon the 19-stone intruder grabbed his clothes and fled. Only when he got downstairs did he realise he had asked for the wrong room key!

We made a point of checking the papers on Monday morning for Eddie's result. He had been beaten five frames to nil. If I had been Anthony's solicitor, I'd have advised him to plead guilty and throw himself at the mercy of the court . . .

But I digress. After Ireland we returned home to face France and lost narrowly, 12–9. At least we were getting closer and, with Alan Davies having agreed to remain after the World Cup, a degree of stability returned at last to team selection. All season we used only eighteen players which was a stark contrast to the hectic comings and goings of previous years.

England at Twickenham coincided with a piece of history which we would have given worlds to have aborted. Their win gave them back-to-back Grand Slams, the first by an English team since the twenties. Wade Dooley, one of those English players suspended by the Rugby Football Union for their part in the match against Wales five years earlier, had the last laugh, celebrating his fiftieth cap with the last of England's three tries.

England were by far the outstanding team and they really ought to have won the Slam four times in five years, a level of consistency which nobody has ever attained. They had such an awesome pack that their domination of the championship during the nineties should have been a case for the monopolies people.

Although we were well beaten, we found some character, admittedly in defeat, which had been sadly lacking. It sounds as though we were clutching at straws but England, fifteen points clear in next to no time, spent the last twenty minutes dominating the match without being able to translate that dominance into points.

By then Will Carling and I had been introduced in less than dignified circumstances. We were wrestling on the ground, chucking handbags at each other much to the amusement of forwards from both sides who gathered round to watch the fun. At that point, Will and I thought better of it and rather sheepishly made our separate ways back to our respective positions. It was hardly a promising beginning to a firm friendship, but we've had many a chuckle since about our initial greeting.

One championship win that year was one more than we had managed in the two previous years. Scotland at home offered us the chance to break even. It was high time we put a stop to people reminding us that we hadn't won a home match in the championship in three seasons. We felt we were winning the battle in terms of restoring our self-respect and confirmation of that came from an unlikely source.

When I picked up a loose kick from Gavin Hastings on the Scottish ten-yard line and counter-attacked, I managed to make a bit of a gap for myself and cut back inside. When I ran out of space, who should be there to carry the move on with an electrifying burst of speed but our tighthead prop, Hugh Williams-Jones. I don't know where he found the extra gears, but once he had put his foot on the accelerator, the Scots had no chance of repairing the damage.

Hugh not only produced his legendary sprint but also put Richard Webster through the last gap and off beneath the posts for the try which made all the difference. Two wins out of four was nothing special but considering what Wales had been through, it amounted to real progress. We were on the way back and somehow it was fitting that Webster should score the try because nobody typified our spirit more than he did.

'Webby' is one of those unforgettable characters, on and off the field. If there is a better team man, I have not met him. He would always put his body on the line, hence all the injuries. Fearless on the field, he was always great fun off it. When the going was tough, and heaven knows we had enough of that, he would always give his best and then make light of whatever predicament we found ourselves in. He would find a bright side to even the dirtiest cloud.

Only 'Webby' could call home in Swansea from a mobile phone in the back of a taxi in Auckland and get away with it. The other Swansea 'Jacks', Tony Clement and Scott Gibbs, would wind him up and egg him on constantly. They would think of something and then say that Richard would never have the nerve to do it but that 'Santa', Alan Reynolds, the other Swansea flanker, would.

They had him going before one match, daring him that he couldn't strike up a conversation with Princess Anne. When I presented Richard to the Princess Royal before the match, blow me if he didn't start talking about one of her horses. He could say the most outrageous things but it was always good, clean fun. Well, most of the time!

The Princess of Wales had started to attend regularly at the Arms Park and her presence always gives the game a special edge. The Princess is always very supportive of the Welsh team and the Princes are big rugby enthusiasts. Before one match, I was presenting the team to her and 'Webby' said something, I can't remember what, which caused her to laugh.

Then there was the day the Princess met Mark Perego, another incredible character who, of course, being a one-off insisted on doing one of his daft handshakes. The Princess giggled nervously, no doubt thinking to herself: 'Who is this lunatic?' I was surprised that Mark had not gone the whole hog and worn a pink beret with a hatchet strapped across his back, the standard gear he wears when he runs knee-deep in the river near his home.

I have to admit that on more than one occasion during the presentation process I have forgotten a player's name. At that stage, immediately prior to kick-off, everyone tends to be so focused and the Princess understands that. She will ask the players how they're feeling and wish them good luck.

Whenever I get a mental block and a name won't spring to mind, I just move on to the next player in the line. It happened once with Tony Copsey, which, I hasten to add, had nothing to do with the Petrocelli bit and it happened once with Hugh Williams-Jones. You can imagine the ribbing I had to put up with over that.

By the end of that season the captaincy was beginning to put a tremendous strain on my relationship with Clare. It wasn't like a normal job where you switch off at five o'clock in the afternoon and you forget about it for the rest of the day. The responsibility of it all had got a hold of me. It wouldn't let me go because I didn't want to let it go.

I felt that I shouldn't be seen drinking, that I shouldn't be drinking anyway, seen or not. Obviously I did drink, but I curtailed it a lot. Instead of going out, I ended up watching television. By this stage, I had become a bit of a bore. Phil Davies kept telling me I was, so it must have been true.

I am sure Clare got pretty fed up. Quite a lot of sportsmen have these problems because of the pressures and because they can't let go. When your social life is not working out to the satisfaction of both parties, then it becomes another psychological burden. It must be the masochist in me, but I loved the rigours of the job which in turn was imposing restrictions on my private life.

The truth of the matter was that I loved being in a position where I was able to face the issues affecting the Welsh rugby team and meet them head-on. As I've said before, nothing in this world is for free. You go from A to B; you pay the toll, as they say. It's all part of life's rich tapestry.

CHAPTER FOURTEEN

Scarlets Supreme

Few players in rugby history can have achieved more in one season than Ieuan Evans did at home and abroad in 1992–93. By the end of it he had left his contemporaries far enough behind as to turn the sport's number-one Oscar, the British Player of the Year, into a one-horse race.

From the beginning, at Pontypool Park in September, to the finish, in New Zealand ten months later, he had done virtually everything, save win the Test series, and he might have achieved that had the Lions only had the nerve to take their wings off the leash from the word go.

In establishing himself as a right wing without peer in Europe, Evans scored 35 tries in 32 matches for Llanelli, Wales and the Lions. What the bald statistics do not tell is how he changed the course of history along the way. His classic try took the Scarlets to victory over the world-beating Wallabies and, if that was more than Wales could manage seven days later, their captain would reappear at the Arms Park in the New Year to ambush the English chariot.

There may have been better tries but none more dramatic than the kick-and-chase with which he scuppered the grand plan for a third English Grand Slam. His shoulder trouble a thing of the past, Evans ensured that Llanelli swept all before them, winning the Heineken League on a torrent of tries before completing three Cup final victories in a row.

Australia may have made him suffer in Brisbane and Sydney but when it came to playing them at Parc y Strade, there was only one winner. Llanelli had beaten the Wallabies eight years before and, when they did it again, only two of that team were still there – Evans and the club's 35-year-old prop, Laurance Delaney.

Phil Davies would have joined them had he not missed the first match because his enrolment in the South Wales Police demanded he switched clubs for a brief period. Now equalling Phil Bennett's record by captaining Llanelli for a sixth season, Davies considers Evans to be the finest European wing of his generation.

'He is one of the greatest the world has ever seen,' Davies says. 'Over the last ten years, I'd put him right up there alongside David Campese and John Kirwan. There is no finer sight in the game than watching Ieuan go thirty or forty yards for a try, beating three or four people along the way. Give him half a chance and he'll score.

'He's always been an inspiration at Llanelli but during that Treble season he was in devastating form. It wasn't only his pace that the opposition couldn't cope with, but his reading of the game: always a step ahead. If it hadn't been for his injuries, he'd have been coming up for a hundred caps by now.'

The pair go back a long way. Davies remembers how it used to be in the early days, when they would meet for a breakfast awash with cholesterol. 'Bacon fry-ups, sausage sandwiches, the lot,' he said. 'Ieuan had a double chin in those days. I'd say to him: "You'll never get rid of that eating breakfasts like these".'

Davies and his wife, Caroline, Jonathan Davies's sister, both remember how it was when they went out on the town as a threesome one summer night in Evans's little brown van. 'We drove to Swansea with the intention of taking a taxi home. He'd throw his jacket, with the keys in the pocket, into the corner of every pub and when it was time to go home he couldn't find the keys anywhere. So we got a taxi back to my house and he got it into his head that he'd go to sleep on the tarmacadam outside my front door. We had a devil of a job dragging him into the house.'

Evans had scored one double hat-trick and three single hat-tricks for his club before running rings round various New Zealand teams. Against the Maoris in Wellington he scored one masterpiece and created another (finished off by Rory Underwood) during the course of a Lions revival which left All Blacks of all shapes and sizes in a state of nervous anxiety.

Bernie Fraser, the most consistent scorer in All Black history, singled Evans out as the best of his breed. Tane Norton, New Zealand's winning captain during the 1977 series against the Lions, went further, tipping the 1993 version to emulate the classic 1971 tourists. 'They have so much pace and craft out wide,' he said. 'Evans's try was a cracker. It's a great pity he has played most of his international rugby in a poor Welsh side.'

If nothing else, he was at least guaranteed access to a Llanelli side good enough to be judged outstanding even by comparison with the revered Scarlets of the seventies. In winning thirty-two of their thirty-six matches that season, they scored 200 tries, including ten from a young giant who would soon command reputedly the largest rugby league signing-on fee for any Union player, Scott Quinnell.

There was no way of telling, of course, but that season even Bath would have been hard pushed to deny them the title 'Best in Britain'. They were certainly the most exhilarating.

This was, without doubt, the best club season of my life. We played a brand of rugby which, for pure excitement, I had never experienced before and certainly not since. The Treble-winning Llanelli of 1992–93 were a mile ahead of the rest.

We won the League by record margins, averaging six tries a match. We won the Cup, averaging six a game there, too, and we also beat the world champions, Australia. We had everything: seasoned internationalists, talented youngsters like Ian Jones, Neil Boobyer and Wayne Proctor, and an ideal coaching partnership in Gareth Jenkins and Allan Lewis.

We had ten of the Welsh team at one stage and a captain from that well-known Scarlet nursery in Walsall, who endeared himself to the Llanelli supporters by the wholehearted way in which he immersed himself in the club, the community and its culture. Rupert Moon never played better than he did that season. He gave us a dynamic edge at scrum-half which has not been matched since, and he always had the back-up which only Phil Davies, one of the club's truly magnificent servants, could provide.

We played a brand of rugby which had not been seen in Wales at that time. We kept the ball alive – we had an open-side wing forward in Lyn Jones with whom the ball never died, and we had another wing forward from whom there would be no escape for the opposition. Mark Perego was the most ferocious tackler I have ever seen. No wonder they called him 'Exocet Swoop'.

That season we played set-piece rugby only when it was absolutely necessary. As a team of all-talents, we would have been a match even for the team of the seventies. It may sound like sacrilege to some but I think we could have beaten the seventies team. Carwyn would have loved it.

The records we set that season may never be beaten. The crowds came flocking back to an extent that we averaged more than 7,000 for the season. For the biggest match of all, Australia, the old place was packed to the rafters – a sell-out 14,000, which was no more than the champions of the world deserved.

Swansea had beaten them a few weeks earlier before a crowd of 10,000 at St Helens, just as the Whites had beaten us in an early First Division match at Stradey, the only competitive fixture we were to lose at home all season. Naturally, we would have to go one better than our dreaded local rivals.

Beating the Wallabies was, after all, a Scarlets' speciality. The club had done it three times before, but what made this one extra special was that the only try of the game came from a move which we had pinched from the Aussies and which, out of respect to them, we had christened 'The Ella'. Their outside half, Mark Ella, had used it to brilliant effect during the 1984 Grand Slam tour of the British Isles.

Marty Roebuck had kicked the Wallabies ahead with three penalties when we hit them with 'The Ella'. We practised the move until we perfected it and anyone looking deep into our arsenal would know that it was our most lethal strike move. The Wallabies were caught unawares simply because they hadn't seen us play.

When the ideal opportunity presented itself in the ideal position, a set-scrum at the Town End, the ploy worked like a dream. Colin Stephens, at stand-off, did a dummy switch with the inside centre, Simon Davies. I came off my blind-side wing and hit the gap between them, just clipping Simon's legs as I took the pass, and over I went, under the posts.

What really set up the victory was the tackling in the first half.

One in particular, by Simon Davies on Roebuck, had such a shuddering impact that it almost put the Wallaby full-back over the stand. Simon's strength is such that I was very glad I never had to be exposed to the risk of him dumping me into the stand. The look in his eyes as he moved in was enough to terrify most opponents.

Colin Stephens then clinched it for us with two drop goals – one low and flat and wobbly, the other high and handsome. After what some of us had taken from the Aussies, it was wonderful to realise that they had been taken aback by the desire of our team and the sheer passion of the occasion. The club's tradition is such that the Stradey faithful expect a victory over a touring team as opposed to hoping for one.

In one sense it was a double-edged sword. No sooner had we started celebrating than people were saying: 'Well, if you can beat them, why can't Wales beat them?' It never works out like that. Test matches are completely different, and by the following Saturday night we knew to our cost exactly how different they are.

Michael Lynagh had been unable to play any part in the Welsh leg of the tour after dislocating his shoulder against Ireland in Dublin so, for the first time in quite a while, they played a Test without either of their established half-backs, Nick Farr-Jones having retired some time before. Once again we had closed the gap but we still weren't close enough to threaten them with defeat.

In two matches since that awful day in Brisbane where we conceded 60-odd points, we had lost 38–3 and, now, 23–6. Not surprisingly, that man Campese had the last word, streaking more than half the length of the pitch along the right-hand touchline for what was a rather fortuitous try. It was as if he was still trying to balance the books after the Lions match in Sydney three years earlier.

Jason Little's touch-kick slid off his boot into Campese's hands, who happened to be in front of the ball at the time. Once he caught it, nobody was going to stop him and the Aussies can never complain about any lack of generosity on the part of the

Welsh crowd. They gave Campo a standing ovation on his way back to his half of the field as if they sensed that they might not see him at the Arms Park again.

Our plan was to do as Llanelli had done and take them on at a fifteen-man game. We were never able to win enough ball, so there was never any realistic chance of Colin Stephens doing what he had done the previous week. He is a tremendously gifted player who was prone to lapses in confidence before he had the misfortune to suffer the same ankle dislocation which caused me so much bother last season.

The demands of playing outside half for Wales are huge. It's the glory position and sometimes the pressures, as much historical as anything else, prove too much – as can be seen from the list of players who have been chosen No. 10 in recent years. We haven't been able to find many to cope with the peculiar needs of the position.

A number have been given ample opportunity but it has never really become the property of one individual. Neil Jenkins is an indispensable goalkicker but he hasn't always been chosen at outside half. Maybe Paul Turner was discarded too soon. There was a change of coach shortly after he had got into the team and a new coach tends to bring in his own men, as I was to discover a few years later.

With Paul, we will never know whether he could have gone on and flourished. He has done an admirable job at Sale and was still going strong last season at thirty-five, but then others have done admirable jobs for their clubs. Stuart Barnes was the best club outside half in England for a number of years with Bath. But he never quite did it for England or the Lions. There's a big difference between doing it for your club and doing it for your country.

The national debate over the Welsh outside half and who would play there in the Five Nations championship was in full swing when we took off in the first week of January for a week's warm-weather training on the volcanic Canary Island of Lanzarote. We arrived at a purpose-built sports complex the day England checked out, which was as close as we would get until the Arms Park game on the first Saturday of the following month.

It would be stretching a point to say that we worked out a way to beat England in Lanzarote, but we certainly began developing the right mentality during our seven days there. Team spirit may sound corny to those who have never experienced it but we built it up in a fun way with a sort of mini-Olympic games.

We split the squad into various teams, each with their own leader. We had a swimming gala; we played soccer, basketball, volleyball; we went go-karting; and some took part in the now notorious mountain-bike ride. Richard Webster, surprise, surprise, was the looney of the tour, running everyone off the road in his go-kart like some demented Grand Prix driver. We could blame him for most things, but not for the calamity which occurred the day before we flew back home to prepare for the England game.

A few of the boys took off up a hill on the mountain bikes for a scene which could have come straight out of one of those frightening, bunched crashes on the Tour de France. Unlike Miguel Induran, they stopped for a beer *en route* and it all went horribly wrong as they came down the hill, not realising that they were going at a fair old lick.

It only took one wheel to collide with another for three or four of them to be brought crashing on to the tarmac at high speed. Tony Clement needed several stitches, others had some nasty bumps and bruises but Mike Griffiths suffered the worst blow of all, a dislocated collar bone which knocked him out of action for the entire international season.

It's frustrating enough to lose your place, for whatever reason, but doubly so when it means you run the risk of not getting it back. You are allowing someone else to build a reputation at your expense and Ricky Evans was never going to be content with keeping the place warm for Mike, as subsequent events proved. I suppose you could say it brought a whole new meaning to the expression 'on your bike' . . .

Once again we had suffered from unnecessary, self-inflicted wounds. There were a few home truths spoken at the team meeting and, when the news got out, it must have encouraged England to believe that it was going to be downhill all the way down the M4 to Cardiff – not that any of us had the foresight then to see how a multiple bike crash could actually enhance our prospects of an unexpected victory.

CHAPTER FIFTEEN

Flying in a Chariot of Fire

At no time during post-war competition had any country reeled off ten straight championship wins. The consensus of opinion throughout that opening week of February 1993 was that England would be the first. Nobody was going to stop them, least of all Wales.

England, after all, had won back-to-back Grand Slams – the first since the 1920s – and had embarked on a third, albeit with a fortuitously narrow squeak against France at Twickenham. Against that, hadn't Wales gone three years without winning any more than a single home match?

Cardiff Arms Park may have terrified succeeding English teams since around the time of the Bay of Pigs crisis, but not any longer. Hadn't England won there by a street on their last visit? Of course they had, and hadn't they won their last three matches against the hapless Welsh by the aggregate margin of 83 points to 12? Anyone would have thought they only had to turn up, which was exactly what a great many thought and they would not all be sporting a red rose that Saturday. No team had produced a longer winning championship sequence during almost seventy years since the England of Wavell Wakefield. Lord Wakefield of Kendal, as he was later known, won ten championship matches between March 1922 and January 1925.

Such a run had been put together once before, by Wales during the pre-First World War era, the Grand Slam originals. Now that the big day had dawned, their descendants were supposed to be no better than clod-hopping also-rans in a two-horse race against the champion thoroughbreds; a theory with which the more morose among the natives would find it hard to disagree.

The more cunning locals were more than willing to encourage the belief within enemy ranks that it really was only a question of the width of the winning margin. The English perception of the match, as articulated by one who had learnt his trade in Wales, was that 'the rugby world found the prospect of a Welsh victory inconceivable'.

Stuart Barnes, the most-capped Welsh schoolboy player of his, or any other, generation, until he went to Twickenham as a member of the senior Welsh squad, found himself rooting for England and switched allegiance. He spent part of the day before the match in a not entirely unfamiliar place of business, spending 'a quiet half-hour in a bookmaker's'.

'The Welshmen who recognised me would have taunted me unmercifully in 1973, but in 1993 they wanted to know by how many points I thought England would win.' Barnes wrote in his autobiography, *Smelling of Roses*: 'I used to loathe the infamous arrogance of Welsh rugby but it was a more edifying spectacle than the depression hanging over this once great rugby land like pollution from Port Talbot.

'The weather does occasionally break and the depression can be lifted. In 1993 England assumed that the gloom would be west, not east, of the Severn and match preparation consisted of similar questions to those of the Welsh punters: 'How many points?'

That Barnes should find the 1993 Welsh players stricken by neurotic fear (a 'perpetual look of angst' to quote his phrase) was, of course, one more factor in support of the theory that yes, sir, this really would be only a matter of England by how many. The Welsh captain had heard the talk all week and it gave him an idea. His antennae told him that England's attitude might just leave something to be desired.

When he woke that morning at an hotel on the western outskirts of Cardiff, Ieuan Evans could sense an indefinable something in the air. He couldn't be sure exactly what it was but he was pretty certain it was going to be something special. The Bread of Heaven would arrive, with breakneck speed at eleven minutes past three that afternoon . . .

I never sleep well the night before any big game and this being the biggest of the lot I was flicking through the TV channels in my hotel room until half past one that morning. Six hours' fitful sleep being just about my limit, I woke at 7.30, then dozed off and on for another couple of hours.

It was gone ten by the time I made my way downstairs for breakfast, although you could hardly call a couple of pieces of toast and a cup of tea much of a breakfast. I couldn't have eaten another morsel because by then the old nerves were playing merry hell with my stomach and the next thing I had to do was get something from the doctor to settle them down.

Playing for Wales has always had this kind of effect on me. The first time I played at the Arms Park, in a final trial, I was so nervous about it that I was actually sick in the dressing-room. I wasn't that bad this time but it meant the odd trip to the toilet with the *Western Mail* as compulsory reading.

My main concern was to get an early reminder that the boys were in the mood; that they meant business. They gave me the impression they would be up for this match like no other. They weren't as gregarious as usual. There was a lot less laughter and conversation, a lot more concentration. The signs were good.

I went back to my room, packed and unpacked my kitbag at least five times, making sure, over and over again, that everything was in place: two pairs of boots, towel, washbag, tracksuit and the shoulder harness with all the various straps. It wasn't necessary for me to wear it, but it's become a comfort blanket more than anything else. I tend to feel naked without it.

The team meeting began at midday when Alan Davies and Bob Norster went over the final points. We split into two groups, forwards and backs, then joined up for one last look at the *Feel Good* video. We had it made specially to highlight England's blunders, to underline their fallibility, while emphasising our plus points. For this match it had an extra element, a few thumping shots from American football of crunching tackles. All week we had been hammering home the need for big hits, and the hits we saw were so big you could almost feel the shuddering impact. Richard Webster, for one, loved it.

There would be no problem with motivation, not today of all days. The players had been tuned in hours before. I remember being impressed by their single-mindedness and thinking that England were going to be in for a rougher ride than they imagined. We had almost been accused of cowardice in previous seasons, but this Welsh team were beginning to steam from the fires burning in their bellies.

Our choice of music, a few blasts of Frankie Goes To Hollywood and the rock number *When Two Tribes Go To War*, ensured the stoking-up process continued on the coach journey from the hotel to the Arms Park. It was then that I got the feeling that something big was going to happen. You could sense it in the air.

Normally when we go out for the team photograph some three-quarters of an hour before kick-off, the ground is fairly empty. This time it was fuller than I'd known it and the atmosphere, even then, was such as I had never felt before. It was as if the nation were also anticipating that England were in for the shock of their lives.

They, too, caught the impression that the English considered an English win to be a foregone conclusion. England had won the Grand Slam for the two previous seasons and they were coming down to put us in our place, yet again. They were very up-beat, very jingoistic. They were also very complacent. They thought they just had to turn up.

You always know when teams are smug. Certainly the English supporters that week wore smug, self-satisfied expressions. Bill Beaumont sounded as though he typified their attitude, writing us off as though we had no chance. It was as if BBC *Grandstand* had come down to celebrate another English victory. We were just there as so much cannon-fodder.

They may feel that is doing them an injustice but it was certainly the impression we got, after reading all those England players in their various newspaper columns. The intimation, that they only had to be there at two-thirty on Saturday afternoon to win, got to us in a way which made our adrenalin run overtime. It gave us a desire and hunger which hadn't been there for a long time.

Our preparation, based on minute video analysis, had been meticulous. We identified their weaknesses and worked at ways of exploiting them, of tackling as though our lives depended on it and applying pressure to the more vulnerable parts of their game. England is always the big game. There is no other like it.

They were such overwhelming favourites that nobody was being foolhardy enough to believe that we were going to win. If we got the big hits in first, we would at least give ourselves a chance, which was more than we had the last time England were at Cardiff when Mike Teague gave us a few lessons in the art of tackling from which there was no escape. We had to hit them hard and early, and we had to keep doing it for eighty minutes.

We sensed, too, that all was not well in the English camp. They were niggling about this and that in the days before the game and they were also irked by the campaign which BBC Wales ran on television, highlighting some lapses by Jonathan Webb beneath the high ball to support their slogan that, far from being unbeatable, England were definitely beatable.

In that respect, we were taking full advantage of the support of our own media, which made a welcome change from going to Australia and New Zealand where such propaganda is rammed down our throats. While the BBC Wales trailer created a nice bit of controversy, its real significance was that it helped us realise they were human after all, not the remorseless machine which they had been made out to be and which the English players were beginning to believe.

They had not concentrated as ruthlessly on beating us as they ought to have done. They weren't, to coin a vogue word, focused. As coach, Alan Davies had reintroduced Welsh rugby to another word which had most definitely gone out of vogue: respectability. Now we were ready to prove it to the world at large.

England had probably not reckoned on the crowd. The atmosphere that day was the best I have ever known at Cardiff. It made the blood tingle and the electricity crackle. The anthem was sung as I have never heard it sung before. My instincts had been right all along. Something big *was* going to happen.

We had divided the pitch up into areas and we knew that if we lost the middle fifty yards, we would lose the game. Webb had kicked two penalties to one tremendous long-range kick from Neil Jenkins and Jerry Guscott had fired them six points clear with a left-footed drop goal when the chance we had been fighting for suddenly presented itself.

England were not playing badly. It was simply that our plan was being put so effectively into operation that we did not allow them to get into their stride. The hits were going in as we hoped and when Webby nailed Rob Andrew, the ball went loose and we attacked down the blind-side. Robert Jones fed Emyr Lewis and I wanted the ball early because I found myself in a lot of space.

When he kicked it, I felt like shouting at him for not passing it but it wasn't quite the time or place to make an official complaint! I started to run like the wind, cursing him a bit under my breath which probably made me go faster. In such circumstances you don't know whether it's a hopeless cause. You look up to see where the ball is, hoping it doesn't roll into touch.

Two thoughts flashed through my mind which made me think a try might just be possible. The ball was still bobbling away in play and, more significantly, Rory Underwood was not aware of the danger. He wasn't exactly ambling back after the ball but nor was he running at full tilt. At that stage I was flying and I thought to myself: 'He doesn't know I'm up this quickly.'

The roar of the crowd must have told him someone was coming but it was obvious he didn't hear my footsteps. When Emyr kicked the ball behind him, he must have been ten yards in front of me. By the time he had turned and gone five yards I was up to his shoulder. I don't honestly believe he thought I would get there that quickly. The ball bounced marginally beyond their ten-yard line and once I went past him within a yard of reaching the ball, he knew he wouldn't catch me.

I had twenty-five yards to go, Rory had fifteen but he had to turn. I fly-hacked the ball, knowing I had to kick it away from touch. The minute I got my foot to the ball, I knew I was going to score. I had not seen another England player until I reached the ball. Then I could see a white jersey but nobody was going to stop me now.

I could just about see Webb but he would have had to be a good ten yards in front of me. I was flying so fast that in a flat race I think I would have beaten anyone. I looked at nothing but the ball. There was no point my looking left or right or any other direction. I had enough faith in my soccer skills to know that there was no danger of me kicking the ball too hard for it to go dead. I usually judge that quite well.

When I dived on it, my first emotion was one of relief, then sheer elation, that I had been able to reward the players for their guts throughout the first forty minutes. Neil's conversion put us 10–9 ahead at half-time. The try was either going to galvanise them to greater things or the shock was going to set them back.

The crowd were baying for blood and their singing kept inspiring us. I said to the boys at half-time: 'We're halfway there but the crowd can't win it for us. We've got to make it happen. We've got to tackle and kick and chase and the crowd will lift us. You can sense that something's going to happen. It's ours if we keep our nerve.'

Ironically, it was a Welshman who gave us the biggest fright. Dewi Morris had a magnificent match and caused us enough problems to finish up as England's best player by some distance. 'The Monkey', as he is known, probably still thinks he was denied a perfectly good try in the second half, but the referee refused to allow it, which is all that matters.

Martin Bayfield lost the ball over the line, another example of how we kept the big hits going from start to finish. Scott Gibbs gave such a flawless exhibition of tackling that Will Carling had nowhere to go. Our defence was awesome. It may not have been the best Welsh victory but it was, without doubt, the gutsiest. And this from a team whose attitude and commitment had been questioned to such an extent that the overwhelming opinion was that we were there to be taken to the cleaners.

At the press conference, I was asked whether England should drop certain players, which I thought was nonsense and said so: 'Why castigate one or two players for a moment's lack of attention?' How could you take one game in isolation out of sixty-odd and drop someone like Rory Underwood?

Form may be temporary, class is permanent. Alan Jones, the former Wallaby coach, was fond of talking about the 'Gucci Factor', making the point that quality exists for a long time. Having played with and against him over a long period, I put Rory right up there with the very best. A tremendous player, convivial room-mate and Grand Slam winner.

At the after-match dinner, I made a point of singling Rory out. 'Don't worry about it,' I told him. 'Not after what you've done for your country – more than the vast majority do for theirs.'

The trouble with Wales beating the double Grand Slam champions was that the country went overboard to such an extent that we allowed ourselves to be carried off on a tidal wave of euphoria. Now that England were out of the way, the rest was going to be easy, or so too many of us thought.

A fortnight later we went to Edinburgh thinking we were going to win the Grand Slam. Some 26,000 supporters followed us only for Scotland to bring us back down from the clouds with an almighty bump in a way which left us literally pointless. They were too street-wise for us and too physical, so much so that we allowed them to bully us to defeat. We never competed, which is an awful admission considering how we had played against England.

We had a subtle pre-match plan up our sleeve that day which, quite obviously, counted for nothing. In order to minimise the threat of being intimidated, Alan Davies came up with the idea that we should join in the singing of *Flower of Scotland*, a rugby anthem which has built up a worthy reputation as a powerful source of tartan motivation. Unfortunately, we had overlooked the fact that none of us knew the words which rather killed the notion of turning it into a singalong.

On top of everything else, we misjudged the wind that day. I chose to play against it in the first half only to end up playing against it in the second. The rebuilding of the new stand created a wind tunnel which meant that, above a certain height, it blew in the opposite direction. Like a good golfer, Gary Armstrong proceeded to punish us for our lack of local knowledge, belting the ball high enough for the wind to carry it fifty yards downfield. Damian Cronin had a superb game at the front of the line-out and Gavin didn't miss a kick.

Scotland made us realise that we were not as good as we thought and Ireland confirmed it a fortnight later. England may have fallen, but the Arms Park held no terrors for the Irish and for Eric Elwood least of all. We thought he could be a potential weakness, which shows how wrong you can be – not that I could remember much about it. Concussed early on, I kept going long enough to fly in at the corner before I was persuaded to call it a day.

Nigel Walker won his first cap on the other wing, climaxing his rise from novice to international, from Olympic hurdler to the quickest wing in the game, with our only try of the last match – France in Paris – where Rupert Moon and Andrew Lamerton brought the Llanelli representation to eight. Somehow, Paris in springtime couldn't hold a candle to Cardiff in February.

CHAPTER SIXTEEN

The Day Will Carling Cried

When the 1993 Lions came from 20 points behind to beat the Maoris at Wellington on the second Saturday of the New Zealand tour, at least one All Black feared the worst. If that was a sample of how they intended to play the Tests, then Bernie Fraser figured that nobody would catch the British fliers.

When it came to assessing the strike power of wings, he knew a bit about it. No All Black could match Bernie's record, 46 tries in 55 matches, equivalent to a scoring ratio of some 84 per cent, and the way he saw it that day Ieuan Evans and Rory Underwood were in a class of their own.

'There is nobody in New Zealand with the gas to get anywhere near them,' he said. 'Some of the things they are doing over here make some of our guys look like kids. Evans is so hard to stop because his angles of running are so good.'

The 1993 Lions, like so many of their predecessors, failed. That they ought to have gone down in history as the first such team to make a clean sweep of the Tests was more an indictment of the opposition than testimony to the prowess of the tourists whose first and second teams had about as much in common as Pavarotti and Boy George.

New Zealand, still finding a way out of the ruins of their doomed defence of the World Cup two years earlier, were in some danger of contradicting the old adage that there is no such thing as a poor All Blacks team. The Lions could sense the smell of anxiety that May day in Wellington and Evans was not alone in believing that they had the expertise to run them off their feet.

He had no way of suspecting then that the Lions would never play like that again on the tour. Obsessed by a belief that they would win the series through forward domination, they kept it tight, by and large, until the latter stages of the last Test by which time it was all over. The chance of a lifetime had gone forever.

History will judge them as just another losing team. The harsh statistics disguise a harsher reality, that these Lions carried a few lame ducks. The passenger effect can be gauged by the shocking fate of the mid-week team: beaten by Hawkes Bay, from the Second Division, then outclassed 38–6 by Waikato in successive matches.

Evans is not using journalistic licence when he makes the point about the dirt-trackers being with the Test team in spirits as well as in spirit. Stuart Barnes, a bon viveur and therefore eminently qualified on the subject, makes no bones about admitting to a general level of indiscipline. He had captained the team through the Hawkes Bay catastrophe and felt angry enough about it to toss protocol aside and fire a few broadsides at his own lot during his speech on behalf of the vanquished.

In his book Barnes referred to the 'vast consumption of alcohol' and said he did 'not understand why our management did not play a heavy and early hand'. He wrote: 'The fault clearly lies largely with those players, myself included, who were too ill-disciplined for the rigours of this Antipodean adventure. However, do not judge too harshly those who find the only way to survive New Zealand on a rugby tour is through a two-month period of serious alcoholic obliteration.'

Barnes blames coach Ian McGeechan for neglecting the backs by failing to widen the scope of his strategy: 'Despite McGeechan's reputation, any vision of the broader game seemed to drown in a flood of attention to detail in the art of ball-winning. He certainly taught us how to retain ball but he seemed curiously incapable of suggesting coherent ways of using it. Running lines, alignment and moves to break organised defences were neglected and I confidently assert that he would not be encouraged to lace Brian Ashton's boots as a backs coach [Ashton is Bath's coach]. This explains the deterioration from the bold play of the backs early in the tour to a conservatism that offered total homage to the pack and percentages. It guaranteed the sad final defeat in Auckland.'

Barnes lays the blame for that at McGeechan's feet. 'Preparation was identical to that which had worked in Wellington. When New

Zealand played differently, nobody knew how to react and so the death warrant of the series was signed.'

Gavin Hastings, needless to say, offers a very different verdict on McGeechan, acclaiming the Scottish coach as 'unquestionably, the man of the tour and there is nothing bad that anyone can say against him'. In his autobiography, *High Balls and Happy Hours*, the Lions captain goes on: 'He was entirely responsible for the so-near success of the British Lions. Any of the players on the 1993 Lions tour, or indeed the 1989 Lions tour, can hold their heads up high because of Ian McGeechan.'

Hastings pays worthy tribute to Evans, in the skipper's view the equivalent of Ben Clarke as the outstanding Lion, the pick of the backs who scored 'some scorching tries and always showed himself as a highly dangerous try scorer and potential match winner'.

How odd, then, that during the Test series he was hardly given a single opportunity to score a try, scorching or otherwise. Had they unleashed their backs the way they did during the final half-hour against the Maoris, the course of history might easily have been very different.

Bernie Fraser could not believe New Zealand's luck. Back in Carmarthen that summer, the Player of the Year couldn't believe it either.

A funny thing happened to me at the Player of the Year lunch seven days before the Lions left for New Zealand. If it was meant to be funny, then I for one did not see the joke and there has never been anything wrong with my sense of humour.

To be invited to a star-spangled awards lunch at a posh London hotel and called up for the top award is the sort of thing every player dreams about. When it happened to me, I felt so bad about it that I swore I would never go to the lunch again.

Once again, David Campese was at the centre of it all. I had gone there not knowing whether I had won anything at all. Had it been up to me I probably wouldn't have gone. We were off on tour the following week and a 200-mile trip to London was the last thing I needed, but the Lions had been instructed to attend *en bloc* to coincide with our last get-together before the tour.

When they called me up to receive the Whitbread Player of

the Year award, I should have felt on top of the world. Instead I felt humiliated. I had some idea then of the humiliation Campese is supposed to have felt over the try which cost the Wallabies the series against the Lions in 1989.

My late arrival, brought about by the traffic in London being rather more congested than it tends to be in Swansea, prompted something of a flap among the organisers. I had no sooner arrived in a rush and sat down than I, along with everyone else, was surprised to see Campese being called up and given his award as the International Player of the Year before lunch had been served.

They had flown him in from his winter base in Milan and had bent over backwards to make the presentation earlier than the rest so he could shoot back to Italy as soon as possible. They gave him a brand new set of golf clubs which was said to have been worth £1,500. When I was called up for my award sometime later, they gave me a used golf ball.

It was meant to be a joke but I felt belittled by it. I have never been the type to throw a tantrum, least of all in public, but my treatment that day hurt. At best, I had been treated with disdain. I am sure it was not intentional but I felt very unhappy. I kept my thoughts to myself, which was just as well because I had decided there and then that it would be the last time I would attend this lunch. I have not been back since.

To be voted the best player in the British Isles is a marvellous accolade which I will always cherish. What rankled was the way they handled it and I say that as one who has never had any prima donna tendencies. One consolation was that I felt I could go to New Zealand as the number-one right wing in the party.

Not having had a bad season, I felt slightly more secure about being selected for my second Lions tour than I had for the first one four years earlier. There is always an unexpected element to any Lions party but this one contained more surprises than usual.

Inevitably, it was always going to be dominated by England. They had monopolised the two previous championships to such an extent that the majority of their team deserved to go, despite losing their last match to Ireland in Dublin against all the odds.

Quite a few Irish players thought they would be rewarded on the strength of that performance only for the selectors to decide that it was a bit too late to make any real difference.

Instead, only two made it, Nick Popplewell and Mick Galwey. 'Pops' was always going as the best loosehead prop which left Mick as the one Irish player who had forced his way in when the selectors finalised their thirty for New Zealand at Heathrow airport the morning after the match.

Jeff Probyn must have wondered what more he had to do as the only member of the English pack to be left out. The Irish, though, were not alone in feeling they had been short-changed. A few Welsh players felt hard done by, with Gareth Llewellyn the unluckiest one of all. He had lost out to Damian Cronin, one of those who was never able to do for the Lions what he had done, and continues to do, for Scotland.

Three national captains had been picked, not that it ever occurred to me that the captaincy contest was anything other than a straight choice between Gavin Hastings and Will Carling. I would only have been considered as a compromise appointment had the selectors been divided in their support for the other two.

We had a Scottish coach, Ian McGeechan, and an English manager, Geoff Cooke, who both had excellent relationships with their respective national captains. Whoever got the nod, it was always going to be difficult for the one who didn't and difficult, too, for someone like Cooke, who was used to calling the shots during his very successful period in charge of England.

That was never the case with the Lions. 'Geech' ran the show in a way which left Geoff feeling too far removed from the important issues. He did very little coaching, if any, and at times you could sense a certain tension between them. Both were used to being in total control of their national teams so one was always going to feel out on a limb. The same was true of Will and Gav, so much so that at times it was impossible not to notice that relationships between them had become strained.

Gav didn't take me into his confidence on selection but then I never expected him to. We spoke in the run-up to the big games, but the consultations tended to be brief. After all, you can't afford to have too many cooks spoiling the broth – although some of the English boys would no doubt argue that one Cooke would have been enough!

The early days held no warning of the frustration and embarrassment which was to turn up like two bad pennies in various places round the country. An Indian summer in the beautiful Bay of Islands gave us the perfect setting to prepare for the first match in a relaxing way and I could afford the luxury of going scuba-diving again without having to worry about any shark alert! Balmy days with some barmy moments.

Scott Hastings had been charged with the back-breaking responsibility of dreaming up nicknames for the entire party and having them emblazoned on baseball caps, the wearing of which would be compulsory. Scott Gibbs, who had been involved in a bit of a scrape with a cabbie back home before the tour, was dubbed 'Taxi'. Stuart Barnes, never averse to good beer and wine, was 'Barrel', Jerry Guscott 'Precious', Tony Clement 'Fat Boy', Robert Jones 'Pigeon' and Will 'Bumchin'. For some unearthly reason, I was 'Twinkle Toes'.

Not surprisingly, the barmiest episode involved Richard Webster as a result of which he was banned from using firearms for the remainder of the tour. Webby had gone there as the number-two open-side to Peter Winterbottom and who should he almost blast clean out of the entire tour before we had played the first match but 'Winters' himself!

The classic case of how to shoot yourself in the foot without trying took place during what was meant to be a fun afternoon, a chance for the players to test their marksmanship at a clay-pigeon competition. Webby fired his shot and missed, then waved the gun around in disgust, forgetting that he still had another cartridge to fire.

He managed to fire it about two inches away from Winterbottom's foot. Peter was close enough to feel the blast. Luckily, he lived to tell the tale. Needless to say, the management took a dim view of it and banned Webster from all firearms, a clear case of protecting the Lions from unwarranted attack as opposed to pigeons, clay or otherwise.

The whole party was split for the first two matches, ensuring there would be no immediate split between the Test XV and the mid-week team. It would happen soon enough and with a far more alarming gap than on the previous tour. The first game against the Going clan, alias North Auckland, at Whangeri, ended with a Lions wing being forced out of the tour there and then with a dislocated shoulder. For once, it wasn't me but Ian Hunter. I knew exactly how he felt.

He had gone as cover for full-back/wing and while he was hardly going to push Gav out of the team he had the talent to push Rory and I on to the wings. The freakish nature of the injury made it all the harder to bear. In making a tackle on his opposite wing, Ian got his hand caught in the player's shorts in such a way that it yanked his shoulder out of place.

The second match, North Harbour in Auckland, enabled me to make a flying start in a satisfying win against powerful opponents with a liberal sprinkling of All Blacks, including Frank Bunce whom I had last encountered during our World Cup calamity against Western Samoa two years earlier. The first nasty incident of the tour left Bunce with a few stud marks in his ear and a few fingers were pointed at Dean Richards. I've played with Dean many a time and he's a great man to have on your side. Hard and as rugged as they come, but he does not go stamping on people's heads.

At Wellington the following Saturday we really put the wind up the whole of New Zealand by the way in which we managed to escape from a deep hole and come from 20 points down in what must have been the finest recovery made by any Lions team. The Maoris had an all All Black back row – Jamie Joseph, Arran Pene and Zinzan Brooke – and in next to no time they were so far ahead that we were in danger of being lapped like a middle-distance runner caught out of his depth.

We had set out to play it tight but we had no pattern, no shape, nothing. There was only one thing for it. We spun the ball at every opportunity and the result paid such a spectacular dividend that we scored three terrific tries in less than twenty minutes and turned the match upside down. They simply had no answer to our pace and angles of running.

The first was a good example. We moved it right and Gav came into the line. My wing had me marked fairly tight, so I came short on to Gav's shoulder between his tackler and mine, shot through the gap and ran round the full-back to score ten yards in from the corner. At last we had some momentum and the second try followed almost immediately.

They kicked the ball behind me from a scrum in the centre of the field. I went back, picked up, ran round their back-row defence and linked with our midfield for Rory Underwood to finish it off, running round his wing as though he was standing still. I discovered then that all they had to do was to spread the ball wide and Rory and I had the beating of our men.

It wasn't only the Maoris that day who had nobody to keep up with us. Gav clinched it for us 24–20 with a gem of a try, coming off both feet in a way which showed that his toes could twinkle with the best. For twenty-five minutes that Saturday we played a brand of rugby which no team in New Zealand could have lived with. It created such a buzz among the crowd that even the most patriotic, one-eyed fans in the world stood up and applauded us off the pitch at the end.

The papers the next day drooled over our performance and wrote sombre warnings that if the Lions kept running the ball, the Blacks were in for big trouble. The crying shame of it all was that we never played like that again on the whole tour. A wonderful opportunity to have won the series in breathtaking style had been lost and gone forever.

Why, then, did we let it slip? In retrospect, we were guilty of a tactical blunder. 'Geech' had made up his mind that he wanted to dominate the Tests through the pack as had been the case in Australia in 1989. There was a widespread belief within the team at that stage that we were going to win the series 3–0 by dominating up front and keeping it tight.

The Maori match had shown the whole of New Zealand that we could have done it the other way. Had we spun the ball and made the most of the weaponry at our disposal behind the scrum, I have no doubt we would have made a clean sweep of the Tests. It was a bad mistake not to have made the most of people like Jerry Guscott, then at the very top of his game and far superior to anything the Blacks could offer.

We could have used both styles, changing tack whenever the situation demanded. Instead, we took the negative option when we had all the material to take some calculated risks. Rob Andrew at outside half can play the expansive game when required as he has proved time after time for Wasps, the best English exponents of the fifteen-man game.

The weather, unusually mild and dry, was another powerful reason for attacking them from every possible angle. Conditions, above ground and underfoot, were ideal for running, never more so than in Dunedin, which can be the most inhospitable of places with its raw, wintry climate. Instead, we ran out at Carisbrook Park in warm sunshine and were duly taken to the cleaners by Otago.

It gave us a mighty shock just a week before the first Test. The prospective Test team had lost more than the match. Martin Bayfield, our primary source of line-out possession, suffered a very nasty neck injury, landing with such a fearful bang that we were all greatly relieved that he had escaped a very serious injury. Although Martin made an amazingly swift return, it took him a long, long time to recover.

Otago, with Pene in tremendous form at No. 8 and Stu Forster and Steve Bachop running the show at half-back, responded to early tries from Dean Richards and myself with five of their own. It rocked us to such an extent that we did not have enough time to hammer out the dents to our confidence before we were into the Test series.

The biggest pre-tour selection issue had been over the eternal battle between Andrew and Barnes for the No. 10 spot. Southland at Invercargill gave Stuart one last chance to clinch it. Instead he caught Robert Jones's boot on his head and that was that. Stuart believed he would be the Test outside half when we left London but the longer the tour went on, the clearer it became that Rob was taking control.

He had done enough to have justified selection regardless of Stuart's head injury. Even at that early stage, he had lost the thread. I was surprised, and disappointed, that he did not make more of a challenge. Stuart could, and should, have done a lot more. He never gave the impression that this really was his last big chance and that nobody was going to stop him. Instead, he gave the impression of being more interested in talking to the journalists covering the tour than pushing for a Test place.

Consequently, we never saw him at his brilliant best. Such a shame, but it was as if he had convinced himself that Geech was always going to prefer Rob. Whatever the reason, there was no escaping the fact that he never played the rugby he was capable of, not that he was alone in that respect.

As the split between Test team and the rest began to widen to seriously large dimensions, so a number of players decided that they weren't going to let it spoil their fun. They did so to such an extent that some gave the impression they were on holiday.

There was never the same sense of togetherness and collective pride which the Lions mid-week team had generated in Australia on the previous tour. Attitudes left a lot to be desired. Too many were content with merely being a Lion instead of pushing themselves to the limit. This was the most privileged school of all but too many were simply not interested in enhancing their education.

The Scottish forwards came in for a lot of stick both in New Zealand and back home. Peter Wright, Damian Cronin, Andy Reed and Paul Burnell did not perform as they had done for their country earlier that year. 'Geech' was more than a bit peeved at the attitude of some of his players as results deteriorated to a shocking level.

We would always turn a blind eye to the midweek beatings and argue that winning the Tests was all that mattered. If ever a New Zealand team was there to be beaten it was this one and yet we contrived to lose the first match with more than a little help from Mr Brian Kinsey. Two decisions from the Australian referee at the beginning and the end of the match resulted in our finishing up on the wrong end of a defeat which left us infuriated.

If I live to be a hundred, I will never understand how Mr Kinsey could award the All Blacks a try in the first minute. Grant Fox dropped one of his bombs towards the corner flag on my wing. I went up for it along with the New Zealand centre Frank Bunce and we came down together. I had both hands on the ball, so did he. Despite being driven over the line, I still had both hands on the ball when, to my amazement, the referee awarded a try.

How he could have given it from his position some distance away was beyond my comprehension. Seeing it again on video, he looked for guidance towards the touch-judge who gave the nod for a try. There was no way he could have known because I was going backwards with my back to him. It was to prove the crucial score.

A match which was a complete non-starter in entertainment terms had swung our way at 18–17 when Gav landed his sixth penalty nine minutes before the end. All week we had been hammering home the point that we simply couldn't give Fox anything within a range of fifty yards. Once ahead, therefore, we had to keep the ball out of our own half because if we allowed them within striking distance, there was nothing more certain than that they would be given a penalty.

True enough, it came in the last couple of minutes, against Deano for killing the ball. It is one of his favourite tricks but, ironically, this time he wasn't guilty of that or any other offence. It should have been a scrum with our put-in. It was inevitable that Fox would score and the awful reality that we had allowed a poor New Zealand side to wriggle off the hook followed all too quickly.

Their defence played well that day but as a back line we had a collective off-day when we could least afford it. Again, the Blacks must have been relieved that we failed to spin the ball more than we did. The slide towards under-achievement had begun and our mood was not made any better by the disgraceful treatment of Wade Dooley following the sudden death of his father. Had that treatment been meted out by the New Zealand authorities, it would have been bad enough. That it came instead from our own people made it infinitely worse.

Wade had had to dash home to Blackpool from Invercargill which is about as far as you can get from the Golden Mile without leaving the planet. Bayfield made a miraculously quick return although he was, understandably, far from his old self. The big Scot, Andy Reed, who had had a good Five Nations, filled the vacancy caused by Dooley's bereavement.

The New Zealand Union could not have been more sympathetic. They offered to pay Wade's return flight after the funeral and we were then flabbergasted to learn that the Four Home Unions Tours Committee, the people who run the Lions, had refused to let him rejoin the party on the grounds that a replacement, Martin Johnson, had already been called up.

There are always rules and regulations but we could not understand why they were not waived in this case. Bob Weighill, the honorary secretary of the Four Home Unions, arrived in New Zealand shortly after the decision had been taken and we had blackballed him before he arrived in protest.

Our annoyance ran so high that we agreed unanimously that Mr Weighill would be sent to Coventry. Any player caught talking to him faced an automatic fine of ten New Zealand dollars and again it says everything about our unity of purpose that not a single fine had to be imposed. Mr Weighill complained that he was only the messenger and that it was all grossly unfair, but, as the Four Home Unions representative, he had to take the brunt of our displeasure over the treatment of a man who had given the game wonderful service over a long period.

The following Wednesday brought the mid-week team their last win of the tour, not that 49 points against Taranaki in New Plymouth did anything to alter the fact that there was by now a serious lack of competition for Test places. Scott Gibbs was pushing Carling so hard he pushed him clean out of the side but the vast majority of the Test team felt in no danger. Webster was one of the few other non-Test players playing well and it was certainly through no lack of effort that he was unable to shift the outstanding Peter Winterbottom.

Dick Best, the assistant coach, is renowned for his acidic brand of wit and the more he applied it in his attempts to knock the mid-week team into shape, the harder Webby tried. Dick would ridicule him, at times unmercifully, and with every insult Richard would train that much harder. He loved being shouted at and never minded the mickey-taking. One day after training, he asked: 'Dick, do you fancy a walk to the shops?' To which Dick replied: 'I'd rather have my eyes poked out with a red-hot needle, thank you, Webster!'

Webby has always been a big lad and on another day Dick came out with a classic. 'Webster, when you go back home to Swansea, they're going to paint you white, put you on wheels, take you to the cricket ground and use you as a sightscreen!'

Then there was the day when the Swansea boyo said to Best, 'Dick, my father's coming out tomorrow. Would you like to meet him?'

'Webster, I'd love to meet whoever sired you . . .'

Their exchanges were among the highlights of the tour. Dick tried to get a similar sort of banter going with the Scottish players in the mid-week team but to no avail. A pity. Had they responded the way Webby did, the dirt-tracking Lions might never have gone down like a lead balloon.

To his credit, Webby had forced his way into the Saturday team for the next match, Auckland at Eden Park, which had been billed as the unofficial fourth Test. Considering that they paraded no fewer than twelve All Blacks, it was as near an international as you could get against provincial opposition.

John Kirwan was back on the right wing for a match we still managed to lose, despite Kirwan's inability to match his opposite number, Rory Underwood, for speed. I scored a try from fifty yards that afternoon and we tried desperately to get the ball to Rory so he could expose Kirwan. Not for the first time, we failed to do ourselves justice in a match which we finished with Carling at full-back for an injured Hastings.

He had never played there before which is not to be recommended when someone like Grant Fox is waiting to drop huge bombs on your head with pinpoint precision. Rory and I told him where to stand and Will, to his credit, performed very well without being able to save himself from being dropped the following week to make way for Scott 'Taxi' Gibbs.

Carling, therefore, found himself playing in the next match which will forever be locked away in the black museum of British rugby. Hawkes Bay, a Second Division outfit, made the Lions look third-rate. This wasn't a beating but a humiliation. It was so bad that the locals could afford to miss a whole series of penalties and still win by a convincing margin, 29–17.

At this time the mid-week team had been given up as a bad job. They had been taken to the cleaners and if it hadn't been for Will playing his heart out, it might have been even worse. The lack of spirit and commitment upset him to such an extent that Carling just sat down in the dressing-room and there were tears in his eyes. He had bounced back and come through his personal crisis in fine style, but you could tell he had never experienced anything like this.

He felt that some people had given up and his sheer frustration made him cry at the shame of it all. I understood how he felt. The way I saw it, some of those who played against Hawkes Bay didn't give a monkey's. They simply weren't trying. It was as if they were saying to themselves, 'We're not bothered. We're not going to get a Test place so we may as well enjoy ourselves.'

It was safe to say that they drank too much. I don't know whether they were with us in spirit but they were very much with us in spirits! The moral support was always there. We needed much more than that, however. We needed people to be pushing the Test to greater heights as had happened in Australia.

We needed more Mike Teagues. He was another who, like Webster and Tony Clement, would fight until he dropped, but his kind were in such a minority that there was never any chance of the mid-week team finding the inspiration which Donal Lenihan had provided in Australia four years before. Needless to say, they were being battered from all directions and the fans who had paid a lot of money to follow us around New Zealand were beginning to lose patience.

One of them, an overweight chap in his late fifties, could contain himself no longer after one match. He went up to Andy

Reed in the clubhouse afterwards and told him that he didn't think he had quite given 100 per cent in the match. Andy got uptight about it and suggested that they should go outside.

Who should be sitting in the corner observing the conversation but Teague. And Iron Mike said in that distinctive West Country burr, 'My money's on the old geyser . . .'

The brutal truth was that the mid-week team had been given up as a bad job. A lot of criticism was flying around and there could be no denying that a number of players, most of them Scottish, had not justified the faith the selectors had shown in picking them. How they could play so well for their country in the Five Nations and so poorly for the Lions was something which suggested that more than one mistake was made in selection. There again, it's all too easy to be wise after the event.

All was far from lost as the second Test proved – a stunning victory gained through the kind of forward domination which justified Geech's strategy. Two important changes from the first Test made the pack all the more powerful. Martin Johnson, who had played just once for England, came in at the front of the line-out as if he had been there all his life and Jason Leonard appeared in place of Paul Burnell on the tight-head of the scrum.

Nick Popplewell, especially, had a terrific match, smashing back the All Blacks time and again with his driving runs and generally proving to the most hard-to-please bunch in the world that there is not another loose-head prop to touch him. He doesn't say much but his expressions are worth a thousand words.

Dewi Morris was another whose performance that day I will never forget. He began the trip as No. 2 scrum-half to Robert Jones and typically fought his way into favour. He had a magnificent tour and no match was more superb than the second Test which he played throughout, despite having his knuckle smashed in the opening minute. When Dean Richards treads on you, accidentally, of course, it is hard not to feel it.

Behind a supreme pack, Rob Andrew kicked supremely to the corners and, while I felt we could have won every bit as effectively by running it, the net result took some beating. On the rare occasion that we did move it, Rory swooped for a great try which was made all the more memorable by a dive which would have made Jurgen Klinsmann look like a belly-flopper. He took off five yards from the line and landed five yards beyond it. We thought about fining him but the collective sense of elation allowed him to get off scot-free.

Everything, therefore, rested on the decider at Eden Park on the following Saturday. Sandwiched in between was the small matter of Waikato, and the New Zealand provincial champions were itching to get to work, confident in the knowledge that whatever Hawkes Bay had done to the Lions second string, the Mooloo men would do a great deal more. And so they did.

They won 38–6 and for any Lions team to lose by such a margin brought disgrace to the British game. If some had been suspected of having given up the week before, there was no doubt about it now. The Scottish boys had definitely given up the ghost, well and truly.

It had to be written off as a bad job; the less said, the better. All that mattered was the final Test. I still hoped that we would use our speed and guile behind the scrum but we had decided not to change our tactics. It was naïve of us to think we could do exactly as we had done at Wellington the previous week; that the All Blacks would not have done their homework very carefully.

Geech was in control. Whatever he wanted, he got – which is as it should be. The coach has to be given a free hand even if the others are left out of it and there was no denying that Cooke and Best felt out of it. We had a coaching balance in 1989 which was lacking in New Zealand but comparisons are odious. This was a different tour, a different country, a different time. Geech, very quiet, very determined, very meticulous, has a record which speaks for itself. With a little bit more adventure, it could have been a record beyond compare.

Again it is easy in hindsight but I was convinced at the time that we had to expand on that game, to allow ourselves a get-out clause if we had to change tack. We had become complacent and the fact that we did not consider another option was an illustration of that complacency, a by-product of the overwhelming nature of our victory at Wellington. We were ten points clear with almost half an hour gone, Scott Gibbs ploughing over beside the post, and we were still swept away.

Whenever they needed it most, the Blacks dug deep and came up with a vintage show. They scored 30 points virtually without reply and they achieved them by playing the sort of total rugby which we had played against the Maoris in the second week of the tour. Ironically, we did spin the ball in the end, but by then the match was beyond recall.

There were acres of space for us to have exploited that day. I knew I had the beating of Va'aiga Tuigamala if only I had been given the chance. The same went for Rory against John Kirwan. The All Blacks had no one in midfield to match Jerry Guscott, and Scott Gibbs was dynamite. Even the New Zealanders at large admitted that, if we had been given the ball, they would not have been able to stop us.

It was a gamble we could have afforded to take. Opportunities to win a Test match in New Zealand are rare. Opportunities to make a clean sweep of the series come along once in a century. No wonder we sat slumped in the dressing-room when it was all over.

If ever there was a series the Lions should have won 3–0, this was it. We had the chance to write our names in history. If only we had been bold enough to take it . . .

CHAPTER SEVENTEEN

Champions at Last

Two unusual results from international matches during November 1993 hardly indicated that the pecking order as decreed by the Five Nations championship was about to undergo a radical change. Wales lost at home to Canada, which hardly registered on the Richter scale of upsets given the Welsh tendency towards calamity, and England beat New Zealand which definitely did register with the seismograph.

What happened during the ensuing four months reinforced the Einstein-like theory that it really is a very funny game. Wales, once again reduced to despair by a bunch of comparative upstarts, ended the season doing something they hadn't done since 1979 under the captaincy of J.P.R. Williams. They won the Five Nations title outright, losing to England but still beating them into second place.

In one respect, it was nothing new. By winning at the Arms Park, Canada were merely following almost everyone else bar Japan, Western Samoa and Romania included as well as Ireland who never seem to fail these days where, once upon a time, they would consider anything less than a 20-point defeat as getting off lightly.

What made it worse was that the Canadian stand-off, Gareth Rees, whose father had emigrated from Llantrisant, had told anyone who bothered to listen that it was going to happen. 'We'll beat Wales alright,' he said before the match. 'I don't understand why people think they are going to win.'

Wales, tactically bankrupt, not only failed to put the young colonial in his place but had the galling experience of watching his conversion win the match for the Maple Leaf 26–24. Al Charron, a flanker good enough to hold his own in the highest company, scored the only try of the match, ensuring Wales got what they deserved for allowing themselves to be dragged into a forward battle.

A little later that month, the All Blacks arrived at Twickenham fresh from running riot over Scotland at Murrayfield. England raised the power of their pack to new heights by picking a back-row triumvirate who would win every match they played until the fateful World Cup semi-final against New Zealand in Cape Town. The Tim Rodber/Dean Richards/Ben Clarke union played a huge part in England's 15–9 win, debutant full-back Jon Callard kicking four penalties on a day when New Zealand's new prodigy, Jeff Wilson, missed repeatedly after being pressed into emergency goalkicking duty.

Seven days later the All Blacks rounded off their tour with the traditional finale against the Barbarians at the Arms Park, the crowd unaware that two players would never be seen in the Union game again. One was Va'aiga Tuigamala, bound for Wigan. The other happened to be the best young player in Britain, never mind Wales.

Scott Gibbs's season ended that first Saturday of December with a shattering knee injury. Welsh despair at losing him for the entire Five Nations programme was nothing compared to the gnashing of teeth which greeted his departure to St Helens Rugby League Club before he had time to complete his lengthy rehabilitation.

All of which made Welsh prospects of winning the title increasingly improbable. They opened with a home win against Scotland which was to prove the most entertaining single performance of the championship – Mike Rayer, a replacement left wing, finishing off the classic moves for two of the three tries. Ieuan Evans skinned Gavin Hastings for the third.

The team Wales had crushed 29–6 were then robbed of a worthy home win over England by the last kick, Callard's long-range penalty reducing Hastings and whole battalions of Scots to tears. On the same day, Wales beat Ireland in Dublin and a fortnight later they were rejoicing at one of the most surprising days in the history of the championship.

France had won 12 matches in a row against Wales when they ran into Scott Quinnell. The new Welsh giant smashed his way over into the corner for the first Welsh try, then set Nigel Walker off for the second on what must have been his fastest run since the 1984 Olympics in Los Angeles. The final whistle had no sooner gone than Wales had double cause for celebration.

Ireland's win at Twickenham had left the way clear for Wales to take the title. England responded to their sudden crisis by winning in France and setting up a finale without precedent in the long history of the Five Nations. Wales, for the first time, were going to HQ for the Grand Slam. England, on the other hand, had to win by sixteen points to clinch the title which had been decided on points difference since the award the previous year of a silver trophy.

England went into the decider without a single try to show for their four previous matches. Geoff Cooke, whose organisational flair had galvanised the English game since his appointment – appropriately enough, on the day of the Great Storm in October 1987 – was resigning as manager and the lads would want to see him off in style.

Championship, Grand Slam, Triple Crown: there could not have been any more at stake for the one hundredth match between the most serious rivals in the championship.

During the banquet after our match in Paris at the end of the 1993 championship, I had a photograph taken with the French captain, Jean-Francois Tordo, and the silver Five Nations trophy. When someone sent me a print a few days later, I put it on the mantelpiece and used it as a constant reminder of my major goal for the 1993–94 season.

The odds, as always, were stacked against our winning but this was no pipe-dream. A team of substance had begun to emerge from the rubble of the Australian tour two years before and when we began the international season against Japan that autumn we had begun to develop something of a club atmosphere, not a cosy or cliquey one but a bond which was growing all the time.

Japan, it has to be said, posed far more of a test to my linguistic skills than anything else. Any anxiety we may have had at stumbling into another of those Arms Park nightmares disappeared almost right away. We knocked-on straight from the kick-off, then they more or less dropped a pass at my feet. I picked the ball up on halfway and ran straight to the line without anyone touching me.

Eight more tries followed and we won by 50 points, a Welsh

record margin, for what it was worth. The Japanese had reinforced themselves with a few Australians and South Sea Islanders and, while a 55–5 win was not going to change the world rankings, it served a very useful purpose in strengthening the collective bond which was to underpin our championship challenge that winter.

Embarking on my third season as captain, I found myself taking more and more time to attend to the many off-field aspects of the job, like trying to make your guests feel welcome by addressing them in their native tongue. Thanks to the strenuous efforts of the Japanese department of the Cardiff Business School, I learnt my speech off by heart. Wrestling with the phonetics of the exercise was as tricky as marking Campese.

They can never have heard Japanese spoken with a Carmarthenshire accent. I stood up at the dinner afterwards, thanked them for the game, wished them every success in their bid to qualify for the World Cup and finished off by expressing the hope that one day I would visit their country. It reminded me of an old Max Boyce song, the one about 'Me Welsh-speaking Japanee'.

They seemed pleased that I had taken the trouble, not that I could be sure whether they understood every word. I only hope my enunciation was of a slightly higher standard than the Welsh as spoken by our favourite son from the People's Republic of Walsall, Rupert Henry Barker St John Moon. My next after-match speech would be no laughing matter.

Rupert's arrival at scrum-half had given us a dynamic quality. A larger-than-life character, he gave the game an ebullience as well as the impression that Jimmy Nail did more than get himself into a few scrapes bringing criminals to justice on Tyneside. Rupert immersed himself in the whole Welsh culture and if his mastery of *Mae Hen Wlad Fy Nhadau* is open to debate, it is better than some efforts managed by non-Welsh-speaking Welshmen.

Japan proved that we were still making progress but no Welsh season would have been complete without finding an opportunity to provide severe cause for public ridicule. Yet again

Flat out for the corner. Scoring in forty-five seconds against Japan at the Arms Park,
16 October 1993 (Picturesport)

One of the perks of the job: presenting the team to the Princess of Wales

Making a late bid for a Ryder Cup place: with Mike Catt, Graeme Hick, David Leadbetter and his son, Andrew

Player of the Year, season 1992–93
(David Rogers, Allsport)

A trio of captains. With Gavin Hastings, Will Carling and mascot at the London Irish
ground prior to the Lions' departure for New Zealand, May 1993 (Colorsport)

Creating a try for Rory Underwood in the great Lions recovery against the Maoris at Wellington in 1993 (David Rogers, Allsport)

Eluding Inga during the Lions' record Test win against the All Blacks on the same ground four weeks later (David Rogers, Allsport)

Still plagued by shoulder trouble – this time during the Five Nations game against Ireland, 5 February 1994 (Mark Leech)

Champions at last! Collecting the Five Nations trophy from the Queen at Twickenham, 19 March 1994 (Colorsport)

Winning the Swalec Cup for Llanelli against Neath, 8 May 1993

*With Nigel Davies and the Swalec Cup after a hat-trick of winning Llanelli finals.
Cardiff Arms Park, 1993 (David Rogers, Allsport)*

At Buckingham Palace, October 1996, with Kathryn and my parents after receiving the MBE from Her Majesty the Queen

Lili, before, during and after the Lions tour of South Africa; at home with her parents (left), and on the beach in Durban, helping a wounded Lion relax the day before the historic second Test

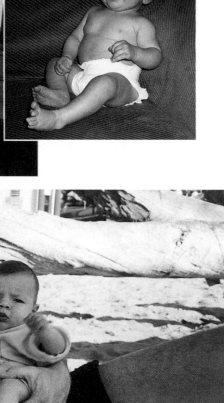

we contrived to bring the wrath of the nation down around our ears and allow a rather bombastic opposition to glory in our predicament.

Losing to Canada was a funny way of letting the public know that we would be going flat out to win the Five Nations. When I got home that night and looked at the photo of me, Tordo and the trophy, I did wonder for a moment or two whether it wasn't really a pipe-dream after all. However, I managed to convince myself very quickly that Canada was a blip, a rather nasty one which would cause a bit of damage to the system. I thought we would be better for the experience, not that an irate public would be in any mood to believe me.

If ever a team brought out the worst in the opposition, Canada did that night under the Arms Park floodlights. Our relationship with the Canadians has remained fairly constant. We seem to hate them, and they seem to hate us. There has never been much in the way of love to cloud the issue. They killed the game and we played into their hands by allowing them to suck us into a physical, forward battle.

Maybe with some the red mist impaired their vision. Whatever the reason, too many of our forwards seemed too eager to get involved in a battering-ram contest. We wanted to move the ball, to exploit their lack of pace and escape their negative clutches. The Canadians love nothing more than hitting anything that moves. We get our buzz from scoring tries, they get theirs from crunching people in the tackle.

Every big hit was greeted with a collective 'yee-hah'. If I had closed my eyes, and heaven knows there were plenty of times I felt like doing so that night, I would have sworn I was at some rodeo in Calgary. Despite being forced to rely solely on Neil Jenkins's boot, it never occurred to me that we would manage to lose until Gareth Rees converted the only try with the last kick of the match and they were home and dry at 26–24.

When you are boiling inside at the way your team has played, it is never easy to stand up at the dinner and say the right things without allowing your emotions to take over. Nor can you be too critical of the other team, lest the victors go away thinking you are a bad loser. On the other hand, I simply could not pretend that our shoddy performance had never happened.

I made it very plain in what I said publicly to the team that it was not good enough and left it at that. As captain, you have to be a bit of a politician. You are representing your Union and your country. You are not there to cause a diplomatic incident. I had seen enough of those in the dining-room at Ballymore in Brisbane to last me a lifetime.

Once the dust had settled, we went into the Five Nations with three changes to our pack which meant two of Llanelli's Treble-winning team dropping out and three more taking their places. Out went Tony Copsey and Lyn Jones; in came Ricky Evans, Mark Perego and the old warhorse himself, Phil Davies.

Scotland at the Arms Park gave us an immediate chance to get our own back for what they had done to us at Murrayfield the previous season. They bullied us out of it that day and I gave the players a final reminder before leaving the dressing-room that they weren't going to find us another soft touch. Considering that it was the start of a championship-winning campaign, the first few minutes were anything but promising.

If we were going to execute our plan to give the Scots the runaround, we would have to do it in a monsoon-like downpour. As if that wasn't daunting enough, we lost one of our main strike weapons in next to no time. Nigel Walker took such a fearful bang in the opening minutes that he had to be almost dragged off the pitch in a severely concussed state. If we had lost our hooker as well, nobody could have complained.

Garin Jenkins was very determined to let the Scottish pack know that he, for one, wasn't going to be pushed around. Unfortunately, he took the command a bit too literally, going over the top with a flurry of blows right under the nose of the French referee. Luckily, Garin lived to tell the tale and his opening onslaught served a purpose, although it caused a stink afterwards.

They realised we meant business. I will admit that we used physical intimidation to impose ourselves in the same way that every team under the sun uses physical intimidation. Let's not pretend otherwise. The risk you run is in being reduced to fourteen men. Garin knew he was lucky to stay on. I had to cool him down and make sure he kept the red mist under control. In taking aggression to the nth degree, he had left Scotland in no doubt that they were in for a rough ride. Now we had to concentrate on playing rugby.

It worked like a treat. The harder it rained, the better we played and nobody splashed through the puddles to reap a richer harvest than someone who had started the match sitting up in the stand. Mike Rayer replaced Walker on the left wing and went aquaplaning in for surely the two best tries of the championship.

While Nigel must understandably have been gnashing his teeth at what he was missing, nobody begrudged Mike his glory. He had been very unfortunate not to have made the Lions tour of New Zealand, losing his place to Tony Clement. The problem with having two outstanding full-backs at the same time is that one is always liable to feel hard done by. Mike had probably suffered enough without breaking his leg in two places playing for Cardiff at Treorchy last season and missing the entire Five Nations as well as the World Cup. His innate footballing ability means that he is very rarely caught out of position and he still has a lot to offer. Wales badly need him back as soon as possible.

By the time we had finished with Scotland we had beaten them more conclusively than they had beaten us twelve months earlier. In completely outplaying them, we spun the ball in defiance of the downpour and, not to be outdone by what was going on along the opposite flank, I managed to sneak over myself with a move straight out of the Llanelli coaching book.

Nigel Davies, drafted back into the team after Scott Gibbs's knee operation, can be a deadly practitioner of the wiper kick, the diagonal punt from midfield towards the touchline. I can always tell from the way he stands when he intends bringing it into play and I deliberately went out wide towards the touchline. The opposition wing had been brought in so when Nigel's kick landed on the proverbial sixpence, it was a straight race between myself and Gavin Hastings.

No disrespect to the captain of the Lions, but there would have been a stewards' inquiry in the Welsh dressing-room had I not got there first. For a start, Gav had been caught so out of position that, when I fly-hacked the ball towards the line, he could do nothing but slide into touch on a sea of spray. Gav struggled badly that season but, when a lot of people thought he was over the hill, he came back and had the season of his life. Only a great player can do that.

On the day we beat Scotland 29–6, France opened the defence of their title in typical style, overwhelming Ireland 35-15. We headed for Dublin confident of extending the established custom in this particular fixture – that the away team always won. With Walker ruled out by the compulsory three-week rest for concussion, we decided against playing two full-backs and opted for a specialist left wing, Wayne Proctor.

The popular theory is that Eric Elwood let us off the hook and that, had he kicked a late penalty instead of seeing it rebound off the post, we would never have won the title – a supposition based on the assumption that we would have lost 18–17 instead of winning 17–15. What people forget is that there were ten minutes left after Elwood's miss and we dominated those ten minutes so completely that we hardly let the ball out of our grasp.

We camped in their twenty-two and if we had needed a drop-goal, all I had to do was give Neil Jenkins the nod. It was probably the best controlled rugby Wales ever played under my captaincy, a period during which one try had to go abegging because my shoulder had popped out, rendering my arm virtually useless. It was so bad I had no alternative but to tell Rupert Moon not to pass me the ball, the only time I ever had to make such a request.

Neil scored all our points. He is probably the best goalkicker in the world and there is not a record that he won't break, provided he stays with us and resists the temptation to go north or anywhere else. People criticise him but he has all the talent you could ask for. He's the best passer I know, a good tackler and he can come off either foot. All he lacks is better support – someone to bring the best out of him.

For the umpteenth time in my life, shoulder trouble forced me to miss the acid test of our championship credentials. France had beaten us home and away annually for so long that by the time they came to Cardiff, they had won twelve in a row. On Wednesday night I finally gave up hope of being there to meet them on Saturday. Nigel Davies had to drop out, too, even though both of us had spent hours on end in a deep-water compression tank.

Despite the double blow we used only nineteen players that season, a sharp contrast to the bad old days when we seemed to get through that many in one match. Twelve of them played in all four matches and what impressed me most of all going into the French match was the attitude of the team. Rayer went to full-back, Simon Hill replaced me on the right wing, Tony Clement filled the gap in the centre, and it was very much a case of business as usual.

The match will be forever remembered as Scott Quinnell's. Probably, there has not been an individual Welsh performance to compare with it since Keith Jarrett made his wonderful début against England during the late sixties. Everything Scott touched turned to gold, in more ways than one. The blockbuster of a try, with Frenchmen bouncing off him all over the place, and the run he gave Nigel Walker for the second try must have been worth £400,000 to Derek's little boy. If ever one match persuaded a club like Wigan to part with so much, this was it.

In some respects it was a performance of Lomu proportions. For most of the match, the French simply couldn't bring him down and when they came back, as they were always going to do from 17–3 down, Scott still had the last word. Olivier Roumat and Philippe Sella crossed our line and suddenly there were only two points in it when Scott sent Nigel clear for the clincher. Neil's touchline conversion completed a day which was already perfect before the word came through from Twickenham that England had lost to Ireland.

England's subsequent win in Paris meant that they could still have pipped us for the title in the last match of the season at Twickenham. They had to win by at least 16 points, but we were totally preoccupied with the prospect of doing the Grand Slam. We had never played at Twickers for such high stakes and we had never experienced as intense a build-up as there was for the match.

The papers, nationally and locally, gave it more column inches than they had ever done, but what really surprised us were the number of calls from radio stations in South Africa, Australia and New Zealand. Television crews turned up at our places of work almost daily and, while it was stimulating to be the centre of attention, there is no doubt that it got to us in the end.

How much it contributed to the net result nobody will ever know. What I do know is that the occasion affected us. We were out of sync from that start of that day. Traffic congestion on the way in from our hotel in Sandhurst meant we arrived twenty minutes late, despite a police escort. We then had to be rushed out of the dressing-room and on to the pitch much earlier than usual to be presented to the Queen and the Duke of Edinburgh.

We were told before kick-off that, whatever happened, both teams would go back to the dressing-room area because, with so many people invading the pitch at the end, it was not advisable for us to hang around on the touchline. Whoever won the game would be first up the steps of the new Royal Box.

England dominated most of the match and we didn't start to play until the last twenty minutes, not that I felt we were in any danger of losing the championship as well. They hadn't scored a try all season and we proceeded to give them two very soft ones. A defensive muddle in midfield where we ended up with Emyr Lewis at outside centre was all Rory Underwood needed to make the most of the mess, and the second try came from a line-out, Tim Rodber taking our throw and diving over. They don't come much softer than that.

At 15–3 England were still one try short. Instead, we had the last word with Walker scoring in the corner after which there was never any doubt that this would be the strangest ending to any championship. We had lost the battle but won the war. There was something missing – the sense of elation which would have come with a Grand Slam.

At the end we headed straight to the dressing-room area as instructed. A couple of RFU officials told us that England would be first up the Royal Box, then we would be called up to receive the trophy. I turned to go into the dressing-room when Will Carling saw me and asked, 'Aren't you going up for the presentation?'

'No. But aren't you going up first?'

He made it clear, not unreasonably, that England would not be going up. After all, they had nothing to collect and, to their credit, they felt it was our day. The officials then began to kick up a bit of fuss. 'Quick,' one of them said to me. 'You're wanted up there now.'

'Hang on a minute,' I said. 'I've got to round up the players.'

At that stage I was not aware that an embarrassingly long time had elapsed between the game ending and my leading the Welsh team up the steps to receive the trophy from the Queen. People have pulled my leg about it: the usual stuff about keeping Her Majesty waiting, but we were entirely innocent. It clearly was not the done thing but I must stress that it was none of our doing.

It had been a warm day and I had to get some of the players back out of the dressing-room. Once people sit down after a hard game, it's sometimes not easy to get them back on their feet quickly. It should have been a perfectly simple matter of the trophy winners congregating in the tunnel and then going straight up for the presentation ceremony.

The Queen congratulated us. I shook hands with the respective presidents, Ian Beer and Sir Tasker Watkins, the secretaries, Dudley Wood and Edward Jones, waited for the rest of the players to shake hands and raised the trophy aloft in the time-honoured fashion. The crowd of Welsh supporters congregating on the touchline loved it but, although we had won the trophy and won it deservedly, it didn't feel quite right.

The look on our faces could not disguise a feeling that it had a slightly hollow ring to it. The question, not unnaturally, cropped up at the press conference. Did I think it was a hollow victory? Well, yes and no. Yes, in that England had beaten us. No, because the title is won over four matches, not one.

It was about all the other games, not just England against Wales. And over all the other games we had done enough to justify our title as Five Nations champions. We had played the best rugby that season. Certainly, England would admit that they had not played anywhere near enough to have deserved the title instead. Besides, they'd won enough to allow us something.

We took the trophy to the dinner at the Hilton in Park Lane followed by a very enjoyable night on the town with the England players, their wives and our wives and girlfriends. For the first time, the RFU threw out the traditional rugby chauvinism and made it a mixed dinner, one effect of which was to lessen the chances of the Five Nations silver trophy being kicked around Hyde Park and given the same treatment as the Calcutta Cup on one riotous occasion following a Scotland–England match!

The trophy came home the next day and was promptly put under lock and key in a bank vault. Never had the Welsh nation been in greater need of reassurance that their rugby team could still win things. Here at last they had tangible evidence of what used to be taken for granted and as one of those who had been through the mill, it gave me immense satisfaction.

Best of all, we were a group of friends who had done well for one another and for the country. People like Rupert, Clem, Robert Jones and my best mate, Phil Davies, had had to endure so much over the years and at last they had won something. And now I had a better picture of the trophy to replace the one on my mantelpiece.

We were a happy camp. Despite at one time having nine Llanelli players in the team, I went out of my way to safeguard against the side being split into cliques. They can develop subconsciously or overtly, as with Wales a few years earlier when it tended to be Neath against The Rest.

The season, though, was far from over. A few weeks later I

was back competing for another piece of silver. Like Twickenham, I wound up on the wrong end of a 15–8 defeat and, unlike Twickenham, we went home empty-handed.

For all our international representation, nothing could save Llanelli from losing the Welsh Cup. One more win would have allowed us to equal the fabulous achievement of the seventies Scarlets in winning four finals in a row, but we were just lucky to be there.

We had played poorly all season and despite my try giving us an early lead, we never deserved to finish anywhere but second. Mike Rayer finished us off with one of his specials and Cardiff had at long last avenged their last-minute defeat by the Scarlets in my first final, way back in the dim and distant past of 1985.

CHAPTER EIGHTEEN

The Worst Day of My Life

On Saturday, 17 September 1994, in a dilapidated soccer stadium in Eastern Europe, the captain of Wales bailed his team out of a nasty spot of bother with the most valuable try in rugby history. It proved to be worth ten points, appropriately so considering that the scorer had broken the Welsh record held jointly since the late seventies by Gareth Edwards and Gerald Davies.

The World Cup qualifier against Romania in the baking heat of Bucharest was in some danger of becoming another Welsh fiasco when Ieuan Evans found himself with half a chance forty yards out. Skinning the opposition in his inimitable style, he dotted the ball down in the corner only to be kneed in the kidney by one of the Romanian centres. When Evans reacted, the Irish referee, David McHugh, told him: 'Leave it to me.'

Neil Jenkins converted, whereupon McHugh, true to his word, restarted the match with a penalty from halfway. Jenkins made it count and Wales, three points down until Evans struck, went into half-time 10–3 ahead. Another exercise in self-destruction had been averted, thanks almost entirely to their captain's enduring ability to lead by example.

The Welsh reign as champions of Europe may have been brief but nobody could accuse them of not showing the flag. A schedule which would have taxed Marco Polo meant seven matches in three continents over a period of exactly four months, starting with their first qualifying competition for the World Cup against Portugal on a chilly May night in Lisbon.

Portugal presented the first, gentle step in the four matches offering the winner the last European place at the finals in South Africa the following summer. It proved ridiculously easy, an away win by 102 points to 11 confirming Jaoa Queimado's prediction that his Portuguese team were in for a hiding. A flood of sixteen tries swept Wales to a World Cup record which lasted fully twenty-four hours until Italy suggested that rugby in the Czech Republic left something to be desired, the Azzurri shading it 104–8.

Evans, captaining Wales for the nineteenth time and thereby overtaking Arthur 'Monkey' Gould's record which had stood since 1897, scored a hat-trick four days later when Wales completed their Iberian romp in Madrid, a 54–0 win over Spain in slightly less of a mismatch guaranteeing their presence in the final qualifying group of the European zone against Romania and Italy, all part of the price to be paid for 'botching up' the 1991 World Cup.

Still the season wasn't over. For reasons best known to themselves, the Welsh Rugby Union decided to send their weary team to Canada and then to the South Pacific for four more matches in a fortnight rather than give them a rest before the World Cup. Fletcher Field, not exactly to rugby what Madison Square Garden used to be to boxing, is where Evans was able to settle a score with the North Americans, erasing the Cardiff result of the previous winter from his memory, if not the record book.

It is true that Gareth and Gerald were never presented with as soft a touch as Portugal and Spain. It is equally true that they were able to help themselves to the rich pickings of a team so overladen with talent that for most of the seventies it was second only to New Zealand. In contrast, Evans has had to eke out an existence by ploughing a lone furrow, often through the most barren team in living memory.

Hugh McIlvanney, *The Sunday Times* award-winning sportswriter, made the point in his inimitable style the week before Evans made his comeback against England, referring to Edwards and Davies as being 'nourished, especially at the zenith of Welsh rugby in the 1970s, by the company of fellow giants. Evans, in contrast, has risen to greatness in a period of dire mediocrity for the Welsh.

'His feats have shown him to be a deadly scoring-machine, a predator who scents and exploits opportunities with the sureness of a born striker. But he has proved himself far more than one of the most penetrative runners rugby has seen. Whether with Llanelli and Wales or on tour with the British Lions, he has emerged as a talismanic influence, an inspiration to everyone alongside him and a turner of the tide in crucial matches.'

Gerald Davies wrote in a similar vein during the course of a generous tribute in *The Times* before his record had been eclipsed.

It is not only his play that is appreciated. He has exhibited strength and dignity at a time when such qualities have been scarce in Welsh rugby. In 1991, a Welsh party touring Australia fell apart under the pressures of repeated failure.

Seventy and sixty-point defeats on the field were followed off the field by brawling among the Welsh players over the dinner table. Evans, a member of that party, took no part in the boorish behaviour, but last year, as captain, made a gesture that went some way to erasing its memory. At the dinner in Paris, after France had beaten Wales, Evans astonished the assembly by making his speech in French, a rare courtesy from a British player. Such graciousness is important to him.

Yet, as a player, Evans has, through perseverance and grasping at the tiniest of possibilities, established himself as a master of deceptive flight and can be ranked in the pantheon. This is an extraordinary achievement for a wing, splendid in isolation, playing in a national team during the worst period in its history.

In Toronto, after the avenging of the Canadian defeat, Evans underlined his knack of being able to make a telling point without raising the hackles of his hosts. Before the match, a Canadian magazine carried an interview with a Canadian player which contained an insulting reference alleging Welsh in-breeding. Evans had it pinned on prominent display in the dressing-room but went out of his way after the match, which Wales won 33–15, to plead for an end to the running feud between them.

'Relationships between the teams have not exactly been a bed of roses,' he told guests. 'We need to put a stop to that. This match could have boiled over at any time and I would hate to see any future matches between our countries erupt into something violent. Our mutual lack of civility must end for the sake of our countries as well as the game.

The never-ending season then switched to the South Pacific and three internationals in seven days – a punishing schedule which ended with Evans leading his weary team through a baptism of fire which caused two players to collapse from heat exhaustion. After wins over Fiji and Tonga, Wales moved on to Apia for another damaging confrontation with Western Samoa.

The match was bad enough, conditions even worse. With the main ground out of use, Wales were dragged to the top of a valley where they changed in a tent. They had no running water and no escape from the unbearable heat, nor from a Samoan roasting to the tune of 34–9. At the end, Ricky Evans, an ex-Royal Engineer renowned for his powers of endurance, collapsed at the touchline. Rupert Moon was then taken ill on the team bus which took an hour to negotiate the one blocked road out of the ground back to their hotel.

Coach Alan Davies protested that lives had been threatened as the heat, scorching into the high nineties, left its mark. Neil Jenkins, with his red hair and face turned the colour of beetroot, ended up, according to his captain, looking 'like a Swan Vesta match'. The dehydration was such that it could all too easily have had far more drastic consequences than a nasty stinging effect on Welsh skins.

Evans reflected on 'a frightening experience'. Flying back for what was left of the close season, he had no way of knowing that an even more frightening one awaited him in the cool of an autumn afternoon back home in South Wales.

Saturday, 1 October 1995. The worst day of my life. Cardiff against Llanelli in the Heineken League, very nearly the last time I ever set foot on a rugby field. The savage irony about it all was that I was never supposed to have been playing in the first place.

I had hurt my shoulder in a tackle the previous Saturday against Pontypool and all week the shoulder hadn't been responding to treatment. I had more or less told everybody that I would give the Cardiff match a miss but fate decreed that I would take a fitness test on the Friday night. Reluctantly, very reluctantly, I decided I would play after all.

I left home that morning shortly after eleven, got a lift towards the motorway and was waiting there when the Llanelli team bus pulled up at the Penllergaer interchange as arranged at

11.30 a.m. The mood on board was strangely subdued and that's how it remained for the hour or so of the journey to Cardiff. Something troubled me from the time I got on until kick-off at 2.30 p.m.

There was a sense of foreboding about the whole day. I'm not claiming to be psychic or to have extra-sensory perception but it was as if I sensed something fairly unpleasant was going to happen; as if somebody was waiting to say, 'Welcome to the twilight zone.' I kept thinking, 'I shouldn't be here. I shouldn't be playing. Well, you'd better shut up because you can't pull out, not now.'

Arriving at the Arms Park, I had a horrible feeling in the pit of my stomach as if I was going to be sick. People were surprised to see me there. They had read about the injury and expected to see someone else in my place. When we ran out for the start, I still didn't feel right. The vibes were still bad. I would not have to wait long to discover the reason for my advanced state of anxiety.

It happened when a long Cardiff drop-out bounced between Colin Stephens and myself. We both started to go for it, Colin decided to leave it to me. I picked it up and ran it back, going in between a couple of backs and beating them. When someone grabbed my shorts, I turned round to offload the ball. Hemi Taylor, the Cardiff flanker, had caught me from behind and tried to haul me down, the sort of routine tackle which is performed up and down the country every Saturday afternoon.

Both my feet were firmly stuck in the ground. I was standing still and suddenly I had this horrible, horrible feeling that something had gone seriously wrong. An expanse opened round me like the parting of the Red Sea as players stepped away, and the crowd went so quiet that an awful hush descended over the place. I shall never forget the deafening silence, nor shall I forget the searing pain which after a few seconds shot up my leg.

I turned to look round to see what was happening to me. Rupert Moon was there alongside me and he immediately grabbed my head and put his hands over my eyes. Emyr Lewis grabbed me, too, but they were both too late. I had looked down and seen this obscene shape which was supposed to have been my foot. I knew then why so many of the players on the field that day had looked away. Someone told me later that at least two spectators had fainted in the stand.

The pain was unbelievable. This was no ordinary dislocation. My left foot was at a right angle to my left leg. It was literally hanging off. If John Fairclough had not happened quite by chance to have been at the match, I would never have played again. Mr Fairclough is an eminent orthopaedic surgeon who had interrupted a game of tennis because he felt he ought to have been at the match, just in case.

When it happened, someone said to John, 'Ieuan's gone down. Looks as though his boot's come off.' 'Yes,' came the reply. 'But his foot's still in it.'

He ran on immediately and tried to settle me down. I was screaming at him to stop the pain but I knew he would have to put it back into place. Rupert, being a compulsive liar, said: 'It's okay, Ieu. He's put it back in.' I relaxed and at that moment John grabbed the foot and all anyone could hear was an awful scraping sound, the sort you get when metal collides with concrete. The noise came from the tendons and muscles as the surgeon put my foot back on to my leg.

The pain went through me like a red-hot poker and then, all of a sudden, it subsided and such a peaceful feeling came over me that I felt like smiling at the sheer relief. The excruciating pain had receded to a dull ache. I thought, 'Thank God, that's over.'

The next fear was whether my career was over. Nobody needed to tell me that I had a serious problem. This wasn't a run-of-the-mill dead leg or a routine groin strain. This was big-time. This was worse than a case entitled 'You may never play again'. This was a case of 'You may never walk again'.

As they carried me off the pitch and into the ambulance it seemed as if half the doctors in South Wales were there. Others were in need of attention. Everyone could hear the crack of the foot going back into place and I heard a huge collective groan from the crowd and then a sympathetic ovation as they carted me off. Two minutes later I was in the Cardiff Royal Infirmary.

As soon as I got into the ambulance, John Fairclough said, 'You'll play again.' At that stage all sorts of thoughts were swimming around in my head and that one remark was to sustain me throughout the long, painstaking rehabilitation. I felt like letting out a whoop of joy. Instead I contented myself with something much more restrained, 'Thank God for that.'

My injuries were so severe that they had a traumatising effect. The bone of my left ankle had sheared away from the shinbone and even in the very short space of time between the accident taking place and Mr Fairclough arriving at the scene, the foot had gone white. The blood supply had been cut off and had it not been put back into place there and then, I would never have played again. In fact, I would have been very lucky to have been able to walk properly, never mind run.

The most frightening aspect of all was that if this had happened at many another venue on the club circuit, I could conceivably have lost the foot. It is not as if an eminent orthopaedic surgeon is in attendance at every club match every Saturday afternoon. In that respect, I was lucky, very lucky.

Within two hours of being admitted to hospital, I was being wheeled into the operating theatre. By then I'd had ample time to reflect on my anxiety that morning. I knew all along that I shouldn't have played. For a while I could hardly get the thought out of my head that I should have paid more attention to my instincts, but there was no point torturing myself.

What was done, was done and what mattered now was that the surgeon who was going to put me back in one piece had assured me that this was not the end and that was more than good enough for me. Admittedly, he was hardly going to be cruel enough to tell me there and then that I was finished. What I desperately needed was reassurance and one of the finest specialists in his field was giving it to me, voluntarily.

It may only have been a throwaway remark designed to lift my spirits but I took it as gospel and, whenever I felt low during the long weeks and months ahead, I used it as a crutch to keep going.

It wasn't the only thing I lent on. My parents, who had both been at the match, were incredible in their support. Many others could not have done enough for me, people like John Fairclough, of course; Roy Bergiers, the Llanelli chairman; Ieuan Harries, the club doctor; Peter Herbert, an inspiration as my fitness trainer; Tim Atter, the physiotherapist at the BUPA hospital in Cardiff; and Moon & Davies (Phil) Ltd, taxi service.

My employers, Forthright Finance, were marvellous. Employers of international rugby players have been the unsung sponsors of the game for many years. As if they hadn't been generous enough with the time they had given me that summer to go on tour with Wales, the post-operation period meant six weeks away from my job as marketing manager but the company gave me all the time I needed without the slightest pressure or hassle for which I shall forever be indebted to chief executive John Skeldon, and my immediate superior in the marketing department, Ian Rone.

On top of all that I could draw on a bottomless reservoir of good will flowing in on a daily basis from what seemed like every corner of the world. Letters and cards poured in from all over the place and it was a tribute to the resourcefulness of the Royal Mail that everything got through despite the vagueness of some of the envelopes. A few letters were addressed: Ieuan Evans, c/o Wales. One or two were even less specific: Ieuan Evans, The World. Not much to go on but they still reached me.

For some time after the accident, 'Dai Dogs', alias Dai Rees, who ran the club shop at Stradey, would deliver a sackful of post to my parents' home at Porthyrhyd near Carmarthen. Children from schools, mainly in Wales but from the rest of Britain and Ireland, went to endless trouble to draw cards for me and send their best wishes. To have such spontaneous support was a humbling experience and I thank everyone for taking the trouble to provide me with such powerful motivation.

Most of all, though, I had the best medical and psychological help available. Will Carling and Gavin Hastings wrote to me and the Welsh boys were always on the phone or calling round, constantly egging me on – and there were occasions when I needed all the egging I could get. I knew how tough the recovery was going to be and at times I struggled to come to terms with what it would demand of me.

Somehow I was going to have to squeeze six months' rehabilitation into not much more than eight weeks. My hopeful aim was to be playing again in three months. In other words, New Year's Day. Instead, I came back on 28 January, which was some going because 1 March had always been a more realistic date for my return.

What I found hard to take was that I had been in the midst of a purple patch, playing better than at any time in my life, and now it had all been taken away from me. I was going to have to start again from scratch and my dream was to be back for the England match in mid-February. Many must have regarded that as an impossible dream, but not to me. The positive vibes of those around me strengthened my resolve.

Within two weeks, the plaster was off and within three weeks, I was doing my first exercise, a daily dose of sit-ups. After five weeks I passed the first major landmark on the way back. The ankle was back in its proper place, the shinbone had knitted together again and there were no complications. I had to walk before I could run and then I began cycling – the first in a series of often painful exercises to rebuild the calf of my left leg. The muscle had wasted away until there was none left.

Neville Southall, the great Everton goalkeeper, had an identical injury a few years ago. Ironically, his happened on a rugby ground, at Lansdowne Road, when the Welsh soccer team played a friendly there against the Republic of Ireland.

By mid-November, six weeks after the accident, I was walking again without any trace of a limp. The operation had changed the way I walked. Before it I had been very splay-footed, ambling along with my feet pointing at ten to two, or ten past ten. Now that the left foot had been straightened out, my walking dial had been advanced ten minutes to two o'clock!

The really hard work began with Peter Herbert putting me through my paces on the running track at the Carmarthen Leisure Centre. The first thing he did was to make sure I didn't lapse back into my old eating habits of scoffing the wrong kind of food. I started running during the first week of December, hopping over a series of ten hurdles which was quite painful given the stress it put on my ankle. The pain, though, was positively pleasant compared to the tortuous business of trying to sprint while dragging a weighted sled behind me.

By Christmas I was so far ahead of schedule that by the New Year I was back at Stradey training with the Llanelli squad. The medical team had given me the full go-ahead to play again, although there was no chance of my being ready for the start of the Five Nations in France where we suffered yet another serious injury in controversial circumstances – a head-butt from the French lock Olivier Merle which caused Ricky Evans to fall over and break his ankle.

My come-back match, 28 January 1995, took me back to grass-roots Welsh rugby for Llanelli's Swalec Cup tie at Glynneath. After eighteen weeks, I was back doing what I like best, playing for the Scarlets, even if on this occasion it meant slogging through a pitch more fit for hippos than humans. The mud must have been about five inches deep and while Max Boyce's home club worked wonders to get the game on, the conditions looked suspiciously conducive to a giant-killing. But we all negotiated the various hazards without mishap, even if the chap with the receding hairline out on the right wing seemed a yard or two off the pace!

A lot more reporters than usual rolled up for the occasion along with the television cameras. They had been with me from day one, filming a documentary about my recovery which Grahame Lloyd produced for BBC Wales television with the appropriate title, *A Wing and a Prayer*. I have never seen the actual video-tape of the events surrounding my injuries. Even to this day, I find it impossible to bring myself to sit down and watch it.

Two more matches for Llanelli and my dream became a reality. I was back as captain for Wales for the home match against England and it is only now I realise that perhaps I did come back a bit too soon. The recovery process had taken far more out of me than I imagined at the time and, inevitably, it was going to take time before I could raise my game to where it was a few minutes before three o'clock on that first Saturday afternoon of October 1994.

Never in my life had I worked so hard to get back. I trained every night, often several hours at a time, invariably in sheeting rain with Peter Herbert keeping me on the straight and narrow. I became so single-minded about it that I blotted everything else out of my life and it wasn't until I took a brief rest from the game after the World Cup last summer that I realised how much of a toll that intensive physical effort had taken.

After missing three games – Italy, South Africa and France – I had at least proved that I wasn't finished even if there was to be no fairytale return. England were in no mood to be caught out at Cardiff again, my sense of achievement suffering as a consequence of a defeat which left me wrestling with a very different kind of emergency.

For reasons beyond my comprehension, the French referee, Joel Dume, sent John Davies off during the second half for supposedly kicking Ben Clarke after the French touch-judge, Patrick Robin, had flagged. Now, whether or not this was a political tit-for-tat following the Welsh Rugby Union's protest over the Merle incident in Paris the previous month, I don't know, but video evidence suggested that John's boot did not make contact with Clarke.

The touch-judge obviously thought it did and at the hearing it was claimed that the Neath player had shown intent. Well, if you are going to send people off because you think they are intent on doing something, there will be very few forwards left on the field after twenty minutes. My immediate concern once John had been dismissed was that we had nobody to prop up the scrum on the tight-head side.

Hemi Taylor was about to step into the breach at the first scrum when I intervened. With something like 850 kilograms coming through from the other side, there was an obvious risk of serious injury which I was not prepared to take under any circumstance. I had to make a decision and make it quickly. In retrospect, I could have exploited a silly loophole in the laws, informed the referee that we were unable to scrummage and he would then have had no alternative but to abandon the match.

Can you imagine the ruction that would have caused, with fifty-five thousand people in the stadium and countless millions watching on television? How stupid that in order for the game to continue and continue without unnecessary risk of serious injury I had to break the rules, replacements only being allowed in the event of an injured player having to leave the field.

I knew I had to make a substitution there and then. I asked Will Carling if England had any objections. He immediately gave me the go-ahead whereupon I sent for our reserve prop, Hugh Williams-Jones, and took Hemi off. He wasn't very happy about it but, in those circumstances, the blind-side flanker is invariably the one to go. At least it enabled us to complete the match without exposing a non-specialist to the risk of breaking his neck simply because the rule said so.

In that case the law really was an ass. Thankfully, the International Board reacted by making provision for a specialist to be brought on at the expense of another player in the event of a prop being ordered off. It was about the only good thing to come out of the incident, not that it offered one iota of comfort to John Davies, distraught enough at being sent off without then being banned for sixty days.

CHAPTER NINETEEN

Sacked and Shattered

A message from Buckingham Palace was among the first to reach Evans as he recovered from the operation to save his career. It came from the Princess of Wales in the form of a telemessage.

> *I was sorry to hear of your accident. Hope you'll soon return to London to continue your shopping expedition with the England captain! Diana.*

Even hard-nosed New Zealanders were moved to write. This letter arrived from Auckland.

> *Dear Mr Evans,*
>
> *I was very distressed to learn you've suffered such a wretched injury; may your recovery be swift and complete. We need you.*
>
> *When I say 'we' I mean New Zealand rugby fans. We need a good strong confident Wales team to knock spots off. Ever since Deans really did make it to the line a mere 89 years ago, Wales has always been the team to beat when on tour in Britain. Since the Edwards/John/Davies/Williams sides of (now) many years ago, that's not been too tough.*
>
> *Now you've put new fire into the reds. Please don't do anything stupid, but I/we want to see you back in business. Especially against the Aussies.*
>
> *Kia Ora,*
> *Don Paterson.*

Of the hundreds of letters which flooded in from nearer home, none caught the mood of schoolchildren across the country better than a get-well card made from half a page of exercise paper. Inside, it read:

'You must get well soon because then my friend Ellie will cheer up and be happy again. Loadsalove, Meg.'

First thing that Monday morning, Frank Burrows, the manager of Swansea City FC, sent a fax to Llanelli Rugby Club. 'Sorry to hear about your bad luck. Be patient and get fit as soon as possible. Best wishes from chairman, directors, manager, players and staff, Swansea City AFC.'

The South African Embassy in London sent a very nice letter, although their wishes, as expressed by First Secretary Henry Short, would prove a bit too much for Wales to manage.

'We hope to see you in South Africa during the World Cup, where we are sure that you will again lead the Welsh rugby team and score a number of very good tries and win famous victories against the other Group C countries – Japan, Ireland and New Zealand. Who knows what may happen in the finals . . .'

Countless letters poured in from the other side of Offa's Dike, underlining how Evans's stature transcended all boundaries. This, from an address in Wimbledon, was typical of them.

> *Dear Ieuan,*
>
> *I am writing to say how saddened I was by the news of your unfortunate injury. I am an Englishman and am fiercely proud of my country's Rugby Union team. Suffice it to say that you have given me many unpleasant moments playing against us (we won't mention the try at the Arms Park in '93) but I have always admired your skill and the manner in which you conduct yourself as player, captain and British Lion.*
>
> *PS: Okay, we will mention that try! In a fit of pre-match exuberance I decided to bet £1 on you to score the first try (the odds were 10–1). My father and I joked about this as we settled down to watch the national anthems. Then you spoilt it! However, the £10 was put to good use in the local hostelry that night.*
>
> *Best of Luck,*
> *John Killoran.*

Nobody took a deeper sense of satisfaction from Ieuan's recovery than John Fairclough, the surgeon whose prompt attention at least gave him the fighting chance of a complete recovery. Having comforted the patient on the way to hospital by reassuring him he would play again, even Fairclough will admit that he feared the worst when it came to playing again on the international stage.

'This was as bad a dislocation as you can get,' he said. 'Most of my surgical colleagues felt the same way. I don't think any of us ever believed he would get back to international level. Yet Ieuan never doubted that he would. Whenever we tried gently to point out how seriously he had been injured, he simply wouldn't listen. He has passed all expectations and we are thrilled to see him back.'

The three-hour operation involved such intricate surgical engineering that Fairclough inserted a three-inch-long stainless steel plate secured by six screws, some as long as one and a half inches. 'When you have a chap who is a national sporting hero, you know your reputation is on the line,' Fairclough, an expert in sporting injuries, said. 'We thought it was the end of an era but Ieuan's response once the surgical work had been done was quite extraordinary.

'I have dealt with many international athletes over the years but he, more than anyone else, had the determination and the hunger to get back. He was so proud of his position as captain of his country. I have never seen motivation like it and to see him back gives us all immense satisfaction.'

Tim Atter took one look at the X-ray plates before being called in to supervise the rehabilitation and thought, 'You don't recover from that.' He was delighted to be proved wrong. 'Ieuan was never desperate and neither were we,' he said. 'He was lucky that the surgery was so good.'

The least the Welsh Rugby Union could have done to show their gratitude was to have sent Mr Atter a ticket for the England match. Instead, he had to scrabble around to obtain one from other sources. If such treatment appeared to be a trifle shabby, it was nothing compared to that meted out to Evans within a month of Wales's departure for the World Cup.

A heavy beating by Scotland at Murrayfield followed by the biennial home failure against Ireland left Wales with their second championship whitewash in five years. They had gone from top to bottom in twelve months, losing five in a row during a season which began promisingly enough against South Africa only to go downhill at an alarming rate of knots.

The Welsh Rugby Union reacted to the crisis by sacking coach Alan Davies, his assistant, Gareth Jenkins, and manager Robert Norster. Alex Evans, the Queenslander then finishing his third season as Cardiff's paid coach, took over, assisted by Mike Ruddock of Swansea and Dennis John of Pontypridd, with Geoff Evans, the former London Welsh lock, as the new manager.

When it comes to forward planning, Wales clearly stick to the principle that the less time the coach has, the better their chance. While some coaches, like Bob Dwyer and Laurie Mains, take four years preparing their team for a World Cup, Wales tend to give theirs months, although even that estimate is generous at times.

Alex Evans had all of six weeks prior to departure for South Africa, which was almost as long as Alan Davies had been allowed when he stepped into the breach. Returning home from Nottingham to rebuild what was left of Welsh rugby, Davies began by appointing a captain who turned out to be an inspired choice. That second week of April 1995 found the captain wondering what on earth was going to happen next.

The phone rang at my office in Cardiff one morning last April and I could tell by the tone of the voice at the other end that he had not called to tell me I had won the lottery. The coaches and manager had been sacked a week or so before but I still did not believe that they would go ahead and sack me as captain.

Geoff Evans, the new manager, was on the line. 'Can we speak?' he said and I knew instinctively what was coming. He asked me how my ankle was and I thought then that something was definitely up because there was nothing wrong with my ankle.

I was like a rabbit trapped in the glare of the headlights of an oncoming vehicle. I knew what was coming but I couldn't do anything about it. Then Geoff got to the point. 'We've decided not to make you team captain for the forthcoming World Cup. Alex Evans wants someone who knows exactly what he wants and can put that over to the squad.'

At that stage I was no longer able to listen properly. I suddenly felt a horrible sense of rejection, that I had let people down, that I had failed. I was shattered and hurt, hurt especially at the inference that after eight years of international rugby, working under five or six different coaches, I was not capable of under-standing a coach's vision and transmitting it to the players. I found that demeaning. It would have taken me two sessions to have got to grips with what Alex wanted of me.

Instead, I was left with the impression that his thoughts were totally beyond me. A whole range of emotions were tumbling around me. Insecurity and paranoia took over. I thought, 'I'm on my way out here.' Then I decided I'd beat them to it. World Cup or no World Cup, I made up my mind to quit there and then.

The funny thing was that I had been on the phone to Mike Hall when Geoff came through on another line connected to an adjoining desk. I said I would call Mike back but he arrived at the office after lunch by which time Geoff had presumably given him the news that he was to captain the team at the World Cup. Whether Mike already knew during our earlier conversation, I don't know.

I told him I wouldn't be going to the World Cup. He implored me not to be foolish, not to cut my nose off to spite my face and then said he would pass my thoughts on to Alex. I began to convince myself that there was some hidden agenda here, that they were going to make me the scapegoat for all the deficiencies in the team.

Nobody knew better than I that something had to be done. The England match, the second of that championship, convinced me that changes had to be made. A lot of people were playing on past glories. We were carrying too many passengers. A comfort zone had been created and too many were sitting back in the middle of it, giving them a sense of security which their performances could not justify.

The selectors had made it too cosy for them. They had gone out of their way to create this false sense of security. If players made mistakes, they would not be castigated for them, let alone thrown out. It had gone too far. In an attempt to foster a happy-family, club atmosphere, we had lost our competitive edge. Training sessions had gone a bit soft. We were in a rut.

Some of us, like Hemi Taylor, Nigel Davies, Emyr Lewis and myself, came back from dramatic injuries and others were not performing. I knew that I wasn't back to top form, that maybe I had come back too soon. But only a few weeks before, I had been under considerable pressure to rush back for the England match as if that was what the country wanted.

I still believe that I should never have been replaced as captain of Wales and in saying that I acknowledge the fact that I am as accountable as the next person. Nor do I want to give the impression that I had some sort of divine right to hold the job for as long as I wanted. I had played in three of the five defeats but the season before I had captained Wales to the Five Nations title and we had come safely through our series of World Cup qualifying matches.

No nation is going to tolerate a whitewash, least of all Wales. I knew something was afoot with the coaches and manager. It still caught me by surprise, despite Bob Norster advising me, 'Watch yourself. Your place might disappear, too.' I weighed it all up and felt the pluses still outnumbered the minuses.

That night I rang my old mate, Phil Davies, and we went out for a drink. Nothing reminiscent of the Carmarthen Cowboy days, just a couple of quiet beers and home. I'd had enough of the whole thing when the chairman of the WRU, Vernon Pugh, learnt of my intentions and invited me to his house in Cardiff. Alex Evans was also there. I knew it was all done and dusted but there were a few things I felt I had to say. More than anything, I wanted an explanation.

As far as I was concerned, I had been judged and found wanting. Now I wanted to know why and I was getting rather emotional about it, more passionate than angry. The job had meant everything to me and I had given it everything I had, often to the exclusion of other considerations. I always felt the captaincy brought out the best in me. Now that I had suddenly been reduced to the ranks, there was some explaining to be done. Alex, being an Aussie, went straight to the point: 'Mike is my club captain. He knows my game plan inside out and I don't have the time to tell you so you can tell the rest.'

I disagreed as Alex expected. Over the years I have worked with all kinds of international coaches, Welsh and non-Welsh, like Ian McGeechan, Dick Best and Roger Uttley. In seeking an explanation, I was also looking for an assurance that there was no hidden agenda. I asked him straight, 'Do you want me out of the team?' He was adamant he didn't. Both Alex and Vernon went out of their way to get my enthusiasm going, insisting that I was the best winger in the world and all that stuff. 'I want you firing on all cylinders,' Alex said. 'I want you to be the best wing in the world again.'

After ninety minutes I left, saying I would think it over for a couple of days and decide. They wanted me to continue but I was still agonising about it. Do I go? Or do I stay? There was a World Cup on the horizon and if I didn't play in that one there wouldn't be another one because I'll be gone thirty-five by the time we host the next one in 1999. The World Cup was a factor, but the decisive factor in the argument came down to one question.

Had I gone through all the pain and heartache to recover from a potentially crippling injury only to give it all up? By packing it in after three come-back matches I would be letting down all those who did so much to help me back on the rugby field. By stripping me of the captaincy, they had given me a new source of motivation, not that I needed it.

If you have nothing to prove, there is no challenge. Now I had something to prove all right. I had not performed at top gear since my return, which was understandable enough in the circumstances, even if I hadn't been given much of an opportunity to show what I could do, but it didn't stop people writing me off. I wanted to show them I could still do it.

I believe I should still be captaining Wales and that they had no good reason to take it away from me. I wouldn't be human if I didn't feel bitter about it but I don't let it show. I keep my head down and concentrate on my own performance. What's gone is gone and while it has reduced the pressures on me to some extent, I take no comfort from that.

With a new broom sweeping clean, players had to start proving themselves again. Training under Alex acquired the harder edge it needed. A few blows were struck, nothing nasty, but enough to keep people on their toes. That, most definitely, had been missing. I am more self-centred than when I was captain but the basic objective will never change.

Wales come first and last. Always have done. Always will.

CHAPTER TWENTY

All Psyched Up for Jonah

When the guillotine fell, Ieuan Evans had captained Wales twenty-eight times, a total which put him fifth in the all-time list behind Will Carling (53), Nick Farr-Jones (36), Jean-Pierre Rives (34) and Wilson Whineray (30). In this case, mere figures do him an injustice.

For Evans, the captaincy of his country went far beyond clapping his hands and exhorting the boys to get stuck in. It meant so much to him that it became less an occasional event and more a way of life, an awareness of the urgent need to create a user-friendly image for a nation sick of seeing its rugby teams dragged through the mud on and off the field.

Unlike Carling, Farr-Jones, Rives or Whineray, Evans was obliged to start knee-deep in rubble, his appointment coming in the aftermath of the internal tribalism provoked by the shocking tour of Australia in the summer of 1991. If many wondered how anyone could captain any team from such a solitary position out on the wing, Evans gave his answer by doing more than anyone else to drag Wales out of the pit.

No player can have gone from extremes of success and failure more often, from clinching a Lions series in Australia to being humiliated there with Wales, from being top of the pile one season and bottom the next. The only consistent world-beater in a team which at best was never much more than moderate, even in winning the Five Nations, Evans responded to the twin impostors of victory and defeat with a stoicism which could have come straight out of Kipling's book of philosophy.

No matter how satisfying or horrific the experience — and there were more than enough of those — he never failed to subject himself to the post-match interrogation and never failed to conduct himself with a dignity which was more than could be said for some of his predecessors.

When he broke the news to Phil Davies the day the new regime stripped him of the captaincy, Llanelli's most-capped forward could hardly believe what he was hearing. 'A total disgrace,' Davies said. 'Here was a man respected the length and breadth of the British Isles and they'd got rid of him. What made it ridiculous was that there was no need for it at all.

'Wherever I went in my travels round the country, nobody could understand it. In my book, Ieuan stood above all the Welsh captains. He brought a charisma to the job which nobody else could match. He worked hard to improve discipline and put an enormous amount of time and effort into all aspects of the captaincy.

'He took it so seriously and gave it so much that I'd try to get him to relax a bit more for his own sake. I once suggested that some day someone might come along and take it away from him which, of course, is exactly what happened. To have done that just before the World Cup was a shocker. Ieuan can be a bit of a loner at times but he was devastated by the business over the captaincy. Sadly, it was typical of the Welsh Rugby Union.'

Davies half-expected, half-hoped they would put Evans back on the bridge after another failed World Cup. 'It's all very well to blood youngsters but you need people of substance who know what it's all about,' he said. 'I thought they'd go back to a caring captain, a renowned player with the right image who worked hard at the job. Everyone in the rugby world respects Ieuan Evans. What more could they want?'

The responsibility of leading his country had pulled him out of his Carmarthen shell. That it helped him develop as a person was one of the most striking aspects of his captaincy, as articulated by the coach who appointed him, Alan Davies. 'At the start, you could see him beginning to grow into the role,' he said. 'And the way he has handled himself and the team on and off the pitch since he became captain has been outstanding.'

What Evans gave Wales, especially in the early years, was spelt out by Stephen Jones in *The Sunday Times* the week before the famous win over England in February 1993.

They made Evans captain of Wales because he was Welsh; not quite burn-those-holiday-homes Welsh, but conspicuously Welsh. Welsh-speaking, he was a man of Carmarthen, where they regard an East Walian as half English.

They needed him because when he became captain, the Welsh team had completely lost the burning dragon passion that renders such mundane matters as playing ability irrelevant. In other ways, Evans did not at first seem much of a choice. His career had always been disrupted by injury, he did not come over as a natural leader and, partly because of the very nature of his position on the wing, he was a peripheral figure.

He owed his elevation to the fact that he was one of very few members of the team not tainted in some way by the faction-fighting into which affairs had degenerated. Robert Norster and Alan Davies invested the whole future in Evans's leadership. Evans and the coaches quickly began to give heritage lessons. They gradually bound players together and succeeded in renewing motivation.

For some, motivation was to become a dirty word. A distinct lack of it when the chips were down at Ellis Park on the first Sunday in June led to Wales being pitched out of the World Cup, their second successive failure to reach the last eight provoking a fresh outpouring of grief over the national sport lurching back into intensive care. From third place in 1987, Wales had been written off by the superpowers of the Southern Hemisphere as third-rate opponents.

Not for the first time, Ireland's unfancied team had found Welsh hwyl less than irresistible. Not satisfied at condemning Wales to the wooden spoon at the Arms Park barely three months earlier, the Irish surprised themselves at the comparative ease with which Wales allowed them to take the match by the throat and cause just enough immediate chaos to see them through.

The only home country not to survive the opening stage of the competition, Wales still wound up as the only one not obliged to qualify for the next World Cup in 1999 when they will be hard pushed to maintain the tradition that the host team always reaches the final. The irony of it all was not lost on their best player, denied what would almost certainly be his last opportunity of a principal role on the grandest stage.

After a week of wallowing in self-pity, I reaffirmed my undying belief in the Welsh cause and immersed myself in preparations for the third World Cup. It was one of those major adjustments of attitude which all of us have to make from time to time, a case of 'stop feeling sorry for yourself and show them what you can do'.

Even at my lowest ebb, I never lost sight of the fact that, having worked so hard to get back in time for the World Cup, I would now be competing in an event which had become one of the biggest in the global sporting calendar. Losing the captaincy was not going to dilute my desire for Wales to succeed.

Drawn in the same pool as New Zealand, Ireland and Japan, we considered a place in the quarter-finals to be the bottom line. For all the comings and goings of the previous weeks, we flew out with a genuine sense of optimism, never imagining that instead we would once again be the first of the home countries to be eliminated.

Never having played there before, South Africa was always going to be a novel experience. Bloemfontein, our base for the opening match against Japan, at least ensured that our challenge would not suffer from any local distractions. Set in the Afrikaaner heartland of the Orange Free State, the town is so quiet that it could make a morgue sound rowdy by comparison.

For all that, they made us very welcome throughout our stay. Nothing was too much trouble and the welcome even extended to the players having armed guards wherever we went. We played golf and we also ventured into the townships to coach the local kids and the raw talent is such that when they start to take the game seriously, the world had better look out.

Given our capacity for skidding on banana skins, Japan could have been a very tricky first match. Instead, we got off to a flying start and finished up topping the 55 points we had scored against them at Cardiff in October 1993. Winning 57-10 sent us off in good heart during the short flight to Johannesburg and the ultimate test of our hoped-for recovery from a losing domestic season.

After Bloemfontein, Jo'burg came as a cultural shock; a huge urban sprawl with such a reputation for street violence that we were under orders never to leave the hotel without an armed guard. Wherever we went, therefore, the men with the Smith & Wessons went with us and while we heard horrific tales of people being robbed at gunpoint, the only disturbance we encountered was from the All Blacks as soon as we set foot on Ellis Park.

It was the night when I had expected to be introducing myself to a very large gentleman by the name of Jonah Lomu. He, alas, had switched to the other wing and it wasn't until they lined up for the kick-off that I realised he had gone out of his way to avoid a direct confrontation! It rather messed up my plan for a friendly attempt to break the ice immediately after the Haka. Different players respond to it differently.

Campo, for instance, always goes behind the posts to do his warm-ups and on that famous occasion in Dublin some years ago, Willie Anderson, then captain of Ireland, gave Wayne Shelford a real eyeballing which left 'Buck' looking as though he was about to explode with anger. I've always believed in facing my opposite number, not as an overt act of aggression but by giving him the respect of paying attention to the pre-match ritual.

The last time I lined up for the traditional Maori war dance, during the Lions tour of New Zealand, I found myself at close quarters with a young man who went through the routine with all the eye-popping fury of an enraged rhino, Va'aiga Tuigamala. Marking him gave me some experience of conceding four or five stone to my opponent.

With Tuigamala, I would smile and wink at him once the Haka had been done. He had such a frightening expression that I wanted to get him to smile and also let him know that I was not the least bit bothered about taking him on. He did smile, once I think, which only seemed to make him run all the harder.

Lomu had already made a huge impact with the trail of damage he had carved through the Irish defence during the Blacks' first match the previous weekend. I had built myself up for the challenge by hatching a plan to mark him so closely that

I'd almost be sitting on him, and if I could get away with living offside, so much the better. Against Lomu, you take whatever advantage you can.

My plan was to hold on to him for grim death until the cavalry could come to the rescue and haul him down. A giant who can run so quickly carrying such awesome power is a frightening prospect, the like of which I had not seen before. Now you may find this hard to believe, but I was not doing cartwheels at discovering that he had switched to the other wing. Any international player wants to play against the best and I had psyched myself up for Jonah in a way which left me as much disappointed as relieved, honestly!

Once again, it must have been the old story of our being overawed by the sight of the black jersey. There could not really be any other explanation for our failure in the first twenty minutes when they hit us and hit us hard, which was all very unfortunate especially after Geoff Evans, as manager, had gone out of his way to talk up our chances. He subsequently came in for some criticism but in claiming that we were the equal of the opposition he was only trying to strengthen our often fragile self-confidence.

Andrew Mehrtens, the new outside-half, kicked towards the corners, tiring our pack in the process and ensuring a productive platform for the magnificent Ian Jones, surely the best line-out jumper in the game. The defeat, 34–9, would have been bigger had it not been for a super performance by the Cardiff flanker, Mark Bennett, on the openside of the scrum.

We also became aware that New Zealand had unearthed another outstanding player. Josh Kronfeld brought such a dynamic touch to their back row that, for all the mania about Lomu, I rated him the outstanding player of the 1995 World Cup. We managed to keep Lomu fairly quiet until the last All Black try where the big man managed to hold on long enough for Kronfeld to come flying through for the finishing touch.

Now everything hinged on our final pool match, against Ireland at the same stadium four days later. The equation was brutally simple. The winner was through to the quarter-finals, the loser on the first plane home. Even judged by the most disastrous matches of Welsh rugby over the last ten years, Ireland at Ellis Park in June 1995 ranks with the worst of them.

The questions still nag away as though it happened yesterday. Why were we half-asleep for the first twenty minutes? Why did we panic? How come we couldn't live with the pace of modest opponents? And, worst of all, where was the hwyl, the will to win?

I don't know whether it was a lack of desire, a lack of ability, a lack of courage or an amalgamation of all three. There was a deathly hush in the dressing-room afterwards. The awful reality had crowded in on us, that we had botched-up another World Cup and for some of us there would never be another opportunity.

In many respects, our failure in South Africa was worse than that of the previous World Cup. Then, we had been caught unawares by the surprise team of the tournament, Western Samoa. This time we had been caught out by our own ineptitude and no single incident summed it up in a more shocking way than the second Irish try. Dennis McBride was left free to walk out of a tackle and then found that there was nobody standing between him and the line.

We started to run the ball in the last twenty minutes only to find that we had given them one point too many. I had three passes and made one of them count towards a late try as Jon Humphreys, our new hooker, gave us belated hope of a reprieve. Sadly, not even some New Zealand expertise, from Gwent's favourite Maori, Hemi Taylor, could save us disappearing down the plughole, beaten 24–23.

It left me with a shameful sense of déjà vu. I felt extreme embarrassment, shame and a sense of grief for our national sport – all sentiments which reminded me of the worst moments in New Zealand in '88 and Australia in '91. To have worked harder than I had ever worked in my life in recovering from a crippling injury only to end up being a party to this was desperately hard to take.

Dr Louis Luyt, the provocative president of the South African Rugby Union, didn't make me or any other member of the

Welsh party feel any better. During his speech at the after-match function, he spoke about New Zealand and ignored Wales so completely that he never gave us a single mention, dishonourable or otherwise. Perhaps it was just as well, given his track record for putting his foot in it during after-dinner speeches.

Our image was bad enough without some of our players being seen on television having a bit of a sing-song with Irish fans in a bar the following night. A few of the boys got conned into taking part – an innocent event but it would not have gone down at all well with the folks back home, depressed enough by our failure.

Had we won, it would have been France in Durban the following Saturday. I went there anyway, then along with Tony Clement and Mike Hall headed off to Mauritius. A week's holiday on the island paradise in the Indian Ocean eased the pain but nothing could compensate for the grim prospect that my last World Cup chance had gone for good.

All being well, I shall be thirty-five when the next one comes round. If that is an unlikely scenario, I have no intention of retiring just yet. I lost so much time earlier in my career that I have yet to reclaim it all. I still have enough left in the tank to keep going for another season, at least.

★   ★   ★

The season could hardly have started on a more demanding note. We spent our first Saturday in the lion's den, back at the altitude of Ellis Park against South Africa. The Boks had won the World Cup there ten weeks previously and the local bookmakers gave us no chance, which suited us just fine.

A Welsh team bristling with youthful energy and no little skill gave them a game for an hour before running out of steam which, on the first day of the season, was understandable. One game at the wrong time of the year was a very small price to pay for South Africa helping Wales win the right to stage the 1999 World Cup.

It took me to a very special landmark, my 55th cap, equalling the Welsh record set by J.P.R. Williams. For me to be up there among the legends takes some believing and J.P.R., who was at the match in his role as a selector, was the first to offer his congratulations – the same J.P.R. whom I saw at the zenith of his career the first time my Dad took me to the Arms Park when I was eight years old.

CHAPTER TWENTY-ONE

The Packer Circus

Had Will Carling got his way, Ieuan Evans would have been spotted in different gear this season. Wearing light blue, magenta, chocolate, French grey, light green – the official colours of the kaleidoscopic Harlequins Football Club.

The England captain makes no secret of the fact that he had hoped to persuade the former Wales captain to join London's richest club and see out his career in the English First Division. 'I think he came very close to joining Quins and I'm sure he would have enjoyed himself in London,' Carling said. 'He is probably the most widely respected Welsh player in England.

'I certainly encouraged him to join us and there is no doubt he would have done Quins a lot of good. It wasn't just a case of switching clubs but about the broader aspects of living and working in a place like London. He weighed everything up and decided not to move.'

Weary of the Heineken League being clogged by an almost annual rise in the amount of dross, Evans considered widening his horizons by heading beyond the near east of London to the Far East of Tokyo. The chance of a challenging new career, combining rugby and business, seemed too good to miss until the Japanese Rugby Union raised various objections.

Leaving Llanelli was never going to be easy, as Quins coach Dick Best discovered to his cost. Wasps made it clear that they, too, were in the market before Evans decided that there was still no place quite like Stradey. Club chairman Stuart Gallacher, anxious to reward his loyalty in a practical way, was only too willing to put the facilities at his disposal for a testimonial match.

He could always count on Carling's support. Their friendship had blossomed from that distinctly unpromising introduction, the 'hand-bagging' session at Twickenham during an England–Wales match a few years before. They became firm friends during the Lions tour of New Zealand in 1993 and therein hangs a tale.

They had supposed to be rooming together during the approach to the Canterbury match in Christchurch where the future Mrs Carling was staying in a nearby hotel during a brief visit. Carling tells the story. 'Ieuan and I were meant to be rooming when Julia turned up without anyone knowing and I spent some time with her. Puzzled as to my absence, Ieuan said, "Will, you've got to be honest. What have I done to upset you?"'

Their friendship had survived one momentous event earlier that year, on 6 February 1993, when Evans sprang the ambush which destroyed the English bid for a hat-trick of consecutive Grand Slams. 'He has produced some magical moments and unfortunately too many of them have been against England,' Carling said. 'I really got to know him later that year with the Lions in New Zealand where he had a brilliant tour.'

Just as his demeanour in the early days had inspired someone at Llanelli to dub him 'The Carmarthen Cowboy', so the Lions branded him with a not dissimilar nickname. 'We called him "Randy" because he always wore jeans,' Carling said. 'We used to wonder where he kept his horse!' His sense of humour off the field as well as his performances on it made him a very popular tourist.

'Wales have not had a particularly successful period over the last ten years by their standards and yet Ieuan has produced many great games. To have done that in a team which was often on the back foot is quite a feat. It makes me wonder what he would have achieved in a successful side.

'Not being particularly strong by today's standards, he relies on a wide range of skills. He beats opponents and scores tries through guile and balance as opposed to brute force. His speed and his intuition make him a very difficult man to mark. On that last Lions tour, he, Scott Gibbs, Jerry Guscott and Rory Underwood were an awesome three-quarter line and it's a shame they weren't used more often.'

Nobody was more surprised than Carling when Wales relieved his Welsh counterpart of the captaincy. England, too, had changed their manager-coach but Jack Rowell's appointment following Geoff Cooke's resignation did not mean a change of leadership on the field.

'Ieuan was perfectly entitled to feel hurt,' Carling said. 'I thought it was a strange decision considering he had done a very good job in difficult circumstances. He commanded such respect within the Welsh squad that he seemed to be the ideal man to carry on, at least through to the World Cup.'

By the end of it, the sport had been plunged into deeper turmoil in its stampede towards professionalism. On the eve of the World Cup final, the South African, Australian and New Zealand Rugby Unions announced a ten-year deal with Rupert Murdoch's satellite television empire worth £360 million for an annual triangular series of international matches backed by a provincial competition featuring the leading teams from the three Southern Hemisphere powers.

While Murdoch tied up the Unions, his rival was backing a move to tie up all the players. Kerry Packer, embroiled with Murdoch in a Rugby League war, gave World Rugby Corporation the financial clout to pursue its outrageous scheme at a total cost of something approaching £100 million. Ross Turnbull, a former Wallaby prop and once a member of the hierarchy of the Australian Rugby Union, headed the global attempt to seize power of the sport and reduce the South African, Australian and New Zealand Unions to impotency by relieving them of all the best Springboks, Wallabies and All Blacks.

The plan was not merely to launch an international tournament but to buy thirty teams, with the British representation divided on a regional basis – four in England (London, the North, Midlands, South-west) and two in Wales (East and West). Each squad would consist of thirty players and thus, had they succeeded in hijacking the lot, England would have been reduced to picking their ninth-best players in every position for their official matches. Wales, already finding life very hard with everyone at their disposal, would have been down to their fifth XV.

Every player in the Packer circus would be given a contract and a signing-on fee, his value determined by his status. David Lord, an Australian journalist, had tried to launch a circus in the early eighties. He had the players but not the money. Money would not be an object this time, not with Packer around. There had never been anything quite like it which is why Springboks, Wallabies and All Blacks signed up *en masse*. The English, Scots and Welsh signed up, too.

At his home in Gorseinon, a little west of Swansea, one player was poring over the small print of his contract, refusing to be stampeded into signing it. He was not to know that his decision would coincide with the collapse of the World Rugby Corporation.

When the Packer offer came, I was staggered by the amount of money involved. It was worth 800,000 US dollars over three years – £175,000 a season for three seasons, give or take a dime or two. I had a contract to that effect from the World Rugby Corporation and I only had to sign it to join the gold rush.

The grapevine had been humming towards the end of last season that something was going to happen, that once the 1995 World Cup was over the game would never be the same again. Something *was* going to happen but I for one had no idea that it would involve money on such a massive scale. The rumours intensified in July and then the names began to leak out – Ross Turnbull, Kerry Packer and their plan to propel the game into the forefront of professional sport.

I remained sceptical until the awesome figures were actually put to me in black and white. It added up to more than £500,000 – half a million! You can buy an awful lot of bread with that and there was a powerful temptation to sign it without being too concerned about the precise detail of the terms and conditions before they changed their minds.

The money was all very well but, of course, not a cent could be guaranteed. Had I signed by early August, I would have been entitled to 10 per cent of my signing-on fee on 22 November, the deadline which the World Rugby Corporation gave themselves to come up with the money to finance the operation. Had they done so, I would have received something like £17,000 but I would then have had to wait almost six months for my next instalment.

It was far too big a decision to be rushed into. I needed expert advice and I referred the contract to my advisers, Masters International, so their legal people could go through it with a fine tooth comb. They examined it and advised me against signing. There were too many imponderables, too many omissions. The drawbacks didn't end with having to wait six months between the first and second payments.

There was the question of insurance, in my case no small matter. I would have to insure myself against loss of earnings and my case history of dislocated shoulders meant the annual premium would cost me £30,000. Then there was a clause which said that any player could be relocated anywhere in the world which presumably meant that I could have been shunted anywhere.

The players still found it a very attractive proposition and while I was no exception in that respect, I did have niggling doubts which my advisers had reinforced. I thought about it long and hard. I thought about what would happen if I signed the contract and sent it off, then took cold feet and asked to have it torn up. I would have had to be very naïve to believe that they would have been perfectly happy to do that.

No, they would have held my contract as a bargaining chip and rightly so. These people were not benefactors out to give the players a golden handshake. They were hard-headed businessmen and the stakes for this venture would be massive. I had to be careful that I didn't end up as a pawn in a political struggle for power. I took a fortnight making up my mind, then sent my contract back unsigned.

It may be too late for me but I can see subsequent attempts being made to set up an alternative to the established game. Rugby Union has become a major sport and it gets bigger with the passing of each season. It generates huge sponsorship with blue-chip companies queuing up to pump millions of pounds into the game. The vast worldwide television audiences generated by the 1995 World Cup says everything about its rocketing commercial appeal.

The real challenge for the sport itself is to prove it can meet the demands of administering in a way that it makes the transition from amateur to professional without allowing the game to splinter into various factions. Unless we are careful, rugby could end up like boxing with all sorts of people laying claim to the throne. The administrators have to be able enough to ensure that it does not run out of control, that it is no longer prey to a take-over, that it doesn't end up like athletics where there is a top tier and not a great deal underneath.

At last there is a chance of British and Irish players getting a square deal. With very few exceptions, most of us have been exploited for years. The Unions were only too glad to take whatever was going from sponsors and if their motives were very laudable in terms of paying for the new Twickenham and the new Murrayfield, the result was that the poor old player had to shoulder a greater burden.

The Unions had always talked, often piously, about the need to reduce pressures on top players and keep the game amateur. Yet while they were spouting that theory, their commercial departments were doing exactly the opposite by welcoming new sponsors. Now, they may be jolly good fellows but they do want their pound of flesh and the Unions were only too glad to assure them they would get it.

Yes, the players can train four nights a week instead of three. Yes, the players can play twice a week instead of once. Yes, the players can go on tour for nine weeks instead of a fortnight and never mind their employers. For too long they have been the real sponsors of international rugby in the British Isles.

After years of doing all that for nothing, it was inevitable that sooner or later the players would say, 'Hey, hang on a minute. This isn't fair.' The only surprise was that it took the penny so long to drop. Why, for instance, should I have had to rely on the benevolence of my employers, Forthright Finance? Why should I train until ten o'clock most nights, not get home until nearly midnight, leave early the next morning to get my work done, spend x months away from home and still be treated as an amateur?

A player is like a fossil fuel. In the end it runs out and when that player is no longer of any use, he is discarded. If the average player is lucky, he will have some wonderful memories but apart from a few jerseys he won't have much to show for his commitment to rugby, least of all family security. His wife turns round and says to him, 'I've supported you playing rugby for ten years, the kids are growing up and what have you got from it? A bit of free kit and a couple of quid to buy me a Chinese meal on a Saturday night. Great!'

It wouldn't have been so bad had we all been in the same boat. Every tour I made down under, especially in the eighties, was a real eye-opener. Suddenly you became aware that your opponents were, to all intents and purposes, professionals. For us, the game was a hobby. For many of them, it was a full-time occupation. We had jobs to worry about. Their job seemed to be playing rugby.

Their status as virtual professionals helped widen the chasm between the Northern and Southern Hemispheres. The All Blacks were cashing in way back at the first World Cup in 1987. Andy Dalton, then their captain who ironically missed the tournament because of injury, caused quite a stir with his tractor commercial on television. Anything like that was strictly illegal as far as the Home Unions were concerned yet there was Dalton driving a tractor through the rules and good luck to him.

How, we all asked, could he get away with that? The New Zealand authorities shrugged their shoulders and did nothing, as if to say, 'What's all the fuss about?' Other high-profile players were promoting airlines and they were obviously getting rather more than the odd free ticket. As for David Campese, he hardly spent all those winters in a rugby backwater in Italy because he likes spaghetti.

Now, at last, a more enlightened attitude prevails and, as usual, the Southern Hemisphere spent the summer showing us the way by putting their players under contract and leaving the International Board no alternative other than to declare the game professional. All the top British and Irish players should be contracted to their Unions, guaranteeing them a minimum payment of £100,000 a year which would still leave us some way behind the Southern Hemisphere.

Players on the fringe of national squads in the Home Unions should be on £50,000 a year with the average international player earning £75,000. Anything above that would have to be performance related. The more you win, the more you make. Yet we in Wales were dismayed to learn at the start of the season that our contracts would be worth considerably less. Nobody will give up his job for £10,000. While it is absolutely right that players cannot expect to be rewarded for mediocrity, they ought at least to have the choice of being able to give up their work and concentrate fully on making themselves better rugby players.

There is a real danger that professionalism will cause an exodus of the best Welsh players. Instead of going north along the M6, they will take the M4 east towards London and Heathrow. Far from encouraging the best to stay in Wales, the imbalance in earning potential will drive them out and Transvaal's interest in Derwyn Jones is a case in point.

It is a sobering thought that he could earn £100,000 next year playing for Transvaal in the Currie Cup, an awful lot more than he could hope to make in a good season with Cardiff and Wales. We could quite possibly end up like the Welsh soccer team whose squad, almost without exception, is made up of players drawn from English clubs.

Contrary to popular belief, rugby was never going to pay the mortgage. There used to be a lot of talk about boot money in Welsh rugby and there would be plenty of the nudge-nudge, wink-wink stuff whenever English players would ask us about it. I will admit I received generous expenses and enough to have a nice meal on a Saturday night but the only thing ever stuffed into my boot was the odd page of a newspaper to make my foot feel more comfortable.

The other popular myth about being a Scarlet is that a directorship of the carpark at Stradey automatically goes with first-team selection. I only wish it were true. The carpark is so vast that, had I been given a cut of the proceeds, I'd have been able to tear up the Packer contract without bothering to have it checked out by my solicitor.

People always talk knowingly about the brown envelope being an integral part of the Welsh scene. Well, all I can say is that I, for one, have never had a penny for playing any match although I have no doubt that signing-on fees are paid. If you believe the rumours, they involve several thousand pounds and tend to be more prevalent among the lower divisions of the Heineken League, away from the glare of the media spotlight.

A few months ago I almost left Llanelli to join Harlequins, a transfer which, in a professional sport, would no doubt have meant a handsome fee changing hands. My motivation had nothing to do with money and everything to do with my rugby ambitions. The Heineken League had begun to stagnate and I had become increasingly disenchanted at the falling standards of the competition. It had become too much of a bore.

Harlequins would have been a very appealing escape from the mediocrity. I had lengthy meetings with their coaching director, Dick Best, and I also had the luxury of being able to choose between one of two jobs in the city. The fact that Will Carling wanted me to go and play outside him in the same three-quarter line was very flattering. It left me with a huge decision.

I decided to go. I asked Llanelli to sign a transfer form, which they did, but not before it had caused consternation among the corridors of power at Stradey. I had to sign another transfer form with Harlequins by early February 1995 in order to be eligible to play at the start of the following season's Courage League. I signed that form but never got round to posting it to the club.

After weeks of agonising, I changed my mind about leaving. It was the ultimate borderline decision. The immediate sense of relief convinced me that, deep down, I could not bring myself to make the wrench from Stradey. London would have been very nice for a while but there's no place like home and home for me is West Wales. And with due respect to the Harlequins, there is no club in the world to compare with the Scarlets. It's probably just as well I decided to stay. The culture shock of moving to The Stoop might have been too much for me!

I had another offer on the table, an even more exotic one from Japan. Their clubs are run by companies and one of those companies wanted me to join them with the specific role of playing on a Saturday and spreading the rugby gospel during the week. It sounded like the perfect antidote to my dissatisfaction with the domestic scene and I even went so far as to plan a crash course in Japanese. Unfortunately, the Japanese Rugby Union intervened, insisting, among other things, on a twelve-month qualification period. There were simply too many complications.

It is imperative now that the British game widens its horizons as soon as possible. The Heineken and Courage Leagues were a step in the right direction but no more than that. In Wales they weakened the League by expanding it and there was even a proposal at the AGM last summer of a further expansion of the First Division to 16 clubs. Ludicrous! The present number, twelve, is at least two too many.

A couple of seasons back Llanelli almost scored a century of points in matches against the South Wales Police and Maesteg. I enjoyed running in lots of tries but I didn't gain anything from it. Nor did the paying public. They pay to see their team win but they also pay to see a match. For the top Welsh clubs, 25 per cent of their League fixtures are mismatches. No wonder the crowds are down.

The future now is in Europe and the sooner we have a European club championship the better. Bath, Cardiff, Gloucester, Leicester, Llanelli, Northampton, Swansea and the French élite, among them Toulouse, Toulon, Agen and Racing, will form the heart of it backed by teams representing Ireland, Scotland and Italy. Imagine a European League match between Leicester and Llanelli, a sell-out whether it's 17,000 at Welford Road or 15,000 at Stradey.

It would also generate millions in sponsorship from television, enough to enable all the clubs to pay their players something like £500 a match. One danger of the rugby revolution is that it could easily spawn an official transfer market and with Wales, Scotland and Ireland having to survive in a far smaller market-place than England, their best players could be tempted into chasing the big bucks on offer among the richer provincial teams like Transvaal, Queensland and Auckland.

It is, therefore, imperative that Wales put as many players under contract as they can afford to. They must also ensure the leading clubs have a far more influential voice. Democracy is all very well but too many small clubs have too big a say without having any knowledge of what is entailed at international level.

The WRU has a lot to answer for. Too narrow in its outlook for far too long, it has been guilty of a disturbing lack of foresight and guilty on too many occasions of behaving with a serious lack of dignity. At least now, under the chairmanship of Vernon Pugh, it is coming to terms with the need for a more streamlined operation.

The game has a great future and the fact that it can now offer wonderful opportunities almost makes me wish I could turn the clock back and start all over again. Then I recall the five shoulder dislocations, two broken legs and the horrendous smashing of my left foot and think better of it!

Rugby has opened doors to me which would otherwise have remained shut. It has given me access to all sorts of unlikely places, like the All-England club at Wimbledon, and enabled me to meet all sorts of famous people, like Sir David Attenborough with whom I sit on the Going For Green committee set up by the Ministry of Environment. I plead not guilty to being an ecological terrorist but I am acutely aware that the planet is in a very sick condition and that we all have to do more to improve its health.

One thing rugby has not made me is rich but there again how can you put a price on the thrill of leading your country or the fun of seeing the world? Two companies, Cellnet and Mizuno, pay me for public relations work and while both look after me well, I would never be in a position to afford to give up work.

My success on the rugby field also put me in places I would never dream of, like an advertising hoarding outside Murrayfield extolling the virtues of Scottish Life. Ian Wright, the Arsenal footballer, and I were chosen to spearhead the company's campaign to show they were more than merely a Scottish firm and I was photographed in a traditional Welsh setting, outside the Big Pit in Blaenavon.

Not all commercial ventures are profitable. A few years ago, I and four other Welsh internationals each put £1,000 into launching our own company, Just Players. It proved to be a bit of a disaster, mainly because we couldn't afford a full-time administrator. When a company approached me for permission to launch a new brand of aftershave in my name, I suspect that it, too, must have been a financial disaster.

Why anyone would want to name an aftershave after me, I don't know. I couldn't for the life of me believe that it was going to sell and, sadly, I was right, although it wasn't for any lack of publicity. Radio One made a big thing of it, so did Radio Five and BBC Television. It was a lot of fun but its commercial success was such that I did not receive a bean. However, I do have a few bottles of the stuff and, if say so myself, the aroma is rather fetching, not that I would go so far as to call it the sweet smell of success.

I admire those who have achieved it by pure excellence. Style has always mattered to me, which is why I particularly admire Brian Lara, Pete Sampras, Alan Shearer, Roberto Baggio and, most of all, Michael Jordan, for me the greatest athlete on the face of the earth. I am a sport-aholic and I love the razzmatazz which the Americans always bring to their big events.

Whether this season is my last in rugby remains to be seen. I have already taken steps towards embarking on an alternative career once the boots have been hung up. During the Open championship at St Andrews last summer, I had a lesson from the teacher whom all the top professionals swear by, David Leadbetter. If that doesn't bring my handicap down, nothing will.

At the end of the championship, who should offer me a lift home in his private jet but Ian Woosnam. Within one hour of take-off, he was dropping me off at Cardiff airport *en route* to his home in the Channel Islands. Maybe if Mr Packer had come along ten years ago, I, too, would have been flying around in my own jet but then I might never have been able to captain Wales to victory against the old enemy at Cardiff Arms Park.

Parker and Murdoch are ready to feed a lot of rugby players until they want no more but neither knows how to bake the real stuff. Bread of Heaven . . .

CHAPTER TWENTY-TWO

Top of the Pile

The rugby war had been won and lost by the time Wales reappeared in South Africa for the first international of the professional era, a classic case of princes against paupers if ever there was one.

The Springboks had won the game's equivalent of the lottery, albeit in circumstances which ultimately prevented almost their entire World-Cup-winning squad from being hijacked by the Packer-backed World Rugby Corporation. Instead of joining New Zealand and Australia in signing for the new rebel venture, as WRC claimed they had done, the South Africans switched sides and put pen to paper for Dr Louis Luyt after the SARFU president had promised to match the Packer offer of £175,000 a year for established internationals.

Once the dam had broken, WRC chairman Ross Turnbull went to court in Cape Town claiming that the South African Union had induced the players to terminate the contracts they had signed with his company. Turnbull went further, producing in court a letter alleging that the Springbok captain, François Pienaar, had been offered $300,000 US as a fee for acting as a WRC agent.

The All Blacks and Wallabies had barely finished spitting blood at South Africa breaking ranks than Pienaar was leading his country back into Ellis Park for their first match since they had beaten the world in the same stadium some seven weeks earlier. It might have been stretching a point to say that he did so as if nothing had happened. The Springbok deals made them the highest-paid players in the game, and there are many Welsh players who will spend the rest of their careers counting the cost of the South African decision.

The best player in Wales had turned his offer down but WRC claimed they had enough signed contracts to account for their quota of 60 players to support a Wales team in their new global operation. The first payment was due on 22 November of the same year, 1995, a date which came and went without any money changing hands. The players are still waiting.

The dream that they would be joining the fat cats overnight vanished once the Springboks had broken ranks. In doing so they saved Murdoch the ultimate humiliation of paying £366 million to the New Zealand, Australian and South African Unions for a period of ten years and then finding that the players had bolted, to the Packer-financed WRC.

The old game would never be the same again, a fact which hit Wales between the eyes when they dutifully returned to the Republic that August, guaranteeing their hosts an extra pay day in return for the South African vote which helped tilt the scales in favour of Wales hosting the 1999 World Cup.

Whatever the politics, the trip was not exactly designed to enhance Welsh reputations overseas. Even by their limited standards in the Southern Hemisphere, the supposed warm-up for the Test turned out to be another of those touring horror shows, a 47–6 beating inflicted by a provincial team ranked 11th in the Republic, South-east Transvaal.

The international one week later proved, from a Welsh perspective, to be far less of a rout, even if there was never any serious danger of a courageous Welsh team qualifying for their first win bonus. It did at least bring an early example that crime in the new professional era was liable to be a costly business. Kobus Weise's brutal punch from behind eliminated Derwyn Jones, removing at a stroke the biggest single source of Welsh possession. Referee Joel Dume missed the incident, which happened right under the nose of a touch judge, but that, at least, cleared the way for Weise to be cited for foul play.

He was banned for 30 days and SARFU, ever mindful of its image under the direction of its then chief executive Edward Griffiths, issued a statement claiming that Weise, one of the heroes of the World Cup, had been fined £9,000 – which was £9,000 more than Wales fined the Swansea hooker Garin Jenkins, sent off three minutes from time for punching Joost van der Westhuizen.

He may have had many more enjoyable matches, but for Wales's most enduring player the match brought him level with J.P.R. Williams as the most-capped Welsh player of all time.

The Johannesburg trip left me feeling psychologically challenged, to such an extent that the question of retirement did flit across my mind as I weighed up the pros and cons of the future as I saw it.

It had not been a good few months. I had lost the captaincy and been part of a very poor World Cup campaign. Although the captaincy issue nagged away at the back of my mind, I had at least come to terms with it and accepted the reality that it was something I would not be given back. I had always wanted to go out on a high note, certainly something a lot higher than failing to make the last eight of the World Cup. I found myself asking the same question: Is the time right? I also wondered how much time I had left.

Throughout my career I have, from time to time, felt the need for an ego-booster. I consulted various people, not least Kevin Bowring, who had succeeded Alex Evans as Wales coach, a position which has changed hands all too frequently over the years. I had played under six other coaches, starting with the late John Bevan. Then there was Tony Gray, fired for losing in New Zealand in 1988 after very nearly landing the Grand Slam a few months earlier, John Ryan, Ron Waldron, Alan Davies and Alex Evans.

Bowring convinced me that the time was not right for me to go, that he was not exactly spoilt for choice in terms of alternative right wings and that, even if there had been, he had no wish at this stage to lose an experienced player. It was nice to feel wanted and to be part of a new coaching philosophy based on a daring approach to the game where the unexpected almost became the norm. Alex Evans had been technically sound although very much forward-orientated, yet I don't believe we made the most of the squad at his disposal for that World Cup campaign.

Rather like Ron Waldron before him, Alex had tried to transform club success into success at international level and, just as Ron had found out a few years earlier with a lot of Neath players, so Alex discovered that what worked for Cardiff fell a long way short of working at international level for Wales. His liking for Cardiff players probably cost me the captaincy – not that I harbour any grudges, least of all towards Alex. As he said to me after Mike Hall had taken over, 'Nothing personal, mate. I just want to have my own man in there.'

Hall lasted only as long as the World Cup, which wasn't very long. It is always easy to be wise after the event but I have always believed that Bowring's appointment should have coincided with Wales taking a long-term view of the captaincy and making an inspirational choice. Rob Howley would have been my man. He was the ideal candidate, and you didn't need to be Einstein to work out that, all things being equal, he would be at the peak of his powers in time for the event which mattered most of all, the 1999 World Cup.

Just as England had invested in the young Will Carling, so Wales could have done the same with Howley. Jonathan Humphreys, the Cardiff hooker, was another obvious candidate, a captain who would lead from the front, but I had my doubts about the job affecting his form. Eventually it did, hence the decision to replace him with another of the young brigade, Gwyn Jones. By the time he made his debut, against Italy in January 1996, I had overtaken J.P.R.'s total of 55 international appearances which had stood for some 15 years. I had played my 56th international and, to my considerable relief, I survived to tell the tale.

Fiji at the Arms Park on Armistice Day 1995 ought to have been the perfect occasion for the climax of my very long journey from nowhere to the most-capped Welsh player. A crowd of 50,000 turned out, they gave me a standing ovation when I ran out – and from then on everything went downhill at a rate of knots.

I don't know whether the emotion of the occasion got to me but, for whatever reason, I had as near to the proverbial stinker as you can get without actually losing your place. We struggled badly to beat a very ordinary team and nobody needed to tell me that I had done myself less than justice.

When I recovered, I knew I had to put the Fijian game behind me and make the most of my next opportunity, if only to ensure that it would not be my last one. Italy, always dangerous opponents, had been brought to Cardiff in the New Year as a dress rehearsal for the 1996 Five Nations championship, and it turned out to be quite a day.

We not only won in some style but introduced a batch of young players who brought their flair to the national stage without being the least bit inhibited by any emotional baggage. Leigh Davies made the first of my two tries, Justin Thomas marked his debut with a try of his own, Gwyn Jones got amongst them from start to finish and we had a new outside-half who seemed to me to have come from another planet!

Arwel Thomas, perhaps more than any other young player, is so completely without fear that he does things which virtually nobody else would think of, let alone attempt, and, what's more, he does them on the international stage where the audience invariably amounts to six or seven million.

What he did against England in the opening minutes of his first match in the Five Nations championship is a classic example. When we were awarded an early penalty within kicking range, I thought I saw someone running on to the field with a kicking tee and assumed that we were going for goal.

The same thought must have struck almost the entire England team. Arwel, to his enormous credit, saw the opportunity in a flash and had the nerve to go for the try. Unfortunately, he caught me almost as unawares as the opposition before switching direction after realising that I couldn't get there in time to finish off the move. Hemi Taylor did the job instead on the other side of the field, and we were off to a flying start, thanks to the ingenuity of a young man who refused to be the least bit intimidated by Twickenham, a ground which, by its sheer size, can be the most intimidating place of all.

Arwel looks like a little schoolboy but plays like a man. England would never make the mistake again of being deceived by his outwardly frail appearance. He typified the new Welsh style of playing it off the cuff in such a way that nobody, least of all the opposition, had a clue what would happen next.

It was a case of 'I don't care who we're playing, let's have a pop'. Inevitably, there was a price to be paid for such a high-risk, cavalier attitude, in our case losing the first three matches of the championship. For all the fun we had put back into the international game, we certainly deserved something better.

If at times we played our rugby with the abandon of schoolboys, then, regrettably, we made mistakes, and that was never more evident than at Lansdowne Road, where we scored some lovely tries only to end up conceding 30 points to Ireland for the first time in our history.

I came off the blindside wing to score my first try beside the post with a little help from Leigh Davies, and he played a part in creating the second. Unfortunately, the Irish then punished our naivety and Arwel, in particular, was made to suffer after taking a heavy bang early in the match.

It left us to prepare for the last match of the championship, France at home, in a state of mounting bewilderment. Nobody could quite understand how a team capable of creating something out of nothing could also be capable of dropping so many clangers.

So, not for the first time, we were threatened with a Five Nations whitewash. France, surprisingly, turned out to be more than slightly off the pace by their own high standards and in the end we won a real battle by a single point thanks to the blistering speed which took Rob Howley down the blindside and in at the corner for another great try.

Like everyone else, I cannot understand why it took various selectors so long to recognise his talent, remarkable even for a country which has produced scrum-halves admired the world over such as Gareth Edwards, Terry Holmes and Robert Jones. When Rob eventually won his cap, against England at Twickenham, he was already 25, but, right from the start, he played with the maturity of a seasoned international. He and a few others gave Wales cause for renewed optimism at the end of a season which took us back to Australia for the first time since the infamous tour there five years earlier.

I should never have gone, not because it proved to be another punishing experience but because I wasn't fit. All sorts of doubts had crowded in on me in the weeks before departure and, in the end, I was talked into going. It was a mistake.

The domestic season had ended for me in circumstances which were all too familiar. A bang on the shoulder during the last match of the campaign for Llanelli against Neath put me in hospital and raised fears that I might have dislocated it for the sixth time. Mercifully, the X-rays revealed nothing worse than severe bruising, but the lengthy recovery period raised immediate doubts about my fitness for the Australian tour. My view was that I saw no point in going because I could not guarantee my fitness. Bowring made it clear that he wanted me to go and convinced me accordingly.

In retrospect, there is no doubt that I would have done myself more of a favour had I stayed at home. I wasn't happy about going in the first place and, having gone, I didn't do myself any favours. I needed a summer off to recharge my batteries and Kevin would be the first to admit that it would have been better had I done so.

The best that could be said about the tour was that we avoided the disasters of 1991, which meant that I could revisit the scene of the most notorious incident, the dining room at Ballymore in Brisbane, without any row breaking out between the soup course and dessert. The Australian press, inevitably, dragged the subject up once or twice, which was fair game, but the topic had been laid to rest for so long that it never caused the slightest embarrassment. There were so many new faces on the tour that it meant nothing. Of the old crew from six years earlier, only two had survived, myself and Gareth Llewellyn.

The trip did coincide with another milestone in my life which I saw as further recognition for Welsh rugby. A few weeks earlier, before leaving London, I had been informed by letter from Buckingham Palace that I had been made an MBE for services to rugby. I had to keep it quiet until the formal announcement was made in the Queen's Birthday Honours list, and by that time I was in Moree preparing for the first of our two Tests against the Wallabies.

It turned out to be the wettest day in the history of Moree, which did not exactly ease my homesickness. By then I had met someone who was going to change my life . . .

CHAPTER TWENTY-THREE

Falling in Love

Friday, 24 November 1995

For Kathryn Smith, another long day's commuting began almost like any other, on board the 8.25 a.m. Inter-City from Cardiff General to Paddington. Quite by chance, Ieuan Evans caught the same train. He, too, had some business to attend to at the end of the line, a personal appearance at Harrod's, signing copies of his newly published autobiography. An hour earlier or later and the British Rail romance would probably never have happened. He was in first class ('someone else is paying'), she in second, making the familiar two-hour journey for another modelling assignment.

At 31, Evans was beginning to wonder when he would meet the girl of his dreams. A long-term relationship had finished a few months earlier and the thought had struck him, more than once, that it would soon be time to settle down and start a family.

Kathryn had heard of him, of course, but she never had any reason to give one of the most eligible bachelors in the country a second thought – at least, not until a little later that morning. Somewhere between Reading and Paddington she went for a little ritual refreshment in the buffet car. As fate would have it, Ieuan was already there. The buffet car manager did the introductions, the first in a chain of events which led to their marriage at St Teilo's church in Pontardulais on 22 August 1997.

We met over a British Rail cup of coffee, which only goes to show that romance can flourish from even the most unlikely beginnings! I don't know about love at first sight, but there was far more than a mutual attraction. The amazing thing about that first, chance meeting was how well we got on from the start, how comfortable we felt with each other, and before we knew it the train had pulled into Paddington.

I have never been one to open up very easily, least of all with people I have never met, no matter how attractive. I tend to put up a lot of barriers, but there was a chemistry between us from the word go – although it would be the best part of six months before anything came of it.

We went our separate ways at the tube station and, while it would be stretching a point to say that I had decided there and then that I had finally met the girl with whom I wanted to spend the rest of my life, I hoped that something might come of it – not that the odds were exactly stacked in my favour.

I had wanted to settle down. I had gone out with Claire for nearly five years and you can't get a much more serious relationship than that. But, for whatever reasons, it didn't work out. After that there were a few short-term relationships before I met Kath. Three full months elapsed before we met again. By then I wasn't exactly flapping about the identity of the future Mrs Evans, whoever she may have been, but I was aware of time drifting by. I had not exactly reached the desperation stage where I had to find a wife quickly. I knew that, sooner or later, I would meet her.

While I had split up with Claire a few months before, Kath was involved with someone else and so we did not see each other until a second chance meeting in a Cardiff bar called Henry's one night the following March. I went off to play for Wales in the Hong Kong Sevens and it was after my return that we started going out.

By then I knew for sure that this was the woman I wanted to be with for the rest of my days. I had never met anyone like Kath before. She was so warm and caring and I hated being away from her – which was one very good reason why I wanted to avoid spending some six weeks with Wales that summer, on the other side of the world in Australia.

Kathryn had also fallen in love. 'I wasn't sure that anything would come of that first meeting, but I had an idea it might,' she said. 'When we got off the train that morning, he pretended that he didn't know how to get from Paddington to Knightsbridge by tube, so I told him to change at High Street Kensington!

'What struck me about Ieuan was that he was just such a nice guy. Lovable, hairy, extremely attractive and rugged. What more could a girl want? There was definitely a spark there right from the start.'

My attitude to life had already changed in many respects. Before I had been able to be very self-centred about my life as a professional rugby player. Now my priorities were changing – and changing rapidly – to those of a family man. Back home from Australia, we went to Barbados for a fortnight's holiday that August and by then we both realised that the relationship had developed into something very special. We were getting very serious by then, serious enough to talk about marriage.

Home again in Cardiff we went out for an Italian meal one Saturday night and I had made up my mind that this would be the night when I popped the question. Being an incurable romantic, I took Kath to Roath Park Lake and, beneath the brightest of moons, asked her if she would marry me. I don't know what it was about my proposal, or Kath's acceptance, but a lot of ducks suddenly made such a racket that we could hardly hear ourselves! I have never been one to leave anything to chance if I can possibly avoid it, and I had a fairly good idea that Kath wasn't going to turn my offer down. She had me in an arm-lock at the time, so I wasn't exactly taking a chance!

We had discussed marrying and had chosen an engagement ring, a fairly strong hint, even for me, that the answer would be in the affirmative. We were so thrilled that we could hardly contain ourselves. We told our respective parents and then I called two of my oldest friends, Phil Davies and Jonathan Davies.

We fixed the wedding for the following August, got on with our busy lives and certainly did not plan to start a family quite so soon. Lili arrived at 5.27 a.m. on Good Friday, 28 March 1997, weighing in at eight pounds, six ounces. I was there at Llandough hospital for her birth and it was the greatest experience of my life.

The baby had been due 11 days earlier. Kath had to be induced and we both had a feeling it was going to be a girl, although we didn't know. Had it been a boy, then we were fully prepared. We had discussed a whole host of names and agreed on Joseff. For a girl, we were down to a short-list of four names: Lili, Ffyion, Eleri and Caitlin. We were still undecided as to which one when I took Kath to the hospital at five o'clock that afternoon, drove to Llanelli for a training session and was back at Llandough by half-past eight.

Kath went into labour around midnight and when Lili came into the world some five and a half hours later, I was there to cut the umbilical cord. To be strictly accurate, I cut it twice. I picked her up and showed her a glimpse of the big wide world and it never looked better than it did on that wonderful Good Friday morning.

A few days later we finally settled on her full name: Lili Ffyion Eleri Evans. Having set a date for the wedding, we saw no point in bringing it forward and disrupting all the arrangements merely for appearance's sake because, all of a sudden, there were three of us instead of two.

Events on the field were not going quite as smoothly. The international season started as it had never started before with a match in August which the Welsh Rugby Union, in their wisdom, had elevated to full international status despite the fact that the opposition were no more than an invitational club side.

Wales had given caps for a match against the Barbarians a few years earlier, when the famous touring club were celebrating their centenary. Their decision then had caused a bit of a stink over the value of the Welsh cap, and, not surprisingly, there was even more of a stink over the latest international fixture. Not to put too fine a point on it, I considered it a travesty of justice. For all the good the Baa-baas had done the game world-wide, not even they would pretend to be anything other than an invitation XV, albeit it a very special one. I felt a touch embarrassed at adding one more cap to my total.

It was not my only potential source of embarrassment at the start of a season which would end with the Lions going to South Africa. My major goal was to make my third Lions tour and complete the set after going to Australia in 1989 and New Zealand four years later. The Welsh Rugby Union had offered me a one-year deal worth £30,000 which, considering I was then 32, was fair enough. The initial contract had to be changed because it would have caused an immediate conflict with my boot suppliers, Mizuno, to whom I was contracted for all matches.

Reebok, whose money was being used by the WRU to pay for the contracts being offered to the top players, naturally wanted everyone to wear their boots. The subject led to strained relationships between the Union and certain players but I certainly wasn't going to give up my existing arrangement. The Union had told us a few years before that we were free to negotiate our own boot deals. Now they were asking us, in effect, to renege on our own private arrangements. I made it clear that I was not going to break my Mizuno contract and, thankfully, the Union understood my position and we duly reached a compromise which meant that I would wear the official WRU boots for international matches only.

After that first match, I was concerned far more about my form than my footwear. I knew I could only get better. My performance against the Baa-baas had been fairly mediocre which, I suppose, was in keeping with the fixture. It was followed by what amounted to an official warning that my place in the Wales team was under pressure, and there were several subsequent hints that I needed to pull my socks up – or else. Far from bridling at Kevin Bowring's assessment of my form, I had no alternative but to agree with him. My performances had deteriorated considerably, something which merely increased my regret at not having taken the previous summer off.

When France came to Cardiff for another early-season friendly at the end of September, I felt much sharper and proved the point with an early try. We were 14 points up in as many minutes when once again fate intervened and what was nothing more than a routine tackle on Philippe St André left me with a nasty gash all the way down my thigh, a freak injury caused by the Frenchman's studs. With some 25 stitches, I had no alternative but to miss the following month's trip to the Olympic Stadium in Rome for the return match against Italy, and to time my reappearance for Australia at Cardiff that December and the international farewell of an old foe.

David Campese's 101st, and last, match for the Wallabies proved that he had one last trick up his sleeve. It came in the shape of a knock-on so blatant that everyone at the Arms Park that Sunday afternoon must have seen it – with the glaring exception of the Scottish referee. Instead of a scrum to Wales being given in front of our own posts, the game was allowed to continue as if nothing had happened, the Aussies picking the ball up after Campo had dropped and kicking to my corner – and the luck of the bounce enabled him to get the touch down.

Nobody could believe it when the referee, Iain Ramage, in his first international, awarded the try which gave the Aussies a flying start. With Gareth Thomas running the length of the field for the first try I have ever seen run in from all of 100 yards, we had come from 18–6 behind to lead 19–18 when Jonathan Davies, back in the side after an absence of nine years, kicked his fifth goal in five attempts. Regrettably, Campo still had the last laugh, a penalty try given against Wales for collapsing the scrum in the first minute of injury time allowing the Wallabies to complete their tour of Ireland, Scotland and Wales without losing a single match.

Another crowd of almost 50,000 were back at the Arms Park a fortnight later for our latest crack at the one major country whom we have never beaten, South Africa. Once again it proved too tall an order but, despite Joost van der Westhuizen's hat-trick of tries and the final scoreline of 37–20, we came out of the match with considerable credit.

The Springboks, then under André Markgraaff, were a more complete, adventurous side than the one which had won the

World Cup six months earlier. Wales still managed to have the final say right at the end of a match which proved real value for money, Arwel Thomas shooting down the blindside for a try which only he, with his vivid imagination, could have seen as more than a remote possibility.

After warming up for the Five Nations with a decisive home win over the American Eagles, we went to Murrayfield and promptly showed everyone that there was more to this evolving Welsh team than promise and potential. Wales had not won in Edinburgh for ten years and nobody could have envisaged the manner with which that miserable fact would be laid to rest.

We scored four tries in a 20-minute spell either side of half-time. The last three of them came in five of the most amazing minutes even I had ever experienced. Despite Scott Quinnell applying a mighty finishing touch to a move which featured two other former rugby league players, Scott Gibbs and Allan Bateman, we were 16–10 down when the tries began flooding in.

Six players handled in a move which had the Scots run off their feet by the time Neil Jenkins touched down in the corner. We scored again almost straight from the kick-off. It looked as though Arwel was intent on running off the pitch and up into the stand at the far end with the ball under his arm when he remembered to dot it down just before he ran out of the in-goal area.

Another two minutes later I was lucky enough to finish off the hat-trick. Once Neil's chip had left Scottish full-back Rowan Shepherd flat-footed, I reached out for the ball, grabbed it one-handed as it bounded away to my left, and took off on a clear run to the line.

In five minutes we had scored 21 points without reply, transforming a six-point deficit into a commanding lead of 31–16. Even with more than 20 minutes left, the Scots and their fans knew that it was all over. Never, in all my years as an international, had I witnessed a Welsh team produce anything quite as devastating.

With Ireland and England to come at home, there was a lot

of fancy talk about a Welsh Triple Crown or, better still, a Welsh Grand Slam. That's always the problem in Wales. One good win and everyone goes overboard, as if we have found the magical formula. The next match, Ireland at Cardiff, should have been sufficient warning that such optimism might just have been seriously misplaced.

Ireland have probably won more matches at the Arms Park over the last 12 years than they have in Dublin, and they won again, despite my scoring the fastest try for Wales in the history of the Five Nations championship – 33 seconds after the kick-off. In spite of that and a second try, we still contrived to lose by a point. So much for the Triple Crown.

That match and the one which followed a fortnight later, France at the Parc des Princes, provided an extreme example of our bewildering inconsistency. The team which failed to make home advantage count against Ireland responded by scoring four terrific tries in Paris. Had there been any justice at all, we would have been home and dry instead of suffering another heart-breaking defeat.

Although there was a full month before our last match, England at home, I feared even then that I would miss it. I damaged a hamstring in Paris and in the end it left me no alternative but to make the agonising decision to withdraw from the England match, along with Scott Gibbs.

I had a lot on my mind at that time. Our baby daugher, Lili, was due on the Monday after the England game and then there was the question of where rugby now stood in my list of priorities. My increasing family responsibilities made me think long and hard about making myself available for the Lions tour of South Africa. They were meeting to finalise their squad after the England match and they wanted to know whether I would be available.

CHAPTER TWENTY-FOUR

Making Lions History

Fran Cotton always knew that the 1997 Lions tour of South Africa would be like no other. The British Isles Rugby Union Touring Team, to give them their full title, had been competing against the best of the Southern Hemisphere for more than a century, but there had never been a tour quite like this one.

The first professional expedition demanded something which no amount of money could buy: a professional attitude and a collective will to win if the Lions were to succeed where everyone else, New Zealand included, had failed two years earlier at the World Cup.

Even before they appointed him manager, Cotton decided that nothing could be left to chance if the Lions were to have a realistic chance of winning their first Test series in the Republic for 17 years. By the time the tour organisers, the Four Home Unions Tours Committee, chose him to lead the adventure, the former England prop had made it clear that the buck would stop with him.

For a start, he took the job on the condition that he had his own coaching team, as opposed to one foisted on him, as had been the fate of previous managers. This time there would be no horse-trading. Cotton was interested only in the best, regardless of nationality.

Ian McGeechan had already coached the last two Lions tours, to Australia in 1989 and New Zealand four years later. No other coach had ever done it twice, let alone three times. The 49-year-old Scot was planning a summer at home when Cotton asked him to make it three in a row and take strategic control of Operation Springbok.

McGeechan, in turn, knew exactly who he wanted to be his running mate as forwards' coach. Jim Telfer, at 57 a Lions veteran of two memorable tours as a player and a less memorable one as coach, was at home in his native Borders when the call came. It offered Scotland's director of rugby a final opportunity to broaden his horizons and leave a lasting impression on the global stage.

It also gave him the chance to put the record straight, to show that what had happened in New Zealand 14 years earlier had been too bad to be true. An ill-conceived Lions squad had been whitewashed in the four Tests and the mistakes made then in selection were uppermost in Cotton's mind when the three-man hierarchy met for the first time.

Picking the players was one thing. Picking the captain was something else. Whoever he was, he had to be certain of his place in the Test team – a rather obvious tenet of sound selection but one which the Lions had not always adhered to (Ciaran Fitzgerald's appointment for the 1983 tour of New Zealand being a case in point). Nobody questioned his leadership qualities, which had been demonstrated in taking Ireland to the Triple Crown the previous year, but there were immediate questions over whether or not he was good enough to make the Test team given that the Lions' alternative hooker, Colin Deans, had established himself as the best in that year's Five Nations championship.

Cotton would not be making the same mistake. It meant reducing the candidates to a very short short-list. None of the then national captains made it. Indeed, one of them, England's Phil de Glanville, failed to make the 62 listed for the tour in February.

Two other captains, Jon Humphreys (Wales) and Jim Staples (Ireland), could not be sure of making the final 35, let alone the Test XV. Only Rob Wainwright of Scotland made the tour but his captaincy credentials suffered from the formidable presence of Lawrence Dallaglio.

By the time the management trio had looked at every international player in Britain and Ireland, they were down to three: in alphabetical order, Ieuan Evans, Martin Johnson and Jason Leonard. That all three were then considered to be sure of their Test places shows how hazardous a business it can be given the vagaries of form. Leonard, for example, had been everyone's choice, pre-tour, as the Test tighthead and yet even his form turned out to be so transient that he failed to make the starting line-up in all three matches.

Paul Wallace was to win the vote ahead of Leonard, deservedly so, despite the fact that he had not been considered good enough for the original squad. The Irish Saracen had been called up at the last minute after his compatriot Peter Clohessy had flown all the way back from Queensland only to fail a fitness test.

At 33, Evans was still the number one right wing – not that he would have been presumptuous enough to assume such peerless status. Cotton made no secret of his admiration of the Welshman as a potential captain, hence his glowing reference before watching the France–Wales match in Paris.

Until then there had been real doubts as to whether Evans was prepared to wrench himself away from home. The birth of his baby daughter was imminent and he had alerted the Lions to the fact that he could not, at that stage, guarantee his availability.

He left it almost until the last minute. 'I am delighted that a player of his experience and his quality has made himself available,' Cotton said at the time. 'Ten years of international rugby can sometimes leave a question mark about a player's hunger but Ieuan has answered that in the best possible way with his recent performances. He is as hungry and as sharp as ever. As one of our genuine world-class players, he is an obvious candidate for the captaincy. He's done it 20-odd times for Wales, acquitted himself very well on and off the field and he's also a very good bloke.'

The dearth of candidates prompted suggestions from some sources that the Lions take off without naming a captain and thereby keep all options open in the run-up to the first Test. Cotton, thankfully, never gave the notion a serious thought.

In the end, Johnson won the vote. A split-decision or not, the Lions went for sheer physical presence, of which the Englishman has plenty, making him the first player, post-war, to lead the Lions without having first captained his country. By coincidence, the last man to do it had also been a Leicester forward, Doug Prentice in 1930. He proved a less than inspiring choice, playing in only one of the four Tests against the All Blacks.

Johnson, whatever else happened, would not lose his place because he wasn't up to it, but there were concerns about his fitness. Nobody had endured a more punishing season or played as many demanding matches, and there were grounds for real fears as to whether he would be able to go the distance and stretch an already long season by a further six weeks. The anxiety about Johnson was such that before leaving London a specialist had booked him into hospital for a groin operation on his return from South Africa two months later. The Lions would have to nurse him through the opening weeks.

There would be no such worries about their senior professional. The old man of the squad, if only by a month or two, Ieuan Evans had achieved the rarest hat-trick of all, a third successive Lions tour. No Welsh wing, not even his boyhood idol Gerald Davies, had done it before.

How close I came to captaining the 1997 Lions is something I will never know. During the weeks leading to the final selection of the tour party several of those involved in the process informed me that I was under consideration for the captaincy. Derek Quinnell, the Welsh selector, said I was in the running with a very good shout. Ray Williams, chairman of the body responsible for the Lions, the Four Home Unions Tours Committee, also mentioned the possibility, as did one or two others.

It would, of course, have been the greatest honour of all, but it was not a huge blow to find out that it had gone to someone else. Nor was it any surprise to me that the job went to Martin Johnson. He was the right choice. He lead from the front and he did it superbly.

I had read that Ian McGeechan wanted someone of physical stature knocking on the Springbok dressing-room door, a second-row forward of towering height, as opposed to a comparatively little fellow pulled in from out on the wing. History has already judged that 'Geech' got the psychology right in the way that he got every major issue right.

The uncertainty over my availability for the tour would not have enhanced my suitability for the captain's job. I made sure that Derek and Fran were fully aware of the position and they both understood my dilemma. It was my duty to be with Kath for the birth of our first child and, like any father anywhere, I devoted myself to that.

The last thing I wanted was to have Kath worried that I was going to disappear for two months. Lili had been due on 17 March but arrived 11 days later, by which time the Five Nations had been completed and the Lions management were preparing for their final selection meeting. Once all had gone well with the birth, I was able to take a far more positive attitude towards the tour.

After talking it through with Kath, I phoned Fran and told him, 'Count me in.' I knew I had a good chance of going, but I had long since learnt the hard way that nothing could be taken for granted. To go on one Lions tour is to reach a pinnacle which only a tiny percentage ever reach. To go twice is almost unbelievable. To make it three in a row is miraculous and, with my medical record, I had needed a few miracles along the way just to stay in one piece.

In Australia eight years earlier I had been amongst the younger Lions. Now I would be going as the oldest, a fact gleefully seized upon by some of my new colleagues, among them Keith Wood, the bald-as-a-coot Harlequins hooker born and bred in that well-known Harlequins hot bed of Limerick. He called me 'Dad', which was a bit rich coming from someone who looked a darned sight older even than me! I took a fair bit of ribbing from all and sundry. Once, during a lull in conversation at the dinner table, Dai Young turned to me and said, 'Ieuan, what was it really like in the Boer War?'

The tour began before we took off for Johannesburg on the first leg of the adventure. It began the previous Monday at Weybridge, where we assembled amid so many gloomy predictions about our chances of winning the Test series that we quickly realised it would be a case of 47 against 45 million.

In addition to the 35 players, the Lions had assembled a support team of 12 specialists, each responsible for providing expert back-up in a variety of fields ranging from nutrition to public relations. They certainly weren't leaving anything to chance and the support unit extended to the appointment of a company specialising in team-bonding.

They had us doing all sorts of amazing things, from canoeing in the Thames to piling milk crates a mile high and then getting someone to stand on top of them. We were split into teams and everything we did was designed with the sole purpose of welding 35 players from four different countries into one whose sole aim was to beat the Springboks.

There were players whom I had never met, Tom Smith, Jeremy Davidson and Richard Hill to name but three. One or two others I could barely recognise and there were a few more who I knew just well enough to be able to say hello. As an exercise in breaking the ice, the outdoor pursuits at Weybridge worked wonders. It also taught us teamwork and made us appreciate that any team is only as good as its weakest member. When you haul yourself up in a safety-harness to the top of milk crates piled 35 feet high, you learn very quickly that you are entirely dependent on the other members of the team who are there to take the slack. Big Jeremy Davidson standing on top of all those crates was a sight to behold.

We had lots of laughs along the way, like Neil Jenkins getting stuck on a riverbank, one half of him in his canoe, the other half in the Thames. Others, myself included, were not what you could call natural sailors. I was among those who could only paddle in one direction.

The competitive edge which would become one of the hallmarks of the '97 Lions had been sharpened before we left Heathrow. Every player wore a suit of armour in the shape of specially padded jackets, which meant that every practice was for real. Everyone got stuck in to such an extent that the training sessions were often as physical as the matches. On one occasion, in East London before the second match of the tour against Border, the forwards got so stuck in that there was a flare-up between the front rows and even Jim Telfer, the forwards' coach and the supreme taskmaster, had to tell them to cool it.

It was a good sign. When you have 35 highly trained international players fighting for 15 places then it can be no surprise if a few of them have to be dissuaded from literally fighting it out. There was an intensity within the squad which made that sort of thing inevitable, although there was never any danger of the conflict degenerating into a running feud.

Long before then we were all fully aware that the Lions had become a big deal, bigger than ever. There had been open days before previous tours but nothing like the one we had 48 hours before departure. There were journalists, photographers, radio and television crews everywhere, so many, in fact, that it was like Billy Smart's circus. I knew that rugby's popularity had been growing world-wide but I had never seen anything like this. It was all very good news as far as we were concerned, because it left us in no doubt about the huge public interest in the tour.

Very few gave us a chance. As we flew off, the Springboks gave the very strong impression that they had only to turn up to win the series. Joel Stransky and Rudi Straueli, two English-based members of their 1995 World Cup team, were so impressed by the Lions that they backed South Africa to win the series 3–0.

By then we were beginning to think that we were on the verge of doing something famous. 'Geech' had been talking our chances up from the outset, and I could sense even before we had got round to playing a match that there was a collective strength about this Lions squad which had not been there in the last one in New Zealand four years before.

Then the tour had been undermined by the fact that most of those who realised they had no chance of making the Test team gave less than their all for the common cause. No matter how great the individual disappointments, not once during the seven weeks travelling round South Africa did anyone let his personal dissatisfaction affect the common cause.

Having such a competitive element throughout the team in almost every position helped hugely. Every one of the 35 players thought he was in with a chance of making the first Test and that helped us avoid falling into the traditional Lions trap of the party being split, almost immediately, into the Saturday team and the lesser midweek team.

On the '97 tour there was no such thing as a dirt-tracker. Having squeezed an awful lot into our week at Weybridge, we had such a gruelling first week's work under a hot sun in

Durban that it was almost impossible to get to grips with the fact that we were supposedly in the depths of the Natal winter!

Eastern Province threw in a couple of ringers for our first match in Port Elizabeth, beefing up their team with the Transvaal centre Hennie le Roux and our old friend Kobus Weise, both members of the World Cup team. Contrary to popular opinion, neither would get anywhere near the Test line-up. They hardly made much of an impression in that opening match, and while we were some way off being the finished article, that first performance offered us real hope that a brand new team would evolve into one capable of winning the series.

While there was a lot wrong with that first effort, we had made a definite declaration of intent. Win or lose, we were going to play a 15-man game by keeping the ball alive in a way which demanded the highest level of fitness. All the hard work put in at London Irish in the days before departure and again at Durban in that first, exhausting week enabled us to finish the Port Elizabeth match the fitter team, just as we finished every match save for the final Test.

Little did we know after that first Saturday that Weise and le Roux would be the only members of the Springbok squad whom we would encounter outside the Tests. In deliberately withdrawing their international players from all the major provincial fixtures before the first Test, the South African management made a serious mistake.

It was a huge *faux pas*, big enough to be a major contributory factor to our victories in the first two Tests. The fate of the Lions was always going to rest, for better or worse, on the three consecutive matches against Northern Transvaal, Gauteng (formerly Transvaal) and Natal, what Fran Cotton referred to as the 'Bermuda Triangle'.

By refusing to release any of their international players for those matches, the Springboks put themselves at a double disadvantage. In addition to weakening their top provincial teams, they also denied their best players the opportunity to sharpen their match fitness. Heaven knows they needed that after the friendliest of friendlies against Tonga in Cape Town, where the opposition was so poor as to make utter nonsense of the exercise.

In a way they became victims of their own arrogance. They somehow believed that the top teams would take care of us even without their top players, and the initial reaction was to dismiss us as a bunch of pussycats. By the time we persuaded them to think otherwise, it was all a bit too late. It made our job less difficult than it would otherwise have been. After surviving a swamp of a pitch in East London, we were warned that Western Province, in front of a full-house 50,000 at Newlands that Saturday, would see us off. Instead we ran them ragged in a way which forced the Springboks to change their perception of us.

If they expected stodgy opponents playing a stodgy British game, they had another thing coming. Instead we produced a brand of rugby which they knew they would be hard pushed to cope with, and in that respect 'Geech', more than anyone, deserves enormous credit. Anyone who coaches three Lions teams has to have something special, and while I had been critical of his tactics in the final, decisive Test against the All Blacks on the last tour, I welcomed his basic philosophy: to create a game which allowed our runners to run from deep. For producing a winning style which changed the image of our game in South Africa, he deserves everyone's admiration.

It succeeded despite the early setback of losing to Northern Transvaal in Pretoria, not that our problems ended with the final whistle. A few hours later they cited Scott Gibbs for foul play, which was hard to take considering what had been done in the name of rugby a few days earlier by Mpumalanga, formerly South-east Transvaal, in the previous match at Witbank.

What happened there to Doddie Weir midway through the second half was a disgrace to rugby union and sport as a whole. The deliberate kick on Doddie's knee which caused enough damage to raise fears over whether or not he would ever play again was an act of wanton violence. The player responsible, Marius Bosman, should have been banned for life. Our management issued a statement in suitably strong terms, calling for the host Union to take action. While they were presumably still considering the matter, the South Africans chose to get their retaliation in first by citing Gibbs for allegedly punching during the match against Northerns.

We had to be seen to be whiter than white, and this was clearly a tit-for-tat measure. Scott is far too good and powerful a player to resort to any dirty tactics. A South African tribunal met on the Sunday morning and suspended him for one match, which, with Scott still recovering from an ankle injury, did nothing to improve his prospects of making the Test team.

Our ability to cope with the injustice of it all would be tested to the limit 24 hours later with the Mpumalanga verdict on Bosman. Unbelievably, he escaped any suspension despite the fact that his victim was by now back in Newcastle wondering when he would be able to play again. How could someone cripple an opponent like that and carry on playing as if nothing had happened, while one of our players was banned for one match over an alleged punch which caused no damage whatsoever?

We knew we had to turn it to our advantage, take it on the chin, so to speak, and prove we had the inner strength to take whatever they threw at us and not allow it to undermine our resolve. Willie John McBride, whose 1974 Lions had won the series without losing a single match, warned us that we would never succeed unless we could cope with adversity.

Another issue had to be tackled at the same time. Three weeks into the tour and the players felt so tired that they asked the management to throttle back on a very punishing training routine. They agreed and gave us two days off, our first of the tour, although that presented a different problem: what to do with ourselves. Pretoria is a nice enough place but hardly the entertainment capital of the world. It gives you some idea of what was on offer when I say that the highlight of our two days off was a game of crazy golf! Then it was back to business for a match which could easily have resulted in a second successive defeat, Gauteng (Transvaal) at Ellis Park.

Luckily, Austin Healey came up with a superb solo try which

was followed by an even better one from John Bentley, made from 60 metres against all the odds. The whole of South Africa was stunned by it, but not half as stunned as Natal were by the sheer size of our win against them at King's Park that Saturday, by 42 points to 12. Unfortunately, it came at a price, and a savage one at that. Losing Rob Howley with a dislocated shoulder was a huge blow. By then he had, for my money, proved himself to be the world's number one scrum-half and I felt desperately sorry for him that fate had denied him the chance of proving it in the Tests.

Despite Rob's cruel luck, the Natal victory had given us a big psychological boost at just the right time, one week before the first Test. All the top Natal players in the Springbok squad, André Joubert, Gary Teichmann, Henry Honiball, Adrian Garvey and Mark Andrews, could only sit and watch the destruction from their seats in the stand. We had effectively told them: 'We have played your best provincial team, in your backyard, in your own humid conditions, and scored 40 points.'

You could tell what Joubert and company, not to mention the Springbok coaches, were thinking: 'These Lions are going to take some stopping now.' One player in particular they could never stop was Scott Gibbs. Against Natal he produced one of the tackles of the tour, dumping Ollie le Roux on his backside. The big prop, nicknamed 'The Elephant Man' largely because of his 20-stone frame, never knew what hit him.

The team for the following week's Test was taking shape, but not in a way I, for one, could have envisaged. At the start of the tour I would have expected the England pack to go in almost *en bloc*, with Keith Wood and Scott Quinnell as the only serious alternatives. Sadly, Scott was already back home after injuring himself in the warm-up to the Northern Transvaal game.

You would have thought that Jason Leonard and Simon Shaw would be certainties. Instead neither made it, their places taken by Tom Smith and Jeremy Davidson, players whom nobody knew much about but who very rapidly developed into world-class performers.

Elsewhere there was a battle royal for places: Wood and Barry

Williams at hooker; Neil Jenkins and Tim Stimpson at full-back; four class players in Jeremy Guscott, Scott Gibbs, Allan Bateman and Will Greenwood going for two places at centre. There were other big questions, too, like Richard Hill or Neil Back at openside and Eric Miller or Tim Rodber at No. 8?

Going into Test week, a lot of anxious contenders could only wait and wonder, myself included. I had been pleased with my form, having raised my game to a higher level with each appearance, but I was far too long in the tooth to assume that I had booked my place.

It had been agreed with the management that every player would be told of his fate individually rather than all 35 being called to a meeting and the team read out. Once the team had been picked, one of three letters would be pushed under the door of every player's room, depending on whether he had made the team, made the bench or just missed out.

When the big day came, our early belief that, man for man, we were superior to the opposition had been strengthened. 'Geech' told us before the Newlands Test, 'Win this one and the Test series is ours. We can't lose here and still expect to win the series. We can't win the rubber here but, believe me, we can lose it.'

At times it felt as though we were in a remake of *The Alamo*. We must have set a record for the number of tackles, missing only two from start to finish. The first cost us a try and the second would probably have cost us the match had André Venter not mistimed his pass by a second or two with the result that his pass to the wing outside him went forward.

Matthew Dawson then chose the perfect moment to claim his place in history. As if replacing the best scrum-half in the world was not daunting enough, he produced a magnificent solo try which knocked the stuffing out of the 'Boks. I came in off the wing on the scissors and every defender came in with me, leaving Matthew all alone to shoot in at the corner when they should have put him into the stand.

When he went to lob the ball back inside, I expected to receive it. Had he done so, I doubt whether I would have lived to tell the tale. There were at least four of them waiting to tear me from limb to limb – but how naive of the Springboks to fall for one of the oldest tricks in the game. Matthew had never intended it as a dummy until he realised they had all bought it.

Tactically, the South Africans failed in other directions. Neil Jenkins had played only a handful of games at full-back and I was very pleasantly surprised that they didn't bombard him with high kicks. Neil's place-kicking, under immense pressure, was as magnificent as usual, and with Alan Tait skating in at the left corner we were home and dry.

Again, Scott Gibbs had proved worth his weight in gold, which, considering he is the best part of 16 stone, gives you some idea of his value. What amazed me was that they kept running into him even after he had stopped another of their mighty props, Os du Randt, in his tracks with a tackle every bit as big as the one he had made on Ollie le Roux.

It was as if the Springboks felt that Scott was questioning their manhood. They saw his jersey as a red rag and kept taking him on, only to finish second best. Once derailed, they had no alternative game plan. Their sledging throughout that match was the worst I had ever heard on a rugby field. There was an awful lot going on and that made our victory all the sweeter.

I had no way of knowing at the time but I had just played my last match for the Lions. My career was over. Before half-time I had felt a twinge in my groin. I put an ice-pack on it during the ten-minute break, went back out and thought nothing more of it.

While the Test players stayed put in the Durban sunshine, the midweek team flew to Bloemfontein and produced a magnificent performance of all-action rugby in rattling up six tries and 52 points against Orange Free State. It would have been more but for the frightening incident involving Will Greenwood, who came down heavily on his head after a tackle. Watching on television back in Durban was scary enough, but it was far more scary for James Robson, the tour doctor, and the other medics in Bloemfontein. Mercifully, Will made a complete recovery, although it meant he would take no further part in the tour. He will be an England player for many years to come.

Back at base, I had been given three days off to recover from my 'twinge'. The Test team was being selected on the Wednesday and at training that day it was obvious that the team was going to be unchanged – obvious, that is, until the fateful moment on the practice ground behind King's Park when I looped round Neil Jenkins, came off my left foot and shot through a gap between two opponents.

No sooner had I broken the line than there was a horrible tear in my groin, followed by excruciating pain. The sniper had got me, good and proper. The cameras were there at the time but I was in such agony that not even their presence could prevent me swearing like a trooper. I had to be carried off for the very good reason that I couldn't move. I knew my tour was over before the doctor Jim Robson confirmed my worst fears without actually saying as much. 'We'll have a look,' he said in his diplomatic way, but I could tell by his face that there would be no miraculous recovery. I knew it was hopeless before they carted me off to hospital for X-rays. At that precise time, my parents, my fiancée Kath and my baby daughter Lili were touching down at Durban for a week's holiday. My mother and father had never seen me play for the Lions, and now they never would.

Instead of preparing to take my place in one of the most famous matches in the Lions' history, I could do nothing but join my family on the beach. I spent that Saturday night hobbling between the dug-out on the touchline and one of the hospitality boxes, where the rest of the squad were watching probably the most amazing, most wonderful match we have ever seen.

The Springboks will probably never know how they lost that match, but as long as they kept missing their chances and we stayed in touch, I knew we had the discipline and, more to the point, the goalkicker to snatch victory. And so it proved. Neil kept us in the game, hauling us back to 15–15 in another match where South Africa were guilty of tactical naivety.

Jerry Guscott, always the coolest man for the big occasion, ensured our place in history with his late drop goal. At the final whistle, I jumped into the stratosphere with sheer joy – which took some doing, in view of the state of my groin. We had created history and we would forever be part of it, taking our places alongside the '74 Lions.

Back at the hotel 'Geech' had his hair as good as scalped by Keith Wood, who had chosen himself for the job of balding the coach in celebration of winning the series, if only because he had had plenty of practice cutting his own hair! I don't know what Mrs McGeechan thought about her husband's appearance, but I thought he looked rather the better for it.

The last Test proved to be a terrific match, even if it was a game too far for us. It reminded us how right we had been in making sure that the series was won before we finished up back at Ellis Park, high on everyone's list of the world's most intimidating grounds.

I had been on some far from happy tours in my time, but this was unquestionably the happiest I had ever known. It was not a fun tour off the field in the Lions tradition, which meant that no hotels were wrecked and nobody ended up in clink. The professionalism of everyone involved meant there was no room for stupidity. The only 'incidents' were provoked by a nocturnal activity which has been kept secret – until now! Those who had the misfortune to room with the great snorers of the trip would cheerfully have called the police.

Woody topped the snoring league by the proverbial mile, with another of the front row, Tom Smith, proving himself the champion sleepwalker. His tendency in that respect was a constant source of anxiety to Mark Regan, and understandably so. Word has it that on one occasion the English hooker woke up to find Tom alongside him, whereupon Mr Smith was told very forcibly to get back into his own bed!

Then there was Mr Soundbite, alias Fran Cotton. Before the second Test he had gone to the trouble of finding a string of Napoleonic quotes which he considered fitted the occasion. When he came to giving us the Napoleon treatment, the relevant passage had been mislaid, with the result that we had the amusing sight of Fran shuffling through a sheaf of papers trying to find the right one.

Not surprisingly, he appeared before the Players' Court under

Lord Chief Justice Wood on a double charge: 'speaking only when the cameras were rolling' and, as a member of the 1974 Lions, 'living in the past at our expense'. He was found guilty on both counts and given an alcoholic fine in the time-honoured way.

Other charges included Austin Healey, the talkative Leicester scrum-half, for talking too much. He was ordered to sit in the corner for half an hour with a large apple strapped to his mouth! Then there was Tim Rodber, accused of using his mobile phone while acting as a substitute during the Northern Transvaal game. He was ordered to provide free use of the aforesaid phone whenever any other player required it.

More seriously, there was no doubt in my mind that Smith and Davidson were the unexpected stars of the tour and that Allan Bateman was the unluckiest. I have no hesitation in picking Lawrence Dallaglio as the player of the tour. His all-round contribution was terrific, both as a dynamic flanker who prides himself on the intensity of his game and as a leader constantly geeing up those around him to get the best out of them. I will be very surprised if he does not now captain England for many years to come. They may have considered him a bit too young when the job came up last season, but after leading Wasps to the English championship and inspiring the Lions, he is certainly ready for it now.

Having made the biggest move of my rugby life, I shall be bumping into him at some stage later in the season, although, naturally, I will do my best to ensure it doesn't happen on the field! Leaving Llanelli after all these years was a huge wrench. Nothing lasts forever, but I had 13 years at a fabulous club which I would not have swapped for the world. Going back to Stradey on the first day of the season to say farewell after signing for Bath was a really emotional experience.

I had given my all for the Scarlets over the years and I think the supporters recognised that. They recognised, too, that this is now a professional game and that the deal which took me across the Severn Bridge was a good one for all the parties concerned. It all happened very quickly. Bath rang the club on the Wednesday for permission to speak to me and then arranged a secret rendezvous at a service station on the M4, where I met Tony Swift, the Bath chief executive who left Swansea for Bath at around the time I was starting with Llanelli. Stuart Gallacher, the Llanelli chairman, said he was 'more than satisfied' with the transfer fee involved, and that I went with his good wishes. That meant a lot to me. The last thing I wanted was any ill feeling over my departure.

Playing in England means I shall have to get used to paying £3.90 every Saturday night to get back into Wales! Seriously, I could not have wished for a better, more professional club than Bath with whom to see out the last two years of my career. It gives me a fresh challenge, the chance to do something I have never done before, by competing for the English Premiership and the English Cup as well as the Heineken European Cup. First and foremost it gives me the challenge of getting into the Bath team, not easy when you consider they have three high-quality international wings in Jon Sleightholme, Adedayo Adebayo and Simon Geoghegan.

At 33 I still have two good years left. Wales want me to continue but I have been thinking long and hard about retiring from international competition, content in the knowledge that I have been lucky enough to do things beyond my wildest dreams. The temptation is to go on, but I have never wanted to outstay my welcome. I would like to think I will be remembered for what I have done for Wales over the years. The whole Arms Park experience has been a rare privilege, from that very first time I sat in the North Stand, a little boy lost who could not possibly have dreamt that one day he would be out there playing for his country.

Not bad for a cowboy from Carmarthen!

Appendix

IEUAN EVANS'S INTERNATIONAL RECORD

For Wales

1987

7.2	France	Parc des Princes	Lost 9–16
7.3	England	Cardiff Arms Park	Won 19–12
21.3	Scotland	Murrayfield	Lost 15–21
4.4	Ireland	Cardiff Arms Park	Lost 11–15 (1 try)
25.5	*Ireland	Wellington	Won 13–6
3.6	*Canada	Invercargill	Won 40–9 (4 tries)
8.6	*England	Brisbane	Won 16–3
14.6	*New Zealand	Brisbane	Lost 6–49
18.6	*Australia	Rotarua	Won 22–21

1988

6.2	England	Twickenham	Won 11–3
20.2	Scotland	Cardiff Arms Park	Won 25–20 (1 try)
5.3	Ireland	Lansdowne Road	Won 12–9
19.3	France	Cardiff Arms Park	Lost 9–10 (1 try)
28.5	New Zealand	Christchurch	Lost 3–52
11.6	New Zealand	Auckland	Lost 9–54

1989

4.2	Ireland	Cardiff Arms Park	Lost 13–19
18.2	France	Parc des Princes	Lost 12–31
18.3	England	Cardiff Arms Park	Won 12–9

1991

19.1 England	Cardiff Arms Park	Lost 6–25
2.2 Scotland	Murrayfield	Lost 12–32
16.2 Ireland	Cardiff Arms Park	Drawn 21–21
2.3 France	Parc des Princes	Lost 3–36
21.7 Australia	Brisbane	Lost 6–63
4.9 France	Cardiff Arms Park	Lost 9–22
6.10 *W. Samoa	Cardiff Arms Park	Lost 13–16 (1 try)
9.10 *Argentina	Cardiff Arms Park	Won 16–7
12.10 *Australia	Cardiff Arms Park	Lost 3–38

1992

18.1 Ireland	Lansdowne Road	Won 16–15
1.2 France	Cardiff Arms Park	Lost 9–12
7.3 England	Twickenham	Lost 0–24
21.3 Scotland	Cardiff Arms Park	Won 15–12
21.11 Australia	Cardiff Arms Park	Lost 6–23

1993

6.2 England	Cardiff Arms Park	Won 10–9 (1 try)
20.2 Scotland	Murrayfield	Lost 0–20
6.3 Ireland	Cardiff Arms Park	Lost 14–19 (1 try)
20.3 France	Parc des Princes	Lost 10–26
16.10 Japan	Cardiff Arms Park	Won 50–5 (2 tries)
10.11 Canada	Cardiff Arms Park	Lost 24–26

1994

15.1 Scotland	Cardiff Arms Park	Won 29–6 (1 try)
5.2 Ireland	Lansdowne Road	Won 17–15
19.3 England	Twickenham	Lost 8–15
18.5 +Portugal	Lisbon	Won 102–11 (3 tries)
21.5 +Spain	Madrid	Won 54–0 (3 tries)
11.6 Canada	Toronto	Won 33–15 (1 try)
18.6 Fiji	Suva	Won 23–8
22.6 Tonga	Nuku'alofa	Won 18–9
25.6 W. Samoa	Apia	Lost 9–34
17.9 Romania	Bucharest	Won 16–9 (1 try)

1995

18.2	England	Cardiff Arms Park	Lost 9–23
4.3	Scotland	Murrayfield	Lost 13–26
18.3	Ireland	Cardiff Arms Park	Lost 12–16
27.5	*Japan	Bloemfontein	Won 57–10 (2 tries)
31.5	*New Zealand	Johannesburg	Lost 9–34
4.6	*Ireland	Johannesburg	Lost 23–24
2.9	South Africa	Johannesburg	Lost 11–40
11.11	Fiji	Cardiff Arms Park	Won 19–15

1996

16.1	Italy	Cardiff Arms Park	Won 31–26 (2 tries)
3.2	England	Twickenham	Lost 15–21
17.2	Scotland	Cardiff Arms Park	Lost 14–16
2.3	Ireland	Lansdowne Road	Lost 17–30 (2 tries)
16.3	France	Cardiff Arms Park	Won 16–15
8.6	Australia	Brisbane	Lost 25–56
22.6	Australia	Sydney	Lost 3–42
24.8	Barbarians	Cardiff Arms Park	Won 31–10
25.9	France	Cardiff Arms Park	Lost 33–40 (1 try)
1.12	Australia	Cardiff Arms Park	Lost 19–28
15.12	South Africa	Cardiff Arms Park	Lost 20–37

1997

11.1	USA	Cardiff Arms Park	Won 34–14 (2 tries)
18.1	Scotland	Murrayfield	Won 34–19 (1 try)
1.2	Ireland	Cardiff Arms Park	Lost 25–26 (2 tries)
15.2	France	Parc des Princes	Lost 22–27

* World Cup
+ World Cup qualifier

246

Lions Test Matches

1989

1.7	Australia	Sydney	Lost 12–30
8.7	Australia	Brisbane	Won 19–12
15.7	Australia	Sydney	Won 19–18 (1 try)

1993

12.6	New Zealand	Christchurch	Lost 18–20
26.6	New Zealand	Wellington	Won 20–7
3.7	New Zealand	Auckland	Lost 13–30

1997

21.6	South Africa	Cape Town	Won 25–16

Total Record, Country by Country, for Wales and the Lions

	P	W	D	L
Ireland	12	4	1	7
England	10	5	0	5
Australia	10	3	0	7
France	10	1	0	9
Scotland	9	4	0	5
New Zealand	7	1	0	6
South Africa	3	1	0	2
Canada	3	2	0	1
Japan	2	2	0	0
Fiji	2	2	0	0
Western Samoa	2	0	0	2
Argentina	1	1	0	0
Romania	1	1	0	0
Italy	1	1	0	0
Tonga	1	1	0	0
USA	1	1	0	0
Portugal	1	1	0	0
Spain	1	1	0	0
*Barbarians	1	1	0	0
Total	78	33	1	44

* Cap awarded by Welsh Rugby Union

WORLD'S MOST CAPPED TOP TEN
(As at 1 September 1997)

Philippe Sella	France	1982–95	111
David Campese	Australia	1982–96	101
Serge Blanco	France	1980–91	93
Sean Fitzpatrick	New Zealand	1986–	91
Rory Underwood	England	1984–96	91
Mike Gibson	Ireland	1964–79	81
Ieuan Evans	Wales	1987–	78
Rob Andrew	England	1985–97	75
Will Carling	England	1988–97	73
Michael Lynagh	Australia	1984–95	72

WORLD'S TEN MOST CAPPED WINGS
(INCLUDING TEST APPEARANCES FOR THE LIONS)
(As at 1 September 1997)

Rory Underwood	England	1984–96	91
*David Campese	Australia	1982–96	85
Ieuan Evans	Wales	1987–	78
John Kirwan	New Zealand	1984–94	63
Philippe St André	France	1990–	58
Patrice Lagisquet	France	1983–91	46
Ken Jones	Wales	1947–57	44
Keith Crossan	Ireland	1982–92	41
Christian Darrouy	France	1957–67	40
Jean Dupuy	France	1956–64	39

* Played 16 internationals at full-back

WORLD'S TOP INTERNATIONAL TRYSCORERS
(As at 1 September 1997)

David Campese	Australia	1982–96	63
*Rory Underwood	England	1984–96	50
Serge Blanco	France	1980–91	38
John Kirwan	New Zealand	1984–94	35
*Ieuan Evans	Wales	1987–	34
Philippe St André	France	1990–	31
Philippe Sella	France	1982–95	30
Marcello Cuttitta	Italy	1987–	24
Ian Smith	Scotland	1924–33	24
Christian Darrouy	France	1957–67	23
Tim Horan	Australia	1989–	22
Tony Stanger	Scotland	1989–	22
Jeff Wilson	New Zealand	1993–	22

* Including Lions' Test matches

WALES'S MOST CAPPED TOP TEN
(As at 1 September 1997)

Ieuan Evans	1987–	71
Gareth Llewellyn	1989–	59
J.P.R. Williams	1969–81	55
Robert Jones	1986–	54
Gareth Edwards	1967–78	53
Neil Jenkins	1991–	50
Gerald Davies	1966–78	46
Phil Davies	1985–95	46
Ken Jones	1947–57	44
Mike Hall	1988–95	42

IEUAN EVANS'S COMPLETE CAREER RECORD IN SENIOR RUGBY, SEPTEMBER 1984 TO 31 JULY 1997

	Games	Tries
Llanelli	231	193
Wales	71	33
Lions Tests	7	1
Wales, non-Tests	10	5
Lions, non-Tests	12	8
Wales B	3	7
Barbarians	4	5
Crawshay's	4	4
Neath	2	2
National trials	2	1
Total	**346**	**259**

Records
Most international tries by a Welsh player – 33
Most matches as captain of Wales – 28
Most capped Welsh player – 71
Most tries in Welsh Cup – 48 in 45 matches
Most tries in a First Division match – 6
Most tries in Welsh Cup finals – 7 in 7 matches

Six tries in a first-class match
19.04.85 for Wales B v Spain at Bridgend
15.11.86 for Llanelli v Merthyr at Merthyr, Welsh Cup
24.10.92 for Llanelli v Maesteg at Stradey Park, First Division

Four tries in a first-class match
03.06.87 for Wales v Canada at Invercargill, World Cup
27.02.92 for Llanelli v Newbridge at Stradey Park, Welsh Cup
07.12.96 for Llanelli v Newbridge at Stradey Park, First Division

Hat-tricks (20)
14 for Llanelli, 3 for Wales, 2 for Wales B, 1 for Crawshay's

Other honours
1992–93   International Player of the Year
1992–93   Welsh Player of the Year

World Cups (3)
1987
1991
1995

Lions tours (3)
1989 Australia
1993 New Zealand
1997 South Africa

Wales tours (4)
1988 New Zealand
1991 Australia
1994 North America and South Pacific
1996 Australia

Medical case history
24.08.83   broken leg (Llanelli Wanderers Sevens)
22.10.85   dislocated right shoulder (Barbarians v Newport, Rodney Parade)
28.12.85   dislocated right shoulder (Barbarians v Leicester, Welford Road)
31.10.87   dislocated right shoulder (Llanelli v Leicester, Welford Road)
23.07.89   dislocated right shoulder (Lions v Anzac XV, Brisbane)
21.10.89   dislocated right shoulder (Llanelli v London Welsh, Old Deer Park)
1.10.94   dislocated left ankle (Llanelli v Cardiff, Arms Park club ground)

Index